File for Divorce in Florida

File for Divorce in Florida

Ninth Edition

Edward A. Haman

Attorney at Law

Sphinx® Publishing
An Imprint of Sourcebooks, Inc.®
Naperville, Illinois
www.SphinxLegal.com

Ninth Edition: 2007

Published by: **Sphinx® Publishing, An Imprint of Sourcebooks, Inc.®**

Naperville Office
P.O. Box 4410
Naperville, Illinois 60567-4410
630-961-3900
Fax: 630-961-2168
www.sourcebooks.com
www.SphinxLegal.com

This publication is designed to provide accurate and authoritative information in regard to the subject matter covered. It is sold with the understanding that the publisher is not engaged in rendering legal, accounting, or other professional service. If legal advice or other expert assistance is required, the services of a competent professional person should be sought.

From a Declaration of Principles Jointly Adopted by a Committee of the American Bar Association and a Committee of Publishers and Associations

This product is not a substitute for legal advice.

Disclaimer required by Texas statutes.

Library of Congress Cataloging-in-Publication Data

Haman, Edward A.
File for divorce in Florida / by Edward A. Haman. -- 9th ed.
p. cm.
Rev. ed. of: How to file for divorce in Florida. 2004.
Includes index.
ISBN-13: 978-1-57248-598-3 (pbk. : alk. paper)
ISBN-10: 1-57248-598-1 (pbk. : alk. paper)
1. Divorce suits--Florida--Popular works. 2. Divorce suits--Florida--Forms. I. Haman, Edward A. How to file for divorce in Florida. II. Title.

KFF100.Z9H36 2007
346.75901'66--dc22

2007004304

Printed and bound in the United States of America.

SB — 10 9 8 7 6 5 4 3 2 1

Contents

Using Self-Help Law Books

Before using a self-help law book, you should realize the advantages and disadvantages of doing your own legal work and understand the challenges and diligence that this requires.

The Growing Trend

Rest assured that you will not be the first or only person handling your own legal matter. For example, in some states, more than 75% of the people in divorces and other cases represent themselves. Because of the high cost of legal services, this is a major trend, and many courts are struggling to make it easier for people to represent themselves. However, some courts are not happy with people who do not use attorneys and refuse to help them in any way. For some, the attitude is, "Go to the law library and figure it out for yourself."

We write and publish self-help law books to give people an alternative to the often complicated and confusing legal books found in most law libraries. We have made the explanations of the law as simple and easy to understand as possible. Of course, unlike an attorney advising an individual client, we cannot cover every conceivable possibility.

Cost/Value Analysis

Whenever you shop for a product or service, you are faced with various levels of quality and price. In deciding what product or service to buy, you make a cost/value analysis on the basis of your willingness to pay and the quality you desire.

When buying a car, you decide whether you want transportation, comfort, status, or sex appeal. Accordingly, you decide among choices such as a Neon, a Lincoln, a Rolls Royce, or a Porsche. Before making a decision, you usually weigh the merits of each option against the cost.

When you get a headache, you can take a pain reliever (such as aspirin) or visit a medical specialist for a neurological examination. Given this choice, most people, of course, take a pain reliever, since it costs only pennies; whereas a medical examination costs hundreds of dollars and takes a lot of time. This is usually a logical choice because it is rare to need anything more than a pain reliever for a headache. But in some cases, a headache may indicate a brain tumor, and failing to see a specialist right away can result in complications. Should everyone with a headache go to a specialist? Of course not, but people treating their own illnesses must realize that they are betting, on the basis of their cost/value analysis of the situation, that they are taking the most logical option.

The same cost/value analysis must be made when deciding to do one's own legal work. Many legal situations are very straightforward, requiring a simple form and no complicated analysis. Anyone with a little intelligence and a book of instructions can handle the matter without outside help.

But there is always the chance that complications are involved that only an attorney would notice. To simplify the law into a book like this, several legal cases often must be condensed into a single sentence or paragraph. Otherwise, the book would be several hundred pages long and too complicated for most people. However, this simplification necessarily leaves out many details and nuances that would apply to special or unusual situations. Also, there are many ways to interpret most legal questions. Your case may come before a judge who disagrees with the analysis of our authors.

Therefore, in deciding to use a self-help law book and to do your own legal work, you must realize that you are making a cost/value analysis. You have decided that the money you will save in doing it yourself outweighs the chance that your case will not turn out to your satisfaction. Most people handling their own simple legal matters never have a problem, but occasionally people find that it ended up costing them more to have an attorney straighten out the situation than it would have if they had hired an attorney in the beginning. Keep this in mind while handling your case, and be sure to consult an attorney if you feel you might need further guidance.

Local Rules

The next thing to remember is that a book which covers the law for the entire nation, or even for an entire state, cannot possibly include every procedural difference of every jurisdiction. Whenever possible, we provide the exact form needed; however, in some areas, each county, or even each judge, may require unique forms and procedures. In our state books, our forms usually cover the majority of counties in the state or provide examples of the type of form that will be required. In our national books, our forms are sometimes even more general in nature but are designed to give a good idea of the type of form that will be needed in most locations. Nonetheless, keep in mind that your state, county, or judge may have a requirement, or use a form, that is not included in this book.

You should not necessarily expect to be able to get all of the information and resources you need solely from within the pages of this book. This book will serve as your guide, giving you specific information whenever possible and helping you to find out what else you will need to know. This is just like if you decided to build your own backyard deck. You might purchase a book on how to build decks. However, such a book would not include the building codes and permit requirements of every city, town, county, and township in the nation; nor would it include the lumber, nails, saws, hammers, and other materials and tools you would need to actually build the deck. You would use the book as your guide, and then do some work and research involving such matters as whether you need a permit of some kind, what type and grade of wood is available in your area, whether to use hand tools or power tools, and how to use those tools.

Before using the forms in a book like this, you should check with your court clerk to see if there are any local rules of which you should be aware or local forms you will need to use. Often, such forms will require the same information as the forms in the book but are merely laid out differently or use slightly different language. They will sometimes require additional information.

Changes in the Law

Besides being subject to local rules and practices, the law is subject to change at any time. The courts and the legislatures of all fifty states are constantly revising the laws. It is possible that while you are reading this book, some aspect of the law is being changed.

In most cases, the change will be of minimal significance. A form will be redesigned, additional information will be required, or a waiting period will be extended. As a result, you might need to revise a form, file an extra form, or wait out a longer time period. These types of changes will not usually affect the outcome of your case. On the other hand, sometimes a major part of the law is changed, the entire law in a particular area is rewritten, or a case that was the basis of a central legal point is overruled. In such instances, your entire ability to pursue your case may be impaired.

Introduction

Going through a divorce is probably one of the most common and most traumatic encounters people have with the legal system. At a time when you are least likely to have extra funds, paying a divorce lawyer can be one of the most expensive bills. In a contested divorce case, it is not uncommon for the parties to run up legal bills of over $10,000. Horror stories abound of lawyers charging substantial fees with little progress to show for it. This book is designed to enable you to obtain a divorce without hiring a lawyer. Even if you do hire a lawyer, this book will help you to work with him or her more effectively, which can also reduce the legal fee.

This is not a law school course, but a practical guide to get you through the system as easily as possible. The emphasis is on practical information in plain English. Legal jargon has been kept to a minimum. For ease of understanding, this book uses the term *spouse* to refer to your husband or wife (whichever applies) and the terms *child* and *children* are used interchangeably.

Please keep in mind that different judges and courts in different counties may have their own particular procedures, forms, and ways of doing things. The court clerk's office can often tell you if they have any special forms or requirements. Court clerks cannot give legal advice, but they can tell you what their court or judges require.

The first two chapters of this book will give you an overview of the law and the legal system. Chapter 3 will help you decide if you want an attorney, and if so, how to find and work with a lawyer. Chapter 4 will help you evaluate your situation and give you an idea of what to expect if you decide to go through with a divorce. The remaining chapters will show you what forms you need, how to fill out the forms, and what procedures to follow.

You will also find a glossary and two appendices in the back of the book. Appendix A contains selected portions of the Florida law and court rules dealing with property division, alimony, and child support. Although these provisions are discussed in the book, it is sometimes helpful to read the law exactly as it is written.

Appendix B contains the forms you will complete. You will not need to use all of the forms. This book will tell you which forms you will need for your individual situation. Many of the forms in Appendix B are Florida Supreme Court approved forms. Those are also found in the *Family Law Rules of Procedure.* These are more numerous and more complex than the prior approved forms; however, they may be easier to use since they more clearly indicate what information needs to be inserted in the blank spaces.

You will also find an instructive word or phrase in brackets, such as {name} or {address}, just before the blank to tell you what information to insert. (For this reason, it was not always necessary to provide line-by-line instructions as in previous editions of this book.)

AUTHOR'S NOTE:

BE SURE TO READ THE "INTRODUCTION TO LEGAL FORMS" IN CHAPTER 5 BEFORE YOU USE ANY OF THE FORMS IN THIS BOOK.

Marriage Ins and Outs

chapter 1

Several years (or maybe only months) ago, you made a decision to get married. This chapter will discuss, in a very general way, what you got yourself into, how to get out, and whether you really want to get out.

MARRIAGE

Marriage is frequently referred to as a contract. It is a legal contract, and for many, it is also a religious contract. This book will deal only with the legal aspects. The wedding ceremony involves the bride and groom reciting certain vows that are actually mutual promises about how they will treat each other. There are also legal papers signed, such as a marriage license and a marriage certificate. These formalities create certain rights and obligations for the husband and wife. Although the focus at the ceremony is on the emotional and romantic aspects of the relationship, the legal reality is that financial and property rights are being created. It is these financial and property rights and obligations that cannot be broken without a legal proceeding.

Marriage gives each of the parties certain rights in property and creates certain obligations with respect to the support of any children they have together (or adopt). Unfortunately, most people do not fully realize that these rights and obligations are being created until it comes time for a divorce. Florida does not recognize *common law marriage* or *same sex marriage*, so this book does not apply to people in those situations.

DIVORCE

A *divorce* is the most common method of terminating or breaking the marriage contract. In Florida, a divorce is officially called a *dissolution of marriage*. The laws, court rules, and legal papers all use this official term. In this book, the terms *divorce* and *dissolution of marriage* are used interchangeably, and have the same meaning. In a divorce, the court declares the marriage contract broken, divides the parties' property and debts, decides if either party should receive alimony, and determines the custody, support, and visitation with respect to any children the parties may have.

Traditionally, a divorce could only be granted under certain very specific circumstances, such as *adultery* or *mental cruelty*. A divorce may be granted today simply because one or both of the parties want one. The wording used to describe the situation is that *the marriage is irretrievably broken*.

Another ground for divorce is the mental incapacity of a spouse (although it is much easier to use the standard ground that the marriage is irretrievably broken). This requires proving mental incapacity, which may require other court procedures.

ANNULMENT

The basic difference between a *divorce* and an *annulment* is that a divorce says *this marriage is broken*. An annulment says *there never was a marriage*. An annulment is more difficult and often more complicated to prove, so it is not used very often. Annulments are only possible in a few circumstances, usually where one party deceived the other. If you decide that you want an annulment, you should consult an attorney. If you are seeking an annulment for religious reasons and need to go through a church procedure (rather than, or in addition to, a legal procedure), consult your priest or minister.

A divorce is generally easier to get than an annulment. This is because all you need to prove to get a divorce is that your marriage is broken. You prove this by simply saying it is so. The *Petition for Dissolution of Marriage* reads: *The marriage between the parties is irretrievably broken*. That is all you need to do. However, in order to get an annulment, you will need to prove more. This proof will involve introducing various documents into evidence and having other people testify at the court hearing.

Under Florida law, annulments can only be granted under one of the following circumstances.

- One of the parties was too young to get married. In Florida, both parties must be at least 18 years old to get married. (There are a few exceptions, such as the woman being pregnant or the underage person having parental consent; however, these exceptions only apply if the person is at least age 16.)

- One of the parties is guilty of *fraud.* For example, one party just got married in order to have the right to inherit from the other, with no intention of ever living together as husband and wife.

- One party was under *duress* when he or she got married. Duress means that the person was being threatened or was under some kind of pressure, so that he or she did not get married voluntarily.

- One party did not have the mental capacity to get married. This means the person was suffering from mental illness or disability (such as having severe mental retardation) to such an extent that the person did not understand he or she was getting married, or possibly did not even comprehend the concept of marriage.

- One party was already married to another person. This might occur if one party married under the mistaken belief that the divorce from a previous marriage was final.

- The marriage is *incestuous.* Florida law prohibits marriage between certain family members, such as brother and sister, first cousins, aunt and nephew, or uncle and niece.

If your spouse wants to stop an annulment, there are several arguments he or she could make to further complicate the case. This area of the law is not as well defined as divorce. There are no Florida Statutes outlining the procedures to follow. Annulments are much less common than divorces. The annulment procedure can be extremely complicated. It should not be attempted without consulting a lawyer.

LEGAL SEPARATION

Florida does not permit a *legal separation.* This is a procedure available in some states to divide the property and provide for child custody and support in cases where the husband and wife live separately, but remain married. This is usually used to break the financial rights and obligations of a couple whose religion does not permit divorce. Some states refer to this procedure as *divorce from bed and board.* It is an old procedure that is gradually fading. The Florida Statutes specifically state "No dissolution of marriage is from bed and board, but is from bonds of matrimony." (Florida Statutes (Fla. Stat.), Section (Sec.) 61.031.)

Florida law does provide the ability to obtain child support or alimony, and determine custody and visitation rights, without getting a divorce; but it does not allow for the division of property. (Fla. Stat., Secs. 61.09 and 61.10.) Because it does not divide property, it is technically not a legal separation, although it is sometimes mistakenly called a legal separation. The statutes refer to these as proceedings *unconnected with dissolution* and they are beyond the scope of this book.

DECIDING WHETHER TO DIVORCE

Getting a divorce will have an impact on several aspects of your life and can change your entire lifestyle. Before you begin the process of getting a divorce, you need to take some time to think about how it will affect your life. This section will help you examine these things and offer alternatives in the event you want to try to save your relationship. Even if you feel absolutely sure that you want a divorce, read this section so you are prepared for what may follow.

Legal Divorce

A legal divorce is simply the breaking of your matrimonial bonds and the termination of your marriage contract and partnership. The stress created here is that of going through a court system procedure and having to deal with your spouse as you go through it. However, when compared to the other aspects of divorce, the legal divorce does not last as long. On the other hand, the legal divorce can be the most confrontational and emotionally explosive stage. There are generally three matters to be resolved through the legal divorce:

1. the divorce of two people (giving each the legal right to marry someone else);

2. the division of their property (and responsibility for debts); and,

3. the care and custody of their children.

Although it is theoretically possible for the legal divorce to be concluded within a few weeks or months, the legalities may continue for years, mostly caused by the emotional aspects leading to battles over the children.

Social and Emotional Divorce

Divorce will have tremendous impacts on your social and emotional lives that will continue long after you are legally divorced. Some of the major impacts are discussed below.

Lack of companionship. Even if your marriage is one of the most miserable, you may still notice at least a little emptiness or loneliness after the divorce. It may not be that you miss your spouse in particular, but just miss another person being around.

Grief. Divorce may be viewed as the death of a marriage or maybe the funeral ceremony for the death of a marriage. Like the death of anyone or anything you have been close to, you will feel a sense of loss. This aspect can take you through all of the normal feelings associated with grief. You will get angry and frustrated over the years you may believe you have wasted. You will feel guilty because you failed to make the marriage work. You will find yourself saying, "I can't believe this is happening to me." For months or even years, you will spend a lot of time thinking about your marriage. It can be extremely difficult to put it all behind you and get on with your life.

The singles' scene and dating. You may find that you are dropped from friends' guest lists, as your current friends—who are probably all married—no longer find that you (as a single person) fit in with their circle. If you want to avoid solitary evenings before the TV, you will find yourself trying to get back into the *singles' scene*. This can be very difficult, especially if you have custody of the kids. Plus, depending on the length of the relationship, the dating scene may have entirely changed from when you were last in it.

Financial Divorce

Many married couples are just able to make ends meet. After getting divorced, there are suddenly two rent payments, two electric bills, etc. For the spouse without custody, there is also child support to be paid. For at least one spouse, and often for both, money becomes even tighter than it was before the divorce. Also, once you have divided the property, each of you will need to replace the items the other person got to keep.

Children and Divorce

The effect upon your children and your relationship with them can often be the most painful and long-lasting aspect of divorce. Your relationship with your children may become strained as they work through their feelings of blame, guilt, disappointment, and anger. This strain may continue for many years. You and your children may even need professional counseling. Also, as long as there is child support and visitation involved, you will be forced to have at least some contact with your ex-spouse.

Alternatives to Divorce

By the time you have purchased this book and read this far, you have probably already decided that you want a divorce. However, if what you have just read and thought about has made you want to make a last effort to save your marriage, there are a few things you can try. (These are only very basic suggestions. A professional marriage counselor can offer other suggestions and more details on the ones listed here.)

Talk to your spouse. Choose the right time (not when your spouse is trying to unwind after a day at work or is trying to quiet a screaming baby) and talk about your problems. Try to establish a few ground rules for the discussion.

- Talk about how you feel, instead of making accusations that may start an argument.
- Each person listens while the other speaks (no interrupting).
- Each person must say something that he or she likes about the other and about the relationship.

As you talk, you may want to discuss such things as where you would like your relationship to go, how it has changed since you got married, and what can be done to bring you closer together.

Change your thinking. Many people get divorced because they will not change something about their outlook, behavior, or lifestyle. Once they get divorced, they find they make that same change they resisted for so long. Perhaps if they had tried the change first, they could have saved the marriage.

Example: George and Wendy were unhappy in their marriage. They did not seem to share the same lifestyle. George felt overburdened with responsibility and bored. He wanted Wendy to be more independent and outgoing, to meet new people, to handle the household budget, and to go out with him more often. Wendy was more shy and reserved, was not confident in her ability to find a job and succeed in the business world, and preferred to stay at home. Wendy wanted George to give up some of his frequent nights out with the guys, to help with the cooking and laundry, to stop leaving messes for her to clean up, and to stop bothering her about going out all the time. Neither would try change. Eventually, all of the little things built up into a divorce.

After the divorce, Wendy was forced to get a job to support herself. Now she has made friends at work. She goes out with them two or three nights a week. She is successful and happy at her job and is quite competent at managing her own budget. George now has his own apartment. He cooks his own meals (something he finds he enjoys) and does his own laundry. He has also found it necessary to clean up his own messes and keep the place neat, especially if he is going to entertain guests. George has even thought about inviting Wendy over for dinner and a quiet evening at his place. Wendy has been thinking about inviting George out for a drink after work with her friends.

Both George and Wendy have changed in exactly the way the other had wanted. It is just too bad they did not make these changes before they got divorced. If you think some change may help, give it a try. You can always go back to a divorce if your problems are not resolved.

Counseling. Counseling is not the same as giving advice. A counselor should not be telling you what to do. A counselor's job is to assist you in figuring out what you really want to do. A counselor's job is mostly to ask questions that will get you thinking. Actually, just talking things out with your spouse is a form of self-counseling. The only problem is that it is difficult to remain objective and nonjudgmental. You both need to be able to calmly analyze what the problems are and discuss possible solutions.

Very few couples seem to be able to do this successfully, which is why there are professional marriage counselors. As with doctors and lawyers, good marriage counselors are best discovered by word of mouth. You may have friends who can direct you to someone who helped them. You can also check with your family doctor or your clergyman for a referral, or even check the telephone Yellow Pages under *Marriage and Family Counselors* or some similar category. You can see a counselor either alone or with your spouse. It may be a good idea for you to see a counselor even if you are going through with the divorce.

Another form of individual counseling is talking to a close friend. Just remember the difference between counseling and advice giving. Do not let your friend tell you what you should do.

Trial separation. Before going to the time, expense, and trouble of getting a divorce, you and your spouse may want to try just getting away from each other for a while. This can be as simple as taking separate vacations or as complex as actually separating into separate households for an indefinite period of time. This may give each of you a chance to think about how you will like living alone; how important or trivial your problems are; and, how you really feel about each other.

The Legal System

chapter 2

This chapter will give you a general introduction to the legal system. There are things you need to know in order to obtain a divorce (or help your lawyer get the job done) and to get through any encounter with the legal system with a minimum of stress. These are some of the realities of our system. If you do not learn to accept these realities, you will experience much stress and frustration.

THEORY VERSUS REALITY

Our legal system is a system of rules. There are basically three types of rules.

1. *Rules of Law:* These provide the basic substance of the law, such as a law telling a judge how to go about dividing your property.

2. *Rules of Procedure:* These tell how matters are to be handled in the courts, such as requiring court papers to be in a certain form, delivered to the other party in a certain manner, or filed within a certain time.

3. *Rules of Evidence:* These require facts to be proven in a certain way.

The theory is that these rules allow each side to present evidence most favorable to that side. An independent person or persons (a judge or jury) will figure out the truth. Then certain legal principles will be applied to that "truth" that will give a fair resolution of the dispute. These legal principles are supposed to be relatively unchanging so that we can all know what will happen in any given situation and can plan our lives accordingly. This will provide order and predictability to our society. Any change in legal principles is supposed to occur slowly, so that the expected behavior in our society is not confused from day to day. Unfortunately, the system does not really work this way. What follows are some of the problems in the real legal system.

The System Is Not Perfect

Contrary to how it may seem, legal rules are not made just to complicate things and confuse everyone. They are attempts to make the system fair and just. They have been developed over hundreds of years, and in most cases, they do make sense. Unfortunately, our efforts to find fairness and justice have resulted in a complex set of rules. The legal system affects our lives in important ways and it is not a game. However, it can be compared to a game in some ways. The rules are designed to apply to all people, in all cases. Sometimes the rules do not seem to give a fair result in a certain situation, but the rules are still followed. Just as a referee can make a bad call, so can a judge. There are also cases in which one side wins by cheating.

Judges Do Not Always Follow the Rules

Many young lawyers are shocked to discover that judges do not always follow the rules. After spending three years in law school learning legal theory and after spending countless hours preparing for a hearing and having all of the law on your side, you find that the judge is not going to pay any attention to legal theories and the law. Many judges are going to make a decision simply on what they think seems fair under the circumstances. This concept is actually being taught in some law schools now.

Unfortunately, what seems *fair* to a particular judge may depend upon his or her personal ideas and philosophy. For example, there is nothing in the divorce laws that gives one parent priority in child custody; however, a vast majority of judges believe that a child is generally better off with his or her mother. All other things being equal, these judges will still find a way to justify awarding custody to the mother.

The System Is Often Slow

Even lawyers get frustrated at how long it can take to complete a case (especially if they do not get paid until it is done). Whatever your situation, things will take longer than you expect. Patience is required to get through the system with a minimum of stress. Do not let your impatience or frustration show. No matter what happens, keep calm and be courteous.

Not All Cases Are Alike

Just because your friend's case went a certain way does not mean yours will have the same result. The judge can make a difference, and more often the circumstances will make a difference. Just because your coworker makes the same income as you and has the same number of children, you cannot assume you will be ordered to pay the same amount of child support. There are usually other circumstances your coworker does not tell you about and possibly does not understand.

Half of the People Lose

Remember, there are two sides to every legal issue and there is usually only one winner. Do not expect to have every detail go your way, especially if you let the judge decide.

DIVORCE LAW AND PROCEDURE

This section will give you a general overview of the law and procedures involved in getting a divorce. To most people, including lawyers, the law appears very complicated and confusing. Fortunately, many areas of the law can be broken down into simple and logical steps. Divorce is one of those areas.

The Players

The law and the legal system are often compared to games, and just like games, it is important to know the players.

The judge. The judge has the power to decide whether you can get divorced, how your property will be divided, which of you will get custody of the children, and how much the other will pay for child support. The judge is the last person you want to make angry with you. In general, judges have large caseloads and like it best when your case can be concluded quickly and without hassle. This means that the more you and your spouse agree upon and the more complete your paperwork is, the better the judge will like it. Most likely, your only direct contact with the judge will be at the final hearing, which may last as little as five minutes. (See Chapter 5 for more about how to deal with the judge.)

The judge's secretary or judicial assistant. The judge will either have a secretary or a judicial assistant (who frequently holds a law degree). Among many duties, the secretary or judicial assistant sets the hearings for the judge. He or she can frequently answer many of your questions about the procedure and what the judge would like or require.

Once again, you do not want to make an enemy of the secretary or judicial assistant. Do not call often, do not ask too many questions, and do not show any anger, frustration, or annoyance. A few questions are okay, but you may want to start off saying that you just want to make sure you have everything in order for the judge.

The court clerk. While the secretary usually only works for one judge, the court clerk handles the files for all of the judges. The clerk's office is the central place where all of the court files are kept. The clerk files your court papers and keeps the official records of your divorce. Most people who work in the clerk's office are friendly and helpful. While they cannot give you legal advice (such as telling you what to say in your court papers), they can help explain the system and the procedures (such as telling you what type of papers must be filed). The clerk has the power to accept or reject your papers, so you do not want to anger the clerk either. If the clerk tells you to change something in your papers, just change it. Do not argue or complain.

Lawyers. Lawyers serve as guides through the legal system. They try to guide their client while attempting to confuse, manipulate, or outmaneuver their opponent. When dealing with your spouse's lawyer (if he or she has one), try to be polite. You will not get anywhere by being antagonistic. Generally, the lawyer is just doing his or her job to get the best situation for the client. Some lawyers, however, are truly nasty people. These lawyers simply cannot be reasoned with and you should not try. If your spouse gets one of these lawyers, it is a good idea for you to get a lawyer also. Chapter 3 will provide more information to help you decide if you need a lawyer.

This book. This book will serve as your map of the trail through the legal system. In most cases, the dangers along the way are relatively small. If you start getting lost or the dangers seem to be getting worse, you can always hire a lawyer to jump to your aid.

The Law

The law relating to divorce, as well as to any other area of law, comes from two sources. The first source is the Florida Statutes, which are the laws passed by the Florida legislature. This book is designed so that you will not need to look up the law. However, a portion of this law, relating to property division, alimony, and child support, can be found in Appendix A of this book.

NOTE: *Florida has a residency requirement. One basic law you need to be aware of is that either you or your spouse must live in Florida for at least six months immediately before filing for divorce. See the section on "Verifying Residency" in Chapter 5.*

The other source of law is the past decisions of the Florida courts. These are often more difficult to locate. For most situations, the law is clearly spelled out in the statutes and the past court decisions are not all that important. However, if you wish to learn more about how to find these court decisions, see the section on "Legal Research" later in this chapter.

The law is really very simple in many divorce cases. You will need to show the following three things:

1. your marriage is *irretrievably broken* (simply state this fact, which means that your marriage relationship is broken and cannot be saved);
2. division of property between you and your spouse; and,
3. custody of your children and how they should be supported.

The Procedure

The procedural requirements come from the Florida Statutes and the Florida Rules of Court. The basic uncontested divorce process may be viewed as a five-step process.

1. File court papers asking the judge to grant a divorce (and to determine child care and property division).
2. Notify your spouse that you are filing for divorce.
3. File papers explaining your financial situation, and what agreements you and your spouse have made.
4. Obtain a hearing date.
5. Attend a hearing with the judge, and have the judge sign a judgment granting the divorce.

There is a simplified procedure, which some people can use, that allows you to skip some of these steps. These steps are discussed in a little more detail now, and later chapters will tell you how to carry out these steps.

Petition for Dissolution of Marriage. This is simply a written request for the judge to grant you a divorce and divide your property. **PETITION FOR DISSOLUTION OF MARRIAGE (PETITION)** forms are provided in Appendix B of this book and full instructions are provided in later chapters. (see forms 3–6.) Once the **PETITION** that fits your situation is completed, it is taken to the court clerk to be filed.

Notify your spouse. After you have prepared the **PETITION**, you need to officially notify your spouse. Even though your spouse may already know that you are filing for divorce, you still need to have him or her officially notified. This is done by having a copy of your **PETITION** delivered to your spouse. This must be done in a specific manner, which will be explained in later chapters. (This step is eliminated in the simplified divorce procedure.)

Obtain a hearing date. Once all of your paperwork has been filed, you need to set a date for a hearing. A hearing is simply a meeting with the judge so that he or she can give you a divorce. This is usually done by contacting the judge's secretary and asking for a hearing date. This can often be done over the telephone.

The hearing. Finally, you go to the hearing. The judge will review the papers you have submitted plus any additional information you have, and will make a decision about whether to grant the divorce, how your property should be divided, who should have custody of your children, and how the children are to be supported. If it applies to your situation, the judge may also decide whether alimony shall be paid. If you and your spouse agree on these matters, the judge will simply approve your agreement.

The judge can order the husband and wife to mediation when they are having a difficult time reaching agreement on the major issues. Also, marriage counseling can be ordered if the judge believes the marriage can be saved; however, this is an extremely rare situation. The judge can also direct the state *Department of Children and Families* (DCF) to conduct a study and provide the judge with a custody recommendation.

LEGAL RESEARCH

This book has been designed so that you do not need to do research. However, if you need or want to find out more about divorce law in Florida, this section will give you some guidance.

Florida Statutes

The main source of information on Florida divorce law is the *Florida Statutes*. This is a set of books that contain the laws passed by the Florida Legislature. A complete new set is issued in odd-numbered years (2005, 2007, etc.), with a supplement being issued in even-numbered years (2006, 2008, etc.). A set can usually be found at the public library, although check to be sure they have the most recent set. They usually are not available until the beginning of the following year. The Florida Statutes are also available on CD-ROM. Divorce laws are found in Chapter 61 of the Florida Statutes.

You can access the Florida Statutes online through **www.findlaw.com**. Once at the Findlaw site, in the box headed "Legal Professionals," click on "Cases and Codes." Next, scroll down and click on "Florida." Then, scroll down and click on "Florida Statutes." Click on "Title VI," then click on "Part I" under "Chapter 61." This will bring you to a screen where you can either click on "View Entire Chapter" to see all of Chapter 61 or scroll down and click on the specific section of the chapter you wish to see.

Case Law

If you want to avoid navigating through the Findlaw site, you can go directly to **www.flsenate.gov/statutes**.

In addition to the laws passed by the legislature, law is also made by the decisions of the judges in various cases each year. To find this *case law*, you will need to go to a law library. Each county has a law library connected with the court, so you can ask the court clerk where the library is located. Also, law schools have libraries that may be open to the public. Do not be afraid to ask the librarian for assistance. Librarians cannot give you legal advice, but they can tell you where the books are located. Case law may be found in the following sets of books.

Florida Statutes Annotated. The *Florida Statutes Annotated* are volumes that contain the Florida Statutes, followed by summaries (*annotations*) of court cases that discuss each section of the statutes. For example, if you are looking for information about alimony, you would find Section 61.08. This would give you the exact language of the statute and be followed by summaries of court opinions explaining the alimony statute.

Florida Digest. The *Florida Digest* is a set of books that gives short summaries of cases and the place where you can find the court's full written opinion. The information in the digest is arranged alphabetically by subject. Find the chapter on "Divorce," then look for the headings of the subject you want.

Southern Reporter. The *Southern Reporter* is where the appeals courts publish their written opinions on the cases they hear. There are two *series* of the *Southern Reporter*, the older cases being found in the *Southern Reporter* (abbreviated *So.*), and newer cases being found in the *Southern Reporter 2d Series* (*So.2d*). For example, if the digest gives you a reference to *Smith v. Smith*, 149 So.2d 721 (1988), this tells you that you can find the case of *Smith v. Smith* by going to Volume 149 (the first number) of the *Southern Reporter 2d Series*, and turning to page 721 (the second number). It also tells you that the court decided the case in the year 1988.

Florida Jurisprudence

Florida Jurisprudence is a legal encyclopedia. You simply look up the subject you want (e.g., Dissolution of Marriage), in alphabetical order, and it gives you a summary of the law on that subject. It will also refer to specific court cases, which can then be found in the *Southern Reporter*.

Florida Rules of Court

The *Florida Rules of Court* are the rules that are applied in the various courts of Florida. The Florida Rules of Court and the *Florida Family Law Rules of Procedure* may be found at your local library or law library in book form, and may also be found online at **www.flcourts.org**.

Forms

The official forms approved by the Florida Supreme Court for divorce cases are included in Appendix B of this book. These forms are also available online at **www.flcourts.org**.

Once you get to the site, click on the tab for "general public," then click on "Family Law Forms." Next, you may either click on information and instructions for downloading forms, or click on "Or Go Directly to the Family Forms" and scroll down to the form you want. You will then have the option of viewing the forms, completing them online, or downloading them to your computer to be completed later. As the forms may be changed at any time, this website can be valuable in the event that any of the forms have changed since this book was published.

This site will also allow you to get information about local family self-help centers. These local self-help centers are a good source of information about what forms and procedures are used in your particular county.

Other Sources

Four books you may want to ask for at the law library are:

1. *Florida Family Law Practice Manual*, by D&S Publishers, Inc.;

2. *Florida Family Law*, by Abrams (published by Matthew-Bender);

3. *Florida Dissolution of Marriage*, by the Florida Bar Continuing Legal Education; and,

4. *Florida Civil Trial Practice*, by the Florida Bar Continuing Legal Education.

You may also find other books on divorce law at the law library or local bookstore.

Lawyers

chapter 3

Whether you need an attorney will depend upon many factors, such as how comfortable you feel handling the matter yourself, whether your situation is more complicated than usual, how much opposition you get from your spouse, and whether your spouse has an attorney. It may also be advisable to hire an attorney if you encounter a judge with a hostile attitude or if your spouse gets a lawyer who wants to fight. There are no court-appointed lawyers in divorce cases, so if you want an attorney, you will have to hire one.

A general rule is that you should consider hiring an attorney whenever you reach a point where you no longer feel comfortable representing yourself. This point will vary greatly with each person, so there is no easy way to be more definite.

You should get an attorney if your spouse is in the military and is unwilling to either sign an **Answer, Waiver, and Request for Copy of Final Judgment of Dissolution of Marriage** (see form 18, p.253) or a **Marital Settlement Agreement** (forms 13, 14, or 15), or use the simplified divorce procedure that is described in Chapter 6.

Rather than asking if you *need* a lawyer, a more appropriate question is: Do you *want* a lawyer? The next section will discuss some of the pros and cons of hiring a lawyer and some of the things you may want to consider in making this decision.

DECIDING IF YOU WANT A LAWYER

One of the first questions you will want to consider (and most likely the reason you are reading this book) is: *How much will an attorney cost?* Attorneys come in all ages, shapes, sizes, sexes, racial and ethnic groups—and price ranges. For a very rough estimate, you can expect an attorney to charge anywhere from $150 to $1,000 for an uncontested divorce, and from $800 and up for a contested divorce. Lawyers usually charge an hourly rate for contested divorces, ranging from about $75 to $300 per hour. Most new (and therefore less expensive) attorneys would be quite capable of handling a simple divorce; but, if your situation became more complicated, you would probably prefer a more experienced lawyer. As a general rule, you can expect the divorce to cost more than what you think it will cost at the beginning.

Advantages to Hiring a Lawyer

The following are some of the advantages to hiring a lawyer.

- Judges and other attorneys may take you more seriously. Most judges prefer both parties to have attorneys. They feel this helps the case move in a more orderly fashion because both sides know the procedures and relevant issues. Persons representing themselves very often waste a lot of time on matters that have absolutely no bearing on the outcome of the case.

- A lawyer will serve as a *buffer* between you and your spouse. This can lead to a quicker passage through the system, by reducing the chance for emotions to take control and confuse the issues.

- Attorneys prefer to deal with other attorneys, for the same reasons listed above. However, if you become familiar with this book, and conduct yourself in a calm and proper manner, you should have no trouble. (Courtroom manners will be discussed in Chapter 5.)

- You can let your lawyer worry about all of the details. By having an attorney, you need only become generally familiar with the contents of this book, as it will be your attorney's job to file the proper papers in the correct form and to deal with the court clerks, the judge, the process server, your spouse, and your spouse's attorney.

- Lawyers provide professional assistance with problems. In the event your case is complicated, or suddenly becomes complicated, it is an advantage to have an attorney who is familiar with your case. It can also be comforting to have a lawyer to turn to for advice, and to get your questions answered.

Advantages to Representing Yourself

The following are some advantages to representing yourself without the assistance of an attorney.

- You save the cost of a lawyer.

- Sometimes judges feel more sympathetic toward a person not represented by an attorney. Sometimes this results in the unrepresented person being allowed a certain amount of leeway with the procedure rules.

- The procedure may be faster. Two of the most frequent complaints about lawyers received by the bar association involve delay in completing the case, and failure to return phone calls. Most lawyers have a heavy caseload, which sometimes results in cases being neglected for various periods of time. If you are following the progress of your own case, you will be able to push it through the system diligently.

- Selecting any attorney is not easy. As the next section shows, it is hard to know whether you are selecting an attorney with whom you will be happy.

Middle Ground

You may want to look for an attorney who will be willing to accept an hourly fee to answer your questions and give you help as you need it. This way you will save some legal costs, but still get some professional assistance.

SELECTING A LAWYER

Selecting a lawyer is a two-step process. First, you need to decide with which attorney to make an appointment. Then you need to decide if you want to hire that attorney.

Finding a Lawyer

There are several ways to locate a good lawyer. The following are some suggestions to help you locate lawyers for further consideration.

Ask a friend. A common, and frequently the best, way to find a lawyer is to ask someone you know to recommend one. This is especially helpful if the lawyer represented your friend in a divorce or other family law matter.

Lawyer referral service. You can find a referral service by looking in the Yellow Pages phone directory under *Attorney Referral Services* or *Attorneys*. This is a service that is usually operated by a bar association and is designed to match a client with an attorney handling cases in the area of law the client needs. The referral service does not guarantee the quality of work, the level of experience, nor the ability of the attorney. Finding a lawyer this way will at least connect you with one who is interested in divorce and family law matters, and probably has some experience in this area.

Yellow Pages. Check under the heading for *Attorneys* in the Yellow Pages phone directory. Many of the lawyers and law firms will place display ads here indicating their areas of practice and educational backgrounds. Look for firms or lawyers that indicate they practice in areas such as divorce, family law, or domestic relations.

Ask another lawyer. If you have used the services of an attorney in the past for some other matter (for example, a real estate closing, traffic ticket, or a will), you may want to call and ask if he or she could refer you to an attorney whose ability in the area of family law is respected.

Internet. You can search on the various search engines on the Internet. You may also be able to find a lawyer in your area through **www.findlaw.com** or **www.martindale.com**.

Evaluating a Lawyer

From your search, select three to five lawyers worthy of further consideration. Your first step will be to call each attorney's office, explain that you are interested in seeking a divorce, and ask the following questions.

- Does the attorney (or firm) handle this type of matter?

- How much will it cost? (Do not expect to get a definite answer, but he or she may be able to give you a range or an hourly rate. You will probably need to talk to the lawyer for anything more detailed.)
- How soon can you get an appointment?

If you like the answers you get, ask if you can speak to the attorney. Some offices will permit this, but others will require you to make an appointment. Make the appointment if that is what is required. Once you get in contact with the attorney (either on the phone or at the appointment), ask the following questions.

- How much will it cost?
- How will the fee be paid?
- How long has the attorney been in practice?
- How long has the attorney been in practice in Florida?
- What percentage of the attorney's cases involve divorce cases or other family law matters? (Do not expect an exact answer, but you should get a rough estimate that is at least 20%.)
- How long will it take? (Do not expect an exact answer, but the attorney should be able to give you an average range and discuss things that may make a difference.)

If you get acceptable answers to these questions, it is time to ask yourself the following questions about the lawyer.

- Do you feel comfortable talking to the lawyer?
- Is the lawyer friendly toward you?
- Does the lawyer seem confident in him- or herself?
- Does the lawyer seem to be straightforward with you, and able to explain things so you understand?

If you get satisfactory answers to all of these questions, you probably have a lawyer with whom you will be able to work. Most clients are happiest with an attorney with whom they feel comfortable.

WORKING WITH A LAWYER

In general, you will work best with your attorney if you keep an open, honest, and friendly attitude. You should also consider the following suggestions.

Ask Questions

If you want to know something or if you do not understand something, ask your attorney. If you do not understand the answer, tell your attorney and ask him or her to explain it again. There are many points of law that many lawyers do not fully understand, so you should not be embarrassed to ask questions. Many people who say they had a bad experience with a lawyer either did not ask enough questions or had a lawyer who would not take the time to explain things to them. If your lawyer is not taking the time to explain what he or she is doing, it may be time to look for a new lawyer.

Give Complete Information

Anything you tell your attorney is confidential. An attorney can lose his or her license to practice if information about your case is revealed without your permission. So do not hold back. Tell your lawyer everything, even if it does not seem important to you. There are many things that seem unimportant to a nonattorney, but can change the outcome of a case. Also, do not hold something back because you are afraid it will hurt your case. It will definitely hurt your case if your lawyer does not find out about it until in court and from your spouse's attorney, but if he or she knows about it in advance, he or she can plan to eliminate or reduce damage to your case.

Accept Reality

Listen to what your lawyer tells you about the law and the system. It will do you no good to argue because the law or the system does not work the way you think it should. For example, if your lawyer tells you that the judge cannot hear your case for two weeks, do not try demanding that he or she set a hearing tomorrow. By refusing to accept reality, you are only setting yourself up for disappointment. Remember, it is not your attorney's fault that the system is not perfect or that the law does not say what you would like it to say.

Be Patient

You will need to be patient with both the system (which is often slow, as discussed earlier) and with your attorney. Do not expect your lawyer to return your phone call within an hour. He or she may not be able to return it the same day either.

Most lawyers are very busy and overworked. It is rare that an attorney can maintain a full caseload and still make each client feel like his or her only client.

Talk to the Secretary

Your lawyer's secretary can be a valuable source of information. Often the secretary will be able to answer your questions and you will not get a bill for the secretary's time.

Let Your Attorney Handle Your Spouse

It is part of your lawyer's job to communicate with your spouse or with your spouse's lawyer. Let the lawyer do his or her job. Many lawyers have had clients lose or damage their cases when the client decides to say or do something on his or her own.

Be On Time

Be on time to appointments with your lawyer and to court hearings.

Keep Your Case Moving

Many lawyers operate on the old principle of *the squeaking wheel gets the oil.* Work on a case tends to get put off until a deadline is near, an emergency develops, or the client calls. Many lawyers take more cases than can be effectively handled in order to earn the income they desire. Your task is to become a squeaking wheel that does not squeak too much. Whenever you talk to your lawyer, ask the following questions.

- What is the next step?
- When do you expect it to be done?
- When should I talk to you next?

If you do not hear from the lawyer when you expect, call the following day. Do not remind him or her of the missed call—just ask how things are going.

FIRING YOUR LAWYER

If you can no longer work with your lawyer, it is time to either go it alone or get a new attorney. You will need to send your lawyer a letter stating that you no longer desire his or her services and are discharging him or her from your case. Also state that you will be coming by his or her office the following day to pick up your file. The attorney does not have to give you his or her own notes or other work he or she has in progress, but he or she must give you the essential contents of your file (such as copies of papers already filed or prepared and billed for, and any documents that you provided). If he or she refuses to give you your file for any reason, contact the Florida Bar about filing a complaint, or *grievance,* against the lawyer. Of course, you will need to settle any remaining fees charged for work that the lawyer has already done.

Evaluating Your Situation

chapter 4

The following things should be done or considered before you begin the divorce process.

RELATIONSHIP WITH YOUR SPOUSE

You need to evaluate your situation with respect to your spouse. If you both have not already agreed to get a divorce, what kind of reaction do you expect from him or her? That expected reaction can determine how you proceed. If he or she reacts in a rational manner, you can probably use the simplified or uncontested procedure. However, if you expect an extremely emotional and possibly violent reaction, you will need to take steps to protect yourself, your children, and your property. You will also have to start out expecting to use the contested procedure.

NOTE: *Read the section in Chapter 12 on protecting yourself if you expect a violent reaction from your spouse.*

Unless you and your spouse have already decided together to get a divorce, you do not want your spouse to know you are thinking about filing for divorce. This is a defense tactic, although it may not seem that way at first. If your spouse thinks you are planning a divorce, he or she may do things to prevent you from getting a fair result. These things include withdrawing money from bank accounts, hiding information about income, and hiding assets. So do not let on until you have collected all of the information you will need and are about to file with the court, or until you are prepared to protect yourself from violence, if necessary.

> ***Warning:*** Tactics such as withdrawing money from bank accounts and hiding assets are potentially dangerous. If you try any of these things, you risk looking like the bad guy before the judge. This can result in anything from having disputed matters resolved in your spouse's favor, to being ordered to produce the assets (or be jailed for contempt of court).

Theoretically, the system would prefer you to keep evidence of the assets (such as photographs, sales receipts, or bank statements) to present to the judge if your spouse hides them. Your spouse will then be the bad guy and risk being jailed. However, once your spouse has taken assets and hidden them, or sold them and spent the money, even a contempt order may not get the money or assets back. If you determine that you need to get the assets in order to keep your spouse from hiding or disposing of them, be sure you keep them in a safe place, and disclose them on your **FINANCIAL AFFIDAVIT** (form 8 or form 9). Do not dispose of them. If your spouse claims you took them, you can explain to the judge why you were afraid that your spouse would dispose of them and that you merely got them out of his or her reach.

FINANCIAL INFORMATION CHECKLIST

It is extremely important that you collect all of the financial information you can get. This information should include originals or copies of the following.

- ❏ Your most recent income tax return (and your spouse's, if you filed separately)
- ❏ The most recent W-2 tax forms for yourself and your spouse
- ❏ Any income reporting papers (for interest, stock dividends, etc.)
- ❏ Your spouse's most recent paystub, hopefully showing year-to-date earnings (otherwise, try to get copies of all paystubs since the beginning of the year)

- ❑ Deeds to all real estate and titles to cars, boats, or other vehicles
- ❑ Your and your spouse's will
- ❑ Life insurance policies
- ❑ Stocks, bonds, or other investment papers
- ❑ Pension or retirement fund papers and statements
- ❑ Health insurance card and papers
- ❑ Bank account or credit union statements
- ❑ Your spouse's Social Security number, driver's license number, date and place of birth, and your date and place of marriage
- ❑ Names, addresses, and phone numbers of your spouse's employer, close friends, and family members
- ❑ Credit card statements, mortgage documents, and other credit and debt papers
- ❑ A list of vehicles, furniture, appliances, tools, etc., owned by you and your spouse (See page 30 for forms and a detailed discussion of what to include.)
- ❑ Copies of bills or receipts for recurring, regular expenses, such as electric, gas or other utilities, car insurance, etc.
- ❑ Copies of bills, receipts, insurance forms, or medical records for any unusual medical expenses (including for recurring or continuous medical conditions) for yourself, your spouse, or your children
- ❑ Receipts or a list of child care, educational, and extracurricular expenses for your children
- ❑ Any papers showing what you and your spouse earn, own, or owe
- ❑ The Social Security number, and date and place of birth for each child

Make copies of as many of these papers as possible and keep them in a safe and private place (where your spouse will not find them). Try to make copies of new papers as they come in, especially as you get close to filing court papers, and as you get close to a court hearing.

PROPERTY AND DEBTS

This section is designed to help you get a rough idea of where things stand regarding the division of your property and to prepare you for completing some of the court papers you will need to file. The following sections will deal with the questions of your debts, child support, custody, visitation, and alimony. If you are still not sure whether you want a divorce, these sections may help you to decide.

Property

This section basically assists you in completing the **PROPERTY INVENTORY**. (see form 1, p.178.) This form is a list of all of your property and key information about that property. First, you need to understand how property is divided.

Marital and nonmarital assets. Under Florida's *equitable distribution* law, the assets and debts of the marriage are divided in a way that is *fair* (this does not necessarily mean *equal).* Assets and debts are separated into two categories: *marital property* (meaning it is both your *and* your spouse's) and *nonmarital property* (meaning it is yours *or* your spouse's alone). In making this distinction, the following rules apply.

- If the asset or debt was acquired after the date you were married, it is presumed to be a marital asset or debt. It is up to you or your spouse to prove otherwise.
- A nonmarital asset or debt is one that was acquired before the date of your marriage. It is also a nonmarital asset if you acquired it through a gift or inheritance (as long as it was not a gift from your spouse). Income from nonmarital property is also nonmarital property.

  Example: Rent you receive from an investment property you had before you got married is nonmarital property.

  If you exchange one of these assets or debts after your marriage, it is still nonmarital.

> ***Example:*** You had a $6,000 car before you got married. After the marriage, you traded it for a different $6,000 car. The new car is still nonmarital property.

Finally, you and your spouse may sign a written agreement that certain assets and debts are to be considered nonmarital or marital.

- Marital assets and debts are those acquired during your marriage, even if they were acquired by you or your spouse individually. This also includes the increase in value of a nonmarital asset during the marriage or due to the use of marital funds to pay for or improve the property. All rights accrued during the marriage in pension, retirement, profit-sharing, insurance, and similar plans are marital assets. One spouse can make a gift of nonmarital property to the other spouse, thereby making it marital property.

- Real estate that is in both names is considered marital property, and it is up to the spouse claiming otherwise to prove it.

- Finally, whether an asset or debt is marital or nonmarital and the value of any asset is determined as of the date of the settlement agreement or the date the **PETITION** was filed, whichever is first.

The **PROPERTY INVENTORY** (form 1), **DEBT INVENTORY** (form 2, p.179), and the instructions that follow, call for a rather specific, detailed listing of property and debt items. Some of these will be grouped together and listed as a single amount in the **PETITION** and **FINANCIAL AFFIDAVIT**. However, it is still a good idea to have a more detailed list, such as that provided by using form 1 and form 2. You will notice that the **PROPERTY INVENTORY** (form 1) is divided into nine columns, designated as follows.

- Column (1): "N-M." You will check the box in this column if that piece of property is *nonmarital* property, as described earlier. (Also see Appendix A, Florida Statutes, Section 61.076, on "Equitable Distribution.") Leave this column blank if that piece of property is marital property.

- Column (2): "Description." In this column, describe the property. A discussion regarding what information should go in this column will follow.

- Column (3): "ID#." Write in the serial number, account number, or other number that will help clearly identify that piece of property.

- Column (4): "Value." This is for the current market value of the property.

- Column (5): "Balance Owed." This will show how much money is owed on the property, if any.

- Column (6): "Equity." Subtract the "Balance Owed" from the "Value." This will show how much the property is worth to you (your *equity*).

- Column (7): "OWNER H-W-J." This column will show the current legal owner of the property. (H) designates the husband, (W) the wife, and (J) is for jointly owned property (in both of your names).

- Column (8): "H." This column will be checked for those pieces of property you expect the husband will keep.

- Column (9): "W." This column is for the property you expect the wife will keep.

Use columns (1) through (7) to list your property, including the following.

Cash. List the name of the bank or credit union and the account number for each account. This includes savings, checking accounts, and certificates of deposit (CDs). The balance of each account should be listed in the columns entitled "Value" and "Equity." (Leave the "Balance Owed" column blank.) Make copies of the most recent bank statements for each account.

Stocks and bonds. All stocks, bonds, or other paper investments should be listed. Write down the number of shares and the name of the company or other organization that issued them. Also, copy any notation such as *common* or *preferred* stock or shares. This information can be obtained from the stock certificate itself or from a statement from the stock broker. Make a copy of the certificate or the statement.

Real estate. List each piece of *real property* you and your spouse own. The description might include a street address for the property, a subdivision name and lot number, or anything that lets you know to what piece of property you are referring. There probably will not be an ID number, although you might use the county's tax number. Real estate (or any other property) may be in both of your names (joint), in your spouse's name alone, or in your name alone. The only way to know for sure is to look at the deed to the property. (If you cannot find a copy of the deed, try to find mortgage papers or payment coupons, homeowners insurance papers, or a property tax assessment notice.)

The owners of property are usually referred to on the deed as the *grantees.* In assigning a value to the property, consider its *market value*—how much you could probably sell the property for. This might be what similar houses in your neighborhood have sold for recently. You might also consider how much you paid for the property or for how much the property is insured. DO NOT use the tax assessment value, as this is usually considerably lower than the market value.

Vehicles. This category includes cars, trucks, motor homes, recreational vehicles (RVs), motorcycles, boats, trailers, airplanes, and any other means of transportation for which the state requires a title and registration. Your description should include the following information (which can usually be found on the title or on the vehicle itself):

- the year it was made;
- the make (this is the name of the manufacturer, such as Ford, Honda, Chris Craft, etc.);
- the model (For example, you know it is a Ford; but is it a Mustang, a Taurus, or an Explorer? The model may be a name, a number, a series of letters, or a combination of these.); and,
- the serial number or vehicle identification number (VIN). (This is most likely found on the vehicle, as well as on the title or registration.)

Make a copy of the title or registration. Regarding a value, you can go to the public library and ask to look at the *blue book* for cars, trucks, or whatever it is you are looking for. A blue book (it may actually be yellow, black, or any other color) gives the average values for used vehicles. Your librarian can help you find what you need. Another source is the classified advertising section of a newspaper to see for what price similar vehicles are selling. You might also try calling a dealer to see if he or she can give you a rough idea of the value. Be sure you take into consideration the condition of the vehicle.

Furniture. List all furniture as specifically as possible. You should include the type of piece (such as sofa, coffee table, etc.), the color, and if you know it, the manufacturer, line name, or the style. Furniture usually will not have a serial number, although if you find one, be sure to write it on the list. Just estimate a value, unless you know what it is worth.

Appliances, electronic equipment, yard machines, etc. This category includes such things as refrigerators, lawn mowers, and power tools. Again, estimate a value, unless you are familiar enough with them to simply know what they are worth. There are too many different makes, models, accessories, and age factors to be able to figure out a value otherwise. These items will probably have a make, model, and serial number on them. You may have to look on the back, bottom, or other hidden place for the serial number, but try to find it.

Jewelry and other valuables. You do not need to list inexpensive costume jewelry. You can plan on keeping your own personal watches, rings, etc. However, if you own an expensive piece, you should include it in your list, along with an estimated value. Be sure to include silverware, original art, gold, coin collections, etc. Again, be as detailed and specific as possible.

Life insurance with cash surrender value. This is any life insurance policy that you may cash in or borrow against and therefore has value. If you cannot find a cash surrender value in the papers you have, call the insurance company and ask.

Other big ticket items. This is simply a general reference to anything of significant value that does not fit in one of the categories already discussed. Examples might be a portable spa, an above-ground swimming pool, golf clubs, guns, pool tables, camping or fishing equipment, or farm animals or machinery.

Pensions and military benefits. The division of pensions or military and retirement benefits can be a complicated matter. Whenever these types of benefits are involved and you cannot agree on how to divide them, you will need to consult an attorney or CPA to determine the value of the benefits and how they should be divided. (Be sure to read the section in Chapter 12 on pension plans.) To divide these plans, complicated and highly technical paperwork must be completed and submitted to the court and the employer involved. You will need an attorney who is experienced in this area to handle the paperwork.

What not to list. You will not need to list your clothing and other personal effects. Pots and pans, dishes, and cooking utensils ordinarily do not need to be listed, unless they have some unusually high value.

Once you have completed your list, go back through it and try to determine who should end up with each item. The ideal situation is for both you and your spouse to go through the list together and divide things up fairly. However, if this is not possible, you will need to offer a reasonable settlement to the judge. Consider each item and make a check-mark in either column (8) or (9) to designate whether that item should go to the husband or wife. You may make the following assumptions:

- your nonmarital property will go to you;
- your spouse's nonmarital property will go to your spouse;
- you should get the items that only you use;
- your spouse should get the items only used by your spouse; and,
- the remaining items should be divided, evening out the total value of all the marital property, and taking into consideration who would really want that item.

To somewhat equally divide your property (your marital property), you first need to know what the total value of your property is. First of all, do not count the value of the nonmarital items. Add the remaining amounts in the "Equity" column of form 1, which will give you an approximate value of all marital property.

When it comes time for the hearing, you and your spouse may be arguing over some or all of the items on your list. This is when you will be glad that you made copies of the documents relating to the property on your list. Arguments over the value of property may need to be resolved by hiring appraisers to set a value; however, you will have to pay the appraiser a fee. Dividing your property will be discussed further in later chapters. (See Chapter 9 for information on dividing property in contested cases.)

Debts This section relates to the **DEBT INVENTORY** that will list your debts. (see form 2, p.179.) Although there are cases in which, for example, the wife gets a car but the husband is ordered to make the payments, generally whoever gets the property also gets the debt owed on that property. This seems to be a fair arrangement in most cases.

On form 2 you will list each debt owed by you or your spouse. As with nonmarital property, there is also nonmarital debt. This is any debt incurred before you were married that is yours alone. Form 2 contains a column for "N-M" debts that should be checked for each nonmarital debt. You will be responsible for your nonmarital debts and your spouse will be responsible for his or hers.

> ***Warning:*** If you and your spouse are jointly responsible for a debt, you are not relieved of your obligation to pay just because your spouse agrees to pay (or is ordered to pay) the debt in the divorce proceeding. If your spouse does not pay, the creditor can still come after you for payment. You would then need to take your spouse to court to get him or her to reimburse you.

To complete the **DEBT INVENTORY** (form 2), list each debt as follows.

- Column (1): "N-M." Check if this is a nonmarital debt. Leave this column blank if it is a marital debt.
- Column (2): "Creditor." Write in the name and address of the creditor (the bank, company, or person to which the debt is owed).
- Column (3): "Account No." Write in the account, loan, or mortgage number.
- Column (4): "Notes." Write in any notes to help identify what the loan was for (such as "Christmas gifts," "vacation," etc.).
- Column (5): "Monthly Payment." Write in the amount of the monthly payment.
- Column (6): "Balance Owed." Write in the balance still owed on the loan.
- Column (7): "Date." Write in the date (approximately) when the loan was made.

- Column (8): "Owner H-W-J." Note whether the account is in the husband's name (H), the wife's name (W), or jointly in both names (J).

- Columns (9) and (10): "H" and "W." Note who will be responsible for the debt after the divorce. Each of you will keep your nonmarital debts, and the remainder should be divided, taking into consideration who will keep the property the loan was for, and equally dividing the debt. (See Chapter 9 about dividing debts in contested cases.)

CHILD CUSTODY AND VISITATION

As with everything else in divorce, things are ideal when both parties can agree on the question of custody of the children. Generally, the judge will accept any agreement you reach, provided it does not appear that your agreement will cause harm to your children. The Florida legislature has attempted to replace the traditional terms *custody* and *visitation* with terms such as *parental responsibility*, *primary residential responsibility*, *secondary parental responsibility*, and *time sharing*; but judges, lawyers, and even some of the supreme court forms still use the traditional words.

With respect to child custody, the Florida law makes the following significant statement:

> *It is the public policy of this state to assure that each minor child has frequent and continuing contact with both parents after the parents separate or the marriage of the parties is dissolved and to encourage parents to share the rights and responsibilities of childrearing. After considering all relevant facts, the father of the child shall be given the same consideration as the mother in determining the primary residence of a child irrespective of the age or sex of the child. (Fla. Stat., Sec. 61.13(2)(b)1.)*

In spite of this modern philosophy voiced by the Florida legislature, you may find that many judges are from the old school of thought on this subject and believe that (all things being equal) a young child is better off with the mother. Because of these statements in the law, the judge may go to great lengths to find that all things are not equal, so as to justify a decision to award custody to the mother. It happens every day throughout the state. This is a reality you may have to face.

The Florida law also states that:

> *The court shall order that the parental responsibility for a minor child be shared by both parents unless the court finds that shared parental responsibility would be detrimental to the child. (Fla. Stat., Sec. 61.13(2)(b)2.)*

This indicates that the law favors what is commonly known as *joint custody*. While it is a great idea in its concept, it is usually not a very practical one. Very few parents can put aside their anger with each other to agree on what is best for their child. Joint custody merely leads to more fighting. Even if joint custody is ordered, a child can only have one primary residence. So the judge must still decide with which parent the child will live, as well as how decisions will be made regarding such things as education and medical and dental care.

Custody Factors

If you and your spouse cannot agree on how these matters will be handled, you will be leaving this important decision to the judge. The judge cannot possibly know your child as well as you and your spouse, so it makes sense to work this out yourselves. Otherwise, you are leaving the decision to a stranger.

If the judge must decide the question of custody, he or she will consider the following factors:

- which parent is most likely to allow the other to visit with the child and to develop and maintain a close and continuing parent/child relationship;
- the love, affection, and other emotional ties existing between the child and each parent;
- the ability and willingness of each parent to provide the child with food, clothing, medical care, and other material needs;
- the length of time the child has lived with either parent in a stable environment;
- the permanence, as a family unit, of the proposed custodial home (this relates to where one of the parties will be getting remarried immediately after the divorce, or more often, to change of custody petitions at a later date);

- the moral fitness of each parent;
- the mental and physical health of each parent;
- the home, school, and community record of the child;
- the preference of the child, providing the child is of sufficient intelligence and understanding; and,
- any other fact the judge decides is relevant.

It is difficult to predict the outcome of a custody battle. There are too many factors and individual circumstances to make such a guess. The only exception is where one parent is clearly unfit and the other can prove it. Drug abuse is one of the most common charges against a spouse, but unless there has been an arrest and conviction, it is difficult to prove to a judge. In general, do not charge your spouse with being unfit unless you can prove it. Judges are not impressed with unfounded allegations; they can do more harm than good.

If your children are older (not infants), it may be a good idea to seriously consider their preference for with whom they would like to live. Your fairness and respect for their wishes may benefit you in the long run. Just be sure that you keep in close contact with them and visit them often.

Visitation

Visitation is the time a child spends with the parent who does not have custody (or primary parental responsibility). It can be any length of time, from a few hours per week to an entire summer. Visitation is presumed to be in a child's best interest, and it will be up to the parent with custody to prove otherwise if he or she wants visitation limited or denied.

The most common visitation schedule is alternate weekends and one weekday each week. You and your spouse should find a schedule that makes your child comfortable and allows both of you a significant amount of time with your child. You should take into consideration your child's age and schedule.

In addition to weekly visitation, you will need to work out a schedule for sharing holidays, school vacations, birthdays, and other important events. It is common to alternate holidays. (You have the child for Thanksgiving this year, your spouse has the child for Thanksgiving next year, etc.)

The following is a list of holidays you may want to consider in preparing a visitation schedule. Some of these are listed because they are days that the schools in Florida are commonly closed. Others are listed to remind you of other days that may be important to your family.

- Your child's birthday
- Your birthday
- Your spouse's birthday
- Labor Day
- Rosh Hashanah
- Yom Kippur
- Columbus Day
- Halloween
- Thanksgiving Day
- Hanukkah
- Christmas Eve
- Christmas Day
- School winter vacation
- New Year's Eve
- New Year's Day
- Martin Luther King Jr. Day
- President's Day
- Valentine's Day
- St. Patrick's Day
- Easter
- School spring vacation
- Passover
- Mother's Day
- Father's Day
- Fourth of July
- Other relatives' birthdays
- Other nonschool days
- Summer vacation
- Any other holiday or day important to you, your spouse, or your child

If you and your spouse cannot agree on how these matters will be handled, you will be leaving this important decision up to the judge. The judge cannot possibly know your child as well as you and your spouse do, so it makes more sense for the two of you to work this out. Otherwise, you are leaving the decision up to a stranger.

A visitation schedule is not written in stone. You and your spouse will need to work together and will need to be flexible. You and your spouse can make any adjustments to the schedule as long as you both agree to do so. For example, you might want to go to a party on your scheduled weekend with the kids or you might want to take your children to a family reunion on your spouse's scheduled weekend. These same type of things will come up for your spouse too. Plan on being in frequent contact with your spouse about the schedule. Make an effort to be flexible and polite. Try to avoid involving your children in any disputes.

CHILD SUPPORT

Once again, the judge will probably go along with any agreement you and your spouse reach, as long as he or she is satisfied that the child will be adequately cared for. Even if you have an agreement, you will still need to file the **NOTICE OF FILING CHILD SUPPORT GUIDELINES WORKSHEET**. (see form 11, p.216.) To help you get a rough idea of the amount of child support to expect, make a copy of form 11 and fill it out using the information and instructions on page 56. Later, after you have more accurate income information, you will complete the copy of form 11 to file with the court clerk. As you prepare your form to file, you will refer back to this section for instructions on completing the form. Some of the information required for form 11 comes from the **FAMILY LAW FINANCIAL AFFIDAVIT** (form 8 or form 9). When an agreement on child support cannot be reached, the following procedure will be used.

How Child Support is Determined

Two factors are used to determine the amount of support: (1) the needs of the child and (2) the financial ability of each parent to meet those needs. Florida has established a formula to be used in calculating both the needs of the child and each parent's ability to meet those needs. The following steps are used in determining the proper amount of support.

1. You and your spouse each provide proof of your *gross* incomes.
2. Taxes and other deductions are allowed to determine each of your *net* incomes.
3. Your net incomes are added together to arrive at your *combined income.*
4. The combined income and the number of children you have are used to establish the children's needs. (This is done by reading a chart.)
5. The net income of the parent without custody is divided by the combined income. This gives that parent's percentage of the combined income.
6. That percentage is multiplied by the needs of the children to arrive at the amount of support to be paid by the parent without custody.

This procedure can be used by most people. However, if you and your spouse's combined income is less than $650 per month, these guidelines cannot be used. If your combined income is over $10,000 per month, you will need to add a percentage of the amount over $10,000, depending upon the number of children.

Also, the judge may depart from the guidelines by up to 5%, after considering the needs of the child and each parent's age, station in life, standard of living, and financial status. A written reason must be given in the **FINAL JUDGMENT** (form 45 or 46) if the judge departs by more than 5%. These guidelines will be discussed more below, and their text can be found in Appendix A. (Fla. Stat., Sec. 61.30.)

The judge can also adjust the amount of child support in consideration of the following factors:

- extraordinary medical, psychological, educational, or dental expenses;
- independent income of the child, but not including supplemental security income for a child;
- the payment of support for a parent that regularly has been paid and for which there is a demonstrated need;
- seasonal variations in one or both parents' incomes or expenses;
- the age of the child, taking into account the greater needs of older children;
- special needs, such as costs associated with the disability of a child, that have traditionally been met by the family even though fulfilling those needs will cause the support to exceed the guidelines;
- the total available assets of the parents and the child;
- the impact of the Internal Revenue Service dependency exemption and waiver of that exemption (the judge may order the custodial parent to execute a waiver of the exemption if the noncustodial parent is current in support payments);
- if the child support guidelines would require the noncustodial parent to pay more than 55% of his or her gross income for a single support order; or,

- any other adjustment needed to achieve an equitable result, such as to allow for a reasonable and necessary expense or debt that the parties jointly incurred during the marriage.

Also, when the noncustodial parent has visitation for a *substantial amount of time*, support must be adjusted based upon:

- the amount of time each child will spend with each parent;
- the needs of each child;
- the direct and indirect financial expenses for each child (Direct expenses includes such things as food, clothing, and school activities. Indirect expenses include such things as mortgage, rent, utilities, and automobile expenses);
- the comparative income of each parent, considering all relevant factors, as provided in Section 61.30(2)(a) of the Florida Statutes;
- the station in life of each parent and each child;
- the standard of living experienced by the entire family during the marriage; or,
- the financial status and ability of each parent to pay.

Most cases will be determined by the parents' incomes, using the child support tables in the Florida Statutes. The only exception is if you or your spouse can show that one or more of the factors discussed apply to your case.

Child Support Guidelines Worksheet

The **NOTICE OF FILING CHILD SUPPORT GUIDELINES WORKSHEET** is used to calculate the proper amount of child support. (see form 11, p.216.) On the second and third pages of form 11, you will see that there is a column for the "Father," a column for the "Mother," and a column for the "Total." Be sure to fill in the information under the proper column. This form has fairly detailed instructions for each item, which should be sufficient for you to complete the form. However, if you have any difficulty, the following instructions and examples may further assist you.

- Complete the top portion of the form according to the instructions at the beginning of Chapter 5.

- In the first unnumbered paragraph, type in your name.

- Fill in the Certificate of Service section to indicate how and when you sent or delivered a copy of the form to your spouse (or his or her attorney); fill in your spouse's (or spouse's attorney's) name, address, and telephone information. The form requires that you fill in the date again.

- Sign your name on the line marked "Signature of Party," and fill in your name, address, and telephone information below the signature line.

- In item "1. Present Net Monthly Income," fill in the net income figures from line 27 of your **FAMILY LAW FINANCIAL AFFIDAVIT** (form 8 or 9), and from line 27 of your spouse's **FAMILY LAW FINANCIAL AFFIDAVIT** (form 8 or 9). Add these amounts together, and fill in the total in the column marked "Total." (If you are just evaluating you situation, you will not have your spouse's **FAMILY LAW FINANCIAL AFFIDAVIT**, so you will need to use your best estimate of your spouse's net income.)

  EXAMPLE: The father's net income is $1,800 per month. The mother's net income is $1,200 per month. This would give a total income of $3,000 (1,800 + 1,200).

- In item "2. Basic Monthly Obligation," fill in the number of children subject to the support order on the line beginning "There is (are) *{number}* _____ minor child(ren)..." Next, turn to the child support guidelines chart in Appendix A. Read down the first column to your total income, then read across to the column for the number of children for which support is owed. Write in this amount from the chart.

  EXAMPLE: With a total income of $3,000 per month, find the figure "3,000" in the left column of the child support guidelines chart, then read across for the number of children. For one child the needs are $644 per month; for two children the needs are $1,001; for three children the needs are $1,252, etc. For this example, assume you have two children, so their monthly needs are $1,001.

- In item "3. Percent of Financial Responsibility," you will determine each parent's percentage share of the total income. To get your share, divide your net income from item 1 by the total income in item 1.

  EXAMPLE: To get the father's percentage, divide $1,800 by $3,000, which will give you .6 or 60%. To get the mother's percentage, divide $1,200 by $3,000, which will give you .4 or 40%. The father's percentage goes in column A and the mother's percentage in column B. (You will note that this item of the form calls for a percentage, which means dropping the decimal point. Using our example, ".4" would be shown in item 3, column B, as "40%," not as ".4%.")

- In item "4. Share of Basic Monthly Obligation," multiply the needs (or basic obligation) by the father's percentage share ($1,001 x .6 = $600.60). This gives the amount of the children's needs the father would be expected to contribute. Next, multiply the needs by the mother's percentage share ($1,001 x .4 = $400.40). This is the amount the mother would be expected to contribute. Write in the contribution of you and your spouse in the appropriate columns in item 4.

- In item "5a. 75% of Monthly Child Care Costs," take the total cost of monthly child care and multiply it by .75; fill in the answer.

- In item "5b. Total Monthly Child(ren)'s Health Insurance Cost," if you or you spouse are paying for health insurance for your children, fill in the monthly cost of the insurance. This is only the portion of the insurance cost related to the children.

- In item "5c. Total Monthly Child(ren)'s Noncovered Medical, Dental and Prescription Medication Costs," fill in either the actual or estimated monthly cost of these expenses.

- In item "5d. Total Monthly Child Care & Health Costs," add the amounts from items 5a, 5b, and 5c, and fill in the total.

- In item "6. Additional Support Payments," multiply the figure in 5d by the father's percentage from item 4, column A. Fill in the total in item 6, column A. Next, multiply the figure in 5d by the mother's percentage from item 4, column B. Fill in the total in item 6, column B.

- In item "7a. Monthly child care payments actually made," fill in the amount of child care paid by each party in the appropriate column.

- In item "7b. Monthly health insurance payments actually made," fill in the amount of health insurance payments paid by each party in the appropriate column.

- In item 7c., fill in any "Other payments/credits actually made for any noncovered medical, dental and prescription medication expenses of the child(ren) not ordered to be separately paid on a percentage basis."

- In item "8. Total Support Payments actually made," add the amounts from items 7a, 7b, and 7c, and fill in the totals in each column.

- In item "9. Minimum Child Support Obligation for Each Parent," for each column, add the amounts from item 4 and item 6; then subtract the amount in item 8.

NOTE: *Whether you need to complete the remainder of this form will depend upon your visitation arrangement. If the noncustodial parent will have overnight visitation less than 146 days in the year, you do not need to complete any more of this form. The amount in item 9 will be the child support amount. (Even if this is the case, be sure to read the last instruction for this form regarding deviations from the child support guidelines.) However, if the noncustodial parent will have 146 or more days of overnight visitation, you will need to complete items 10 through 21 as follows.*

- In item 10, take the basic monthly obligation from item 2 and multiply it by 1.5, and write in the answer.

- In item "11. Increased Basic Obligation for each parent," multiply the number in item 10 by the percentage in item 3a, and fill in the answer in item 11a. Next, multiply the number in item 10 by the percentage in item 3b, and fill in the answer in item 11b.

- In item "12. Percentage of overnight stays with each parent," fill in the number of nights the children stay with each parent. Take the number of nights with the father, multiply by 100, then divide by 365. Fill in the answer in item 12a.

Example: If the children will spend 150 nights with the father, you would multiply 150 by 100, which would give you 15,000. Then you would divide 15,000 by 365. That would give you 41.09, which can be rounded off to 41%. Next, take the number of nights with the mother, multiply by 100, then divide by 365. Fill in the answer in item 12b.

- In item 13, multiply the number in item 11a by the percentage in item 12b, and fill in the answer in item 13a. Then multiply the number in item 11b by the percentage in item 12a and fill in the answer in item 13b.

- In item "14a. Total Monthly Child Care Costs," fill in the monthly child care costs if you or your spouse are paying for child care.

- In item "14b. Total Monthly Child(ren)'s Health Insurance Costs," fill in the monthly insurance cost if you or your spouse are paying for health insurance for the children. This is only the portion of insurance that relates to the children.

- In item "14c. Total Monthly Child(ren)'s Noncovered Medical, Dental and Prescription Medication Costs," fill in either the actual or estimated monthly expenses for these items.

- In item "14d. Total Monthly Child Care & Health Costs," add the amounts from items 14a, 14b, and 14c, and fill in the total.

- In item "15. Additional Support Payments," multiply the number in item 14d by the percentage in item 3a and fill in the answer in item 15a. Next, multiply the number in item 14d by the percentage in item 3b and fill in the answer in item 15b.

- In item "16a. Monthly child care payments actually made," fill in the amount of child care paid by each party in the appropriate column.

- In item "16b. Monthly health insurance payments actually made," fill in the amount of health insurance payments paid by each party in the appropriate column.

- In item 16c., fill in any "Other payments/credits actually made for any noncovered medical, dental and prescription medication expenses of the child(ren) not ordered to be separately paid on a percentage basis."

- In item "17. Total Support Payments actually made," add the amounts from items 16a, 16b, and 16c, and fill in the totals in each column.

- In item "18. Total Additional Support Transfer Amount," for each column, take the amount in item 15 and subtract the amount in item 17. Fill in the answer. If the answer is a negative number, enter zero.

- In item "19. Total Child Support Owed from Father to Mother," add item 13a and item 18a, and fill in the total.

- In item "20. Total Child Support Owed from Mother to Father," add item 13b and item 18b Fill in the total.

- In item "21. Actual Child Support to Be Paid," compare items 19 and 20. Subtract the smaller amount from the larger amount. Enter the result in the column for the parent who owes the larger amount of support.

- On the fourth page of form 11, you will see a section with the heading "Adjustments to Guidelines Amount." In most cases you will check line "b. Deviation from the guidelines amount is NOT requested." However, if your child has special needs (such as because of a physical or mental handicap, because the child is in a special private school for gifted children, etc.), or there are any other reasons you think the child support guidelines are not giving a proper result, you can check line "a," and file a **MOTION TO DEVIATE FROM CHILD SUPPORT GUIDELINES**. (see form 12, p.220.)

Motion to Deviate from Child Support Guidelines

If there are unusual circumstances in your case that would make the regular child support guidelines insufficient, you can ask the judge to deviate from the guidelines. You do this by checking line "a" in item 10 of the **CHILD SUPPORT GUIDELINES WORKSHEET** (see form 11, p.216) and filing a **MOTION TO DEVIATE FROM CHILD SUPPORT GUIDELINES**. (see form 12, p.220.) If you read form 12, it will tell you what types of situations will justify deviating from the guidelines.

If one party voluntarily reduces his or her income or quits a job, the judge can determine that it was done to avoid child support and refuse to recognize the reduction or loss of income. The judge will then order support as if that party were still receiving the income. This is called *imputed income*. An exception is made where the parent is required to take such an action to stay home and care for a young, ill, or handicapped child. If this question arises, the judge will decide whether the parent needs to stay home. If you are the one in this situation, be ready to explain your reasons.

Use the following instructions to complete the **MOTION TO DEVIATE FROM CHILD SUPPORT GUIDELINES** (form 12).

- Complete the top portion of the form according to the instructions at the beginning of Chapter 5, page 56.

- In the line immediately above "Section I," check "Petitioner."

- In "Section I," if you are requesting more child support than is called for by the guidelines, check the line for "a." Check any of items 1 through 14 under "a" that apply.

  If you are requesting less child support than is called for by the guidelines, check the line for "b." Check any items 1 through 15 under "b" that apply. Under either of these choices are a few blank lines where you need to explain the items you select. If necessary, you can add additional sheets for your explanation.

- Complete "Section II. Income and Assets of Child(ren) Common to Both Parties," and "Section III. Expenses for Child(ren) Common to Both Parties." Just follow the instructions on the form itself.

  NOTE: *In order for the judge to consider your request to deviate from the guidelines, you will need to file a* **FAMILY LAW FINANCIAL AFFIDAVIT** *(form 8 or 9) and the* **NOTICE OF FILING CHILD SUPPORT GUIDELINES WORKSHEET** *(form 11).*

- Fill in the certificate of service section (beginning with "I have filed, ...") to indicate how and when you sent or delivered a copy of the form to your spouse (or his or her attorney); fill in your spouse's (or his or her attorney's) name, address, and telephone information.

- Sign your name before a notary public or court clerk on the line marked "Signature," and fill in the date, your name, address, and telephone information on the lines indicated.

- File this form with the court clerk.

ALIMONY

Either the husband or the wife may be granted alimony. (See Appendix A for the factors involved in deciding the issue of alimony.) (Fla. Stat., Sec. 61.08.) In reality, there are few cases in which a wife will be ordered to pay alimony to her husband.

Types of Alimony

There are three types of alimony.

1. *Rehabilitative.* This is for a limited period of time and is to enable one of the spouses to get the education or training necessary to find a job. This is usually awarded when one of the parties has not been working during the marriage.

2. *Permanent.* This continues for a long period of time, possibly until the death of the party receiving the alimony. This is typically awarded when one of the parties is unable to work due to age, or on account of a physical or mental illness.

3. *Lump sum.* This is where a fixed sum of alimony is set and is payable either all at once, or in a few installments. It is really more like a property division than true alimony.

During the past decade, some Florida courts have granted what is known as *bridge-the-gap alimony.* Although this is not provided for by the Florida Statutes, the various Florida district courts of appeal have upheld such awards, although with sometimes differing views of when such an award is appropriate. However, the Florida supreme court has not yet ruled on this issue. This type of alimony is for the stated purpose of assisting one spouse "in making the transition from a marital to a single state" (*Shea v. Shea*, 572 So.2d. 558 (1st DCA 1990)). It is usually termed *rehabilitative alimony*, but has been awarded in situations where the spouse receiving it is already employed and is not expected to acquire any rehabilitative education or training. Bridge-the-gap alimony has also been awarded in cases where the marriage was of short duration, where alimony would not traditionally have been awarded.

How Alimony Is Determined

There are really two parts to deciding a request for alimony.

1. Should alimony be awarded?
2. If so, what type of alimony, and how much should be awarded?

The only specific statement in the Florida Statutes as to when alimony may be awarded refers to cases involving "the adultery of a spouse and the circumstances thereof..." However, the factors to be considered in determining the type and amount of alimony also give clues as to when alimony might be awarded.

The law requires the judge to consider the following factors:

- the standard of living established during the marriage;
- the length of time the parties were married;
- the age and the physical and emotional condition of each party;
- the financial resources of each party;
- the time necessary for either party to obtain education and training in order to obtain appropriate employment;
- the contribution of each party to the marriage (such as services rendered in homemaking, child care, and the education and career building of the other party);
- any other relevant economic factor; and,
- any other factor the judge finds necessary to reach a fair result.

As an alternative to alimony, you may want to try to negotiate to receive a greater percentage of the property instead. This may be less of a hassle in the long run, but it may change the tax consequences of your divorce. (See Chapter 12 regarding taxes.)

TYPES OF AVAILABLE PROCEDURES

Technically, there are two divorce procedures (simplified and regular); however, this book refers to four:

1. simplified divorce procedure;
2. uncontested divorce procedure;
3. default procedure; and,
4. contested divorce procedure.

Each of these procedures is discussed in detail later in this book. Chapter 6 explains the simplified procedure; Chapter 7 describes the uncontested procedure; Chapter 8 relates the default procedure; and, Chapter 9 discusses the contested divorce. You should read this entire book once before you begin filling out any court forms, to be sure you know which procedure is right for your situation.

> ***Warning*:** Florida has a residency requirement. Before you can use any procedure, you or your spouse must have lived in Florida for at least six months before filing your **PETITION**.

Simplified Divorce Procedure

To be eligible for the simplified divorce procedure, you must be able to satisfy all of the following requirements.

1. You and your spouse have resided in Florida for at least the past six months.
2. Your spouse agrees to the divorce, and will cooperate in signing the necessary documents and following the required procedures.
3. You and your spouse do not have any minor or dependent children.
4. The wife is not pregnant.
5. You and your spouse agree on how to divide property and debts.
6. Neither you nor your spouse wants alimony.

7. You and your spouse are both willing to give up your right to a trial and to appeal.

8. You and your spouse agree that you do not need to give each other any financial information, except what is given in the Family Law Financial Affidavit each of you will file (these will be explained later).

9. You and your spouse are willing to go to the court clerk's office to sign the **PETITION**.

10. You and your spouse are willing to attend the court hearing.

(Chapter 6 provides more details about the simplified procedure.)

Uncontested Divorce Procedure

If you cannot qualify for the simplified procedure, you will have to use the uncontested procedure, the default procedure, or the contested procedure. The uncontested procedure is used in either of the following situations:

- if you and your spouse are in agreement (or can reach an agreement), but cannot use the simplified procedure because there are children involved (also referred to as a *consent divorce)* or
- when your spouse files a basic response to the petition indicating that he or she will not actively oppose you, but is not willing to sign a settlement agreement or otherwise take part in the divorce process.

(Chapter 7 provides more details about the uncontested procedure.)

Default Procedure

The default procedure is actually another version of the uncontested procedure, but is used in either of the following situations:

- when your spouse does not respond to your petition and summons after being served or
- when you cannot locate your spouse to have him or her personally served with the petition and summons.

In either situation, your case will still be uncontested, in that your spouse will not be actively opposing you, but there will be other procedures you will need to follow. (The default procedure is discussed in more detail in Chapter 8.

Additional information about what to do if you cannot locate your spouse is provided in Chapter 11.)

Contested Divorce Procedure

The contested divorce procedure will be necessary when you and your spouse are arguing over some matter and cannot resolve it. This may be the result of a disagreement over custody of the children, the payment of child support or alimony, the division of your property, or any combination of these items. The section of this book dealing with the contested procedure builds on the uncontested procedure section.

First, you will need to read Chapter 7 to get a basic understanding of the forms and procedures, then read Chapter 9 for additional instructions on handling the contested situation. Be sure to read through both chapters before you start filling out any forms.

If your case becomes contested, it is also time to seriously consider getting a lawyer. If you do not think you can afford a lawyer, you may be able to require your spouse to pay for your lawyer. Find a lawyer who will give you a free initial consultation. He or she will explain your options regarding the lawyer's fees. See Chapter 3 for more information about lawyers. (Chapter 7 and Chapter 9 provide more information about the contested procedure.)

General Procedures

chapter 5

This chapter covers forms and procedures common to all types of divorce cases and serves as a basic foundation for what is explained in later chapters. It covers using legal forms, filing your papers with the court clerk, notifying your spouse that you have filed for divorce, verifying your residency, scheduling a court hearing, conducting yourself before the judge, and basic principles of negotiation.

INTRODUCTION TO LEGAL FORMS

Most of the forms in this book follow forms approved by the Florida supreme court. Some of these official forms are poorly drafted, but their use is required in most counties. A few counties may have their own forms (which you must obtain from the court clerk), but they will be very similar to the forms in this book. Additional forms are included in Appendix B to cover common situations for which there are no supreme court forms.

The forms in this book are legally correct; however, you may encounter a clerk or judge who is very particular about how he or she wants the forms. If you encounter any problem with the forms in this book being accepted by the clerk or judge, try one or more of the following.

- Ask the clerk or judge what is wrong with your form, then try to change it to suit the clerk or judge.

- Ask the clerk or judge if there is a Florida supreme court form or a local form available. If so, find out where you can obtain it, then get it and use it. The instructions in this book will still help you to fill it out.

- Consult a lawyer.

Typing Forms

If you tear the forms out of this book, it is best to make photocopies of the forms and keep the originals blank to use in case you make mistakes or need additional copies.

Although the instructions in this book will tell you to "type in" certain information, it is not absolutely necessary to use a typewriter. If typing is not possible, you can print the information required in the forms. Just be sure your handwriting can be easily read or the clerk may not accept your papers for filing.

> ***Warning:*** Some, if not all, of the counties require the use of *black ink* on the forms. Therefore, whenever you sign a form or if you write in the information instead of typing, be sure to use a pen with black ink.

Form Numbers and Titles

In most places in this book, each form is referred to by both the title of the form and a form number. (The only exception to using the form number will be when there is more than one form of a certain type and the explanation relates to all forms of that type. For example, there are four **PETITION** forms. A statement about *the Petition*, without a form number, means that it applies to whichever **PETITION** form you are using.)

Be sure to check the form number because some of the forms have similar titles. The form number is found in the top outside corner of the first page of each form. Also, a list of the forms, by both number and name, is found at the beginning of Appendix B. These form numbers relate to this book only and should be removed from the corner of the form in the photocopying process.

Case Style

You will notice that most of the forms in Appendix B of this book have the same heading format. This is called the *case style*. The forms without this heading are not filed with the court. The case style portion of these court forms will all be completed in the same manner. The heading at the very top of the form tells in which court your case is filed. You will need to type in the number of the *judicial circuit* and the *county* in which the court is located. You can look in the phone book or call the court clerk's office to find out your court's circuit number.

Next, type your full name on the line marked "Petitioner" and your spouse's full name on the line marked "Respondent."

NOTE: *The simplified forms use "Husband" and "Wife" instead.*

Do not use nicknames or shortened versions of names. You should use the names as they appear on your marriage license, if possible.

You will not be able to fill in the "Case Number" or "Division" designation until after you file your **PETITION** with the clerk. The clerk will assign a case number and a division. He or she will write them on your **PETITION** and any other papers you file with it. You must type in the case number and division designation on all papers you file later.

When completed, the top portion of your forms should look something like the following example:

IN THE CIRCUIT COURT OF
THE ___THIRTEENTH___ JUDICIAL CIRCUIT,
IN AND FOR ___HILLSBOROUGH___ COUNTY, FLORIDA

Case No.: __________
Division: __________

Rhett Butler__________,
Petitioner,

and

Scarlett O'Hara Butler__________,
Respondent.

Signatures and Notaries

At the end of the forms there will be a place for you to sign your name, and type in your name, address, and phone numbers. Space is provided for a "Fax Number," but this can be left blank if there is no fax machine available. Your signature must be notarized on certain forms, in which case there will be a space for the notary public or a deputy court clerk to complete.

Assistance from Nonlawyers

At the very end of most forms, there will be a section beginning with the words "If a nonlawyer," which must be completed by someone who is not a lawyer, but who helps another person complete the form. This is primarily for use by paralegals. If you are filling out your own papers, you do not need to be concerned with this section of the form and should leave it blank.

FILING WITH THE COURT CLERK

Once you have decided which forms you need and have them prepared, it is time to file your case with the court clerk. First, make at least three copies of each form (the original for the clerk, one copy for yourself, one for your spouse, and one extra just in case the clerk asks for two copies or you decide to hire an attorney later).

Filing is actually about as simple as making a bank deposit, although the following information will help things go smoothly. Call the court clerk's office. You can find the phone number under the county government section of your phone directory. Ask the clerk the following questions (along with any other questions that come to mind, such as where the clerk's office is located and what their hours are).

- How much is the filing fee for a dissolution of marriage?
- Does the court have any special forms (other than the Florida supreme court forms) that need to be filed with the **PETITION**? (If there are special forms that do not appear in this book, you will need to go down to the clerk's office and pick them up. There may be a fee, so ask.)
- How many copies of the **PETITION** and other forms do you need to file with the clerk?

Next, take your **PETITION** and any other forms you determine you need to the clerk's office. The clerk handles many different types of cases, so be sure to look for signs telling you which office or window to go to. You should be looking for signs that say such things as "Family Court," "Family Division," "Filing," etc. If it is too confusing, ask someone where you file a petition for dissolution of marriage.

Once you have found the right place, simply hand the papers to the clerk and say, "I'd like to file this." The clerk will examine the papers, then do one of two things: either accept it for filing (and either collect the filing fee or direct you to where to pay it) or point out something that is not correct or that is incomplete (such as you forgot to sign the form, or missed checking a space).

If you are told something is wrong, ask the clerk to explain to you what is wrong and how to correct the problem. It may be possible to correct the problem at the clerk's counter. Although clerks are not permitted to give legal advice, the types of problems they spot are usually very minor things that they can tell you how to correct. It is often possible to figure out how to correct it from the way they explain what is wrong.

NOTIFYING YOUR SPOUSE

A basic sense of fairness (and the law) requires that a person be notified of a legal proceeding that involves him or her. If you are using the simplified divorce procedure, you do not need to worry about the information in this section (your spouse will have to sign the **PETITION**, so it will be obvious that he or she knows about the divorce). Also, you do not need to worry about this section if you and your spouse are in agreement about everything, but do not qualify for the simplified procedure. You will both sign and file a **MARITAL SETTLEMENT AGREEMENT** (form 13, 14, or, 15) or your spouse will sign an **ANSWER, WAIVER, AND REQUEST FOR COPY OF FINAL JUDGMENT OF DISSOLUTION OF MARRIAGE** instead. (see form 18, p.253.) However, in all other cases, you are required to notify your spouse that you have filed for divorce. This gives your spouse a chance to respond to your **PETITION**.

If you are unable to find your spouse (and therefore cannot have him or her personally served by the sheriff), you will need to read Chapter 11. (The notice requirements, as they relate to your particular situation, are discussed in later chapters.)

Notice of Filing the Petition

The usual way to notify your spouse that you filed for a divorce is called *personal service*. This is where the sheriff (or someone else designated by the judge) personally delivers the papers to your spouse.

NOTE: *This section does not apply if you are using the simplified procedure. In such a case, your spouse will sign the* **PETITION FOR SIMPLIFIED DISSOLUTION OF MARRIAGE** *(form 3) with you. It will not be necessary for you to do anything else to notify your spouse.*

Call the sheriff's office in the county where your spouse lives; ask how much it will cost to have your spouse served with divorce papers and what forms of payment they accept (they may not accept personal checks). It will probably cost about $20.

Summons. The **PETITION** will be delivered along with a **SUMMONS**. Check with your court clerk to see if the clerk will prepare the **SUMMONS** or if you need to prepare one. If you need to prepare it, you will need to complete the **SUMMONS: PERSONAL SERVICE ON AN INDIVIDUAL**. (see form 19, p.255.)

To complete form 19, use the following instructions.

- Complete the top portion according to the instructions in the first section of this chapter, on page 56.
- Type your spouse's name and an address where he or she can be found (preferably during the day) on the first two lines (just above the word "Important"). The address you give is where the sheriff will first try to find your spouse, so be as certain as possible that it is a good address.
- Type in the street address of the courthouse on the line in the first paragraph below the word "Important."
- Type in your name and mailing address on the lines in the third paragraph, after the words "{Name and address of party serving summons}."
- Go to the court clerk's office and have the clerk date and sign the **SUMMONS** at the bottom of the third page.

After the clerk signs the **SUMMONS**, you will need to deliver or mail to the sheriff the original and one copy of the **SUMMONS**, a copy of your **PETITION**, and whatever papers you filed along with the **PETITION** (such as your **FAMILY LAW FINANCIAL AFFIDAVIT**, **UNIFORM CHILD CUSTODY JURISDICTION AND ENFORCEMENT ACT AFFIDAVIT**, etc.). The sheriff will deliver these papers to your spouse and file a paper with the court verifying the date and time the papers were *served* (delivered).

Process service memorandum. To assist the sheriff, you should also complete the **PROCESS SERVICE MEMORANDUM**. (see form 20, p.258.) On form 20 you will note that there is a space to give any special instructions, such as the hours of the day your spouse will most likely be at the place you intend for him or her to be served or alternate addresses where he or she might be found.

Other Notices

Once your spouse has been served with the **PETITION**, you may mail him or her copies of any papers you file later. All you need to do is sign a statement (called a **CERTIFICATE OF SERVICE**) verifying that you mailed copies to your spouse. Some of the forms in this book will include a certificate of service section for you to complete. If any form you file does not contain one, you will need to complete the **CERTIFICATE OF SERVICE**. (see form 25, p.269.) The form is rather clear about what information is to be filled in. On the line after the phrase: "I certify that the {name of document(s) served}," type in the title of what you are sending, such as "Motion for Temporary Support and Custody." Form 25 is to be filed with the court clerk as your proof that you sent a copy to your spouse.

There are special forms to notify your spouse that a hearing has been scheduled. These forms are discussed in the next section of this chapter.

VERIFYING RESIDENCY

As stated earlier, either you or your spouse must be a resident of Florida for at least six months immediately before the **PETITION** is filed. You will be required to offer proof of residency at the final hearing. You may prove residency at the final hearing in one of the following ways:

- by showing the judge your valid Florida driver's license, official Florida identification card, or Florida voter registration card, issued at least six months before the date your **PETITION** was filed (check with the court clerk to find out exactly what you need to do, as they may require you to bring a photocopy of your license, etc., to be placed in the court file);
- bring a witness to the final hearing to testify that he or she has known you for at least six months, and knows that you have been a resident of Florida for at least six months; or,
- file an **AFFIDAVIT OF CORROBORATING WITNESS**, signed before a notary by someone who has known you for at least six months, and knows that you have been a resident of Florida for at least six months. (see form 16, p.250.)

Affidavit of Corroborating Witness

To use the **AFFIDAVIT OF CORROBORATING WITNESS** (form 16), you will need to find a friend, relative, coworker, neighbor, or someone else you know (but not your spouse) to sign this form before a notary.

> ***Warning:*** Form 16 must be signed and notarized *after* you have filed your **PETITION**. (It is invalid if signed *before* filing the **PETITION**.)

Complete form 16 using the following instructions.

- Complete the top portion of the form according to the instructions at the beginning of Chapter 5, page 56.
- In the first paragraph, type in the name of the person who will sign the form on the first line.
- On the second line, type in either your name or your spouse's name, whichever of you has lived in Florida for at least six months. If you have both lived in Florida that long, you can just use your name and have the form signed by someone who knows you.
- On the third line, type in the approximate date you (or your spouse, if it is your spouse who meets the residency requirement) have known the person signing the form.
- Leave the "Signature of Corroborating Witness" line blank, but type in the witness's name, address, and phone number on the lines so designated.
- Have your witness take the form to a notary, or go with you to the court clerk's office. The witness will sign and date the form before the notary or court clerk. The notary or clerk will then complete the bottom portion of the form. You will need to make a photocopy of your witness's Florida driver's license or Florida identification card, and staple it to the form. Your witness should also bring identification to show the court clerk or notary.

If you decide to prove residency with form 16, it may be filed at any time after your **PETITION** is filed, as long as it is available for the judge when you go for your final hearing.

SETTING A COURT HEARING

At some point you will need to set a hearing date. Hearings will be necessary to obtain your judgment and for any preliminary matters that require a hearing (such as requests for temporary support or custody, which will be discussed later in this book). You will schedule a final hearing in one of the following situations.

- You and your spouse are using the simplified procedure and have filed all of the required forms.
- Your spouse has filed an answer to your **PETITION** and you are ready for a hearing.
- Your spouse has failed to respond to your **PETITION** within the time allowed by law and you have obtained a **DEFAULT** from the clerk.

Depending upon the procedures used in your county, your hearing may be before the judge, a child support hearing officer, or a *general magistrate* (a general magistrate is an attorney who is appointed by the judge to hear cases and make recommendations to the judge).

If your hearing will be before the judge, you will probably have to get a date from the judge's secretary or judicial assistant. (If you do not know which judge, call the court clerk, give the clerk your case number, and ask for the name and phone number of the judge assigned to your case. The judge's phone number can also be found in the government section of your telephone book.)

You can then either call or go see that judge's secretary and say that you would like to set a final hearing date for a dissolution of marriage (or for whatever preliminary motion needs a hearing). If the hearing will be before a child support enforcement hearing officer or a general magistrate, you may need to schedule the hearing with the hearing officer's or general magistrate's secretary, or with the court clerk. The clerk can tell you what you need to do to set a hearing.

You may be asked how long the hearing will take. If you are using the simplified divorce procedure, tell the secretary or clerk. He or she will probably know how much time to allow (usually about five or ten minutes).

If you are unable to use the simplified procedure, but you and your spouse have agreed on everything (an uncontested divorce), tell the secretary or clerk it is an uncontested divorce and ask for about ten minutes (unless they advise you differently). If you have a contested divorce, it could take anywhere from thirty minutes to several days, depending upon such things as what matters you disagree about and how many witnesses will testify.

One general rule is that the more time you need for a hearing, the longer it will take to get the hearing. Also, it is better to overestimate the time required, rather than not schedule enough time and have to continue the hearing for several weeks. Judges do not go over the time scheduled. The secretary or clerk will give you a date and time for the hearing, but you will also need to know where the hearing will be. Ask for the location. You will need the street address of the courthouse, as well as the room number, floor, or other location within the building.

Motion to Set Final Hearing/Trial

Some judges may insist that you file a motion to set the final hearing or trial. This is simply a paper to let the judge know that you are ready for the final hearing. If your judge requires this, a **MOTION TO SET FINAL HEARING/TRIAL** (see form 40, p.305) and an **ORDER SETTING MATTER FOR FINAL HEARING OR FOR STATUS CONFERENCE** (see form 41, p.306) are provided in Appendix B.

To complete form 40, follow these instructions.

- Fill in the top portion according to the instructions in the first section of this chapter, page 56.

- Check the appropriate boxes next.

- Type in how long you expect the hearing will take in paragraph "2."

- Fill in the date, sign your name on the line marked "Signature," and fill in your name, address, and telephone information on the lines indicated.

- Prepare a **CERTIFICATE OF SERVICE** (form 25) according to the instructions for form 25 on page 269.

- Send a copy of the **MOTION TO SET FINAL HEARING/TRIAL** and the **CERTIFICATE OF SERVICE** to your spouse (or his or her attorney) and file the originals with the court clerk.

In some counties, if you have a contested case, the court will require you to file a **NOTICE FOR TRIAL**. (see form 39, p.304.) This form will be explained further in Chapter 9 on the contested divorce procedure.

Order Setting Matter for Final Hearing or for Status Conference

When you file form 40, you will also need to complete the top portion of form 41 and leave it with the court clerk (along with two extra copies to be returned to you). The clerk or judge will fill in the rest and return a copy of form 41 to you. If your case is contested, the judge may set it for trial or may first schedule a *status conference,* wherein you and your spouse sit down with the judge for a few minutes to make it clear to everyone what issues the judge needs to determine at the trial.

Your next step will be to notify your spouse of the hearing or status conference by sending him or her a copy of the **ORDER SETTING MATTER FOR FINAL HEARING OR FOR STATUS CONFERENCE** (form 41). Then file a **CERTIFICATE OF SERVICE** (form 25) listing the **ORDER SETTING MATTER FOR FINAL HEARING OR FOR STATUS CONFERENCE** (form 41) as the document served. (See the previous section of this chapter on certificates of service.) If this procedure is used, you do not need to send a **NOTICE OF HEARING (GENERAL)** (form 34), as the hearing information is already included in form 41.

Notice of Hearing

If your judge or county does not require you to use the procedure discussed above and you can obtain a hearing date from the judge's secretary or judicial assistant, you will need to send your spouse a **NOTICE OF HEARING (GENERAL).** (see form 34, p.294.) If your hearing will be before a child support enforcement hearing officer, you will use the **NOTICE OF HEARING (CHILD SUPPORT ENFORCEMENT HEARING OFFICER)**. (see form 35, p.296.)

Use the following instructions to complete the **NOTICE OF HEARING (GENERAL)** (form 34) or **NOTICE OF HEARING (CHILD SUPPORT ENFORCEMENT HEARING OFFICER)** (form 35).

- Complete the top portion according to the instructions in the first section of this chapter, page 56.
- Type in your spouse's name and address after the word "To:"
- Complete the main paragraph by typing in the information requested, relating to where and when the hearing will be held. For example:

> There will be a hearing before Judge *{name}* ___Barry D.___ on *{date}* ___June 23___, ___2008___, at *{time}* ___9:30 a.___ m., in Room ___16___ of the ___Hillsborough___ Courthouse, on the following issues:
> ___Dissolution of marriage___.

On form 35, you will insert the name of the hearing officer instead of the judge.

- After you have scheduled a hearing date, fill in the amount of time you reserved for the hearing.
- Call the court clerk to obtain the information you need to complete the section relating to the *Americans with Disabilities Act.*
- Complete the certificate of service section (beginning with "I certify..."), indicating how and when you sent or delivered a copy of the form to your spouse, and filling in your spouse's name, address, and telephone information. If your spouse has an attorney, you will send or deliver a copy to the attorney, and fill in the attorney's name, address, and telephone information.
- Fill in the date, and sign your name on the line marked "Signature of Party." Type in your name, address, and telephone number information on the lines indicated.
- Make three copies of the **NOTICE OF HEARING** and mail one copy to your spouse (or his or her attorney). If you are seeking to modify alimony or child support, also send a blank **FAMILY LAW FINANCIAL AFFIDAVIT** (form 8 or form 9). File the original **NOTICE OF HEARING** with the court clerk and keep two copies for yourself.

Motion for Referral to General Magistrate

If your circuit court has a *general magistrate,* either you or your spouse may ask the judge to refer the case to the general magistrate; the judge may take the initiative and refer the case to the general magistrate. If you want the case referred to a general magistrate, you will need to complete the **MOTION FOR REFERRAL TO GENERAL MAGISTRATE**. (see form 36, p.298.) You may be able to get a hearing scheduled before the general magistrate earlier than a hearing with the judge. For example, the general magistrate may be scheduling hearings two weeks away, where the judge's heavy trial schedule may not allow you to get a hearing with the judge for two months.

To complete the **MOTION FOR REFERRAL TO GENERAL MAGISTRATE** (form 36), use the following instructions.

- Complete the top portion of the form according to the instructions at the beginning of this chapter, page 56.

- In the main paragraph, fill in your name and and the issues that the general magistrate will need to resolve (such as "child custody and child support" or "property division").

- Fill in the certificate of service section (beginning with "I certify…"), indicating how and when a copy of this form will be sent or delivered to your spouse, and filling in your spouse's name, address, and telephone information. If your spouse has an attorney, you will need to send or deliver a copy of the form to the attorney, and fill in the attorney's name, address, and telephone information.

- Fill in the date, and sign your name on the line marked "Signature of Party." Fill in your name, address, and telephone information on the lines below your signature.

Order of Referral to General Magistrate

If the judge refers your case to a general magistrate (either upon a request from you or your spouse, or on the judge's own referral), you will need to complete the **ORDER OF REFERRAL TO GENERAL MAGISTRATE** and submit it to the judge for his or her signature. (see form 37, p.300.) Read this entire form carefully because it spells out your rights and provides other important information regarding referrals to general magistrate.

To complete form 37, follow these instructions.

- Complete the top portion according to the instructions at the beginning of this chapter, page 56.

- Fill in the name, address, and phone number information for you and your spouse on the second page of the form.

- Check with the judge's secretary or the court clerk to find out if you need to complete more of this form. If so, you will need to list the matters being referred to the general magistrate in items 1 through 4 at the top of the form, type in the name of the general magistrate in the first paragraph, and fill in any other information as instructed. However, the judge or clerk may fill in these items.

Notice of Hearing before General Magistrate

Once signed by the judge, a copy of form 37 will be sent to you, your spouse, and the general magistrate. The general magistrate will then schedule a hearing date. Once the general magistrate sets a hearing date, you will need to notify your spouse by sending him or her a **NOTICE OF HEARING BEFORE**

General Magistrate (form 38). This is very similar to the **Notice of Hearing (General)** (form 34), and **Notice of Hearing (Child Support Enforcement Hearing Officer)** (form 35), so see the instructions for those notice of hearing forms beginning on page 65.

COURTROOM MANNERS

There are certain rules of procedure that are used in a court. These are really the rules of good conduct or good manners, and are designed to keep things orderly. Many of the rules are written down, although some are unwritten customs that have just developed over many years. They are not difficult, and most of them do make sense.

Following the suggestions below will make the judge respect you for your maturity and professional manner, make your case go more smoothly and quickly, and possibly even make the judge forget for a moment that you are not a lawyer. It will also increase the likelihood that you will get the things you request.

Show Respect for the Judge

Showing respect for the judge basically means, do not do anything to make the judge angry at you, such as arguing with him or her. Be polite. Call the judge "Your Honor" when you speak, such as "Yes, Your Honor," or "Your Honor, I brought proof of my income." Although many lawyers address judges as "Judge," this is not proper. Showing respect also means wearing appropriate clothing, such as a coat and tie for men and a dress or suit for women. This especially means no T-shirts, blue jeans, shorts, or revealing clothing.

When the Judge Talks—Listen

Anytime the judge is talking, you need to be listening carefully. Even if the judge interrupts you, stop talking immediately and listen. Judges can become rather upset if you do not allow them to interrupt.

Only One Person Can Talk at a Time

Each person is allotted his or her own time to talk in court. The judge can only listen to one person at a time, so do not interrupt your spouse when it is his or her turn. As difficult as it may be, stop talking if your spouse interrupts you. (Let the judge tell your spouse to keep quiet and let you have your say.)

Talk to the Judge—Not to Your Spouse

Many people get in front of a judge and begin arguing with each other. They actually turn away from the judge, face each other, and begin arguing as if they are in the room alone. This generally has several negative results. The judge cannot understand what either one is saying since they both start talking at once, and they both look like fools for losing control. As a result, the judge gets angry with both of them. Whenever you speak in a courtroom, look only at the judge. Try to pretend that your spouse is not there. Remember, you are there to convince the judge that you should have certain things. You do not need to convince your spouse.

Talk Only When It Is Your Turn

The usual procedure is for you, as petitioner, to present your case first. When you are done saying all you came to say, your spouse will have a chance to speak. Let your spouse have his or her say. When he or she is finished, you will get another chance to respond to what has been said.

Stick to the Subject

Many people cannot resist the temptation to get off the track and start telling the judge all the problems with their marriage over the past twenty years. This just wastes time and aggravates the judge. Stick to the subject and answer the judge's questions simply and to the point.

Remain Calm

Judges like things to go smoothly in their courtrooms. They do not like shouting, name calling, crying, or other displays of emotion. Generally, judges do not like family law cases because they get too emotionally charged. Give your judge a pleasant surprise by keeping calm and focusing on the issues.

Show Respect for Your Spouse

Even if you do not respect your spouse, act like you do. All you have to do is refer to your spouse as "Mr. Smith" or "Ms. Smith" (using his or her correct name, of course).

NEGOTIATING

It is beyond the scope of this book to fully present a course in negotiation techniques. However, a few basic rules may be of some help.

Ask for More than You Want

Asking for more than you want always gives you some room to compromise by giving up a few things and ending up with close to what you really want.

Property. With property division, you will review your **PROPERTY INVENTORY** (form 1) and decide which items you really want, which items you would like to have, and those about which you do not really care. Also try to figure out which items your spouse really wants, which items he or she would like to have, and those about which he or she does not really care.

At the beginning you will say that you want certain things. Your list will include: (a) everything you really want; (b) almost everything you would like to have; (c) some of the things about which you do not care; and, (d) some of the things you think your spouse really wants or would like to have. Once you find out what is on your spouse's list, you begin trading items. Generally, you try to give your spouse things that he or she really wants and that you do not care about, in return for your spouse giving you the items you really care about and would like to have.

Child custody. Child custody tends to be something that cannot be negotiated. It is often used as a threat by one of the parties in order to get something else, such as more of the property or lower child support. If the real issue is one of these other matters, do not be concerned by a threat of a custody fight. In these cases, the other party probably does not really want custody and will not fight for it. If the real issue is custody, you will not be able to negotiate for it and will end up letting the judge decide anyway.

Child support. If child support is involved in your case, you should first work out what you think the judge will order based upon the child support guidelines discussed in Chapter 4. Do this before discussing the matter with your spouse. If you will be receiving child support, you may want to ask for more than the guidelines call for and negotiate down to what the guidelines require. If you will be paying child support, you may want to try for slightly less than the guidelines call for, but keep in mind that the judge will probably look at the schedule and ask questions if you and your spouse are agreeing to less. This does not mean the judge will reject your agreement, but you may need to offer an explanation as to why you are not following the guidelines.

You can tell your spouse that there is little room for negotiation on child support as the court will probably require it be set according to the statute. If your spouse will not agree on something very close to the guidelines, give up trying to work it out and let the judge decide.

Be Patient

One of the basic rules of negotiating is: the first person to mention a dollar figure loses. Whether it is a child support figure or the value of a piece of property, try to get your spouse to name the amount he or she thinks it should be first. If your spouse starts with a figure close to what you had in mind, it will be much easier to get to your figure. If your spouse begins with a figure far from yours, you know how far in the other direction to begin your bid.

Give Your Spouse Time to Think and Worry

Your spouse is probably just as afraid as you about the possibility of losing to the judge's decision and would like to settle. Do not be afraid to state your *final offer* and walk away. Give your spouse a day or two to think it over. Maybe he or she will call back and make a better offer. If not, you can always reconsider and make a different offer in a few days. Do not be too willing to do this or your spouse may think you will give in even more.

Know Your Bottom Line

Before you begin negotiating, try to set a point that you will not go beyond. If you have decided that there are four items of property that you absolutely must have and your spouse is only willing to agree to let you have three, it is time to end the bargaining session and go home.

Remember What You Have Learned

By the time you have read this far, you should be aware of two things.

1. The judge will roughly divide your property equally.

2. The judge will probably come close to the child support guidelines.

This awareness should give you an approximate idea of how things will turn out if the judge is asked to decide these issues. This knowledge should help you set your bottom line on these issues.

Simplified Divorce Procedure

chapter 6

In certain circumstances, you may take advantage of Florida's *Simplified Dissolution of Marriage* procedure. In order to use this procedure, you must meet the following basic requirements.

1. You or your spouse have resided in Florida for at least the past six months.

2. Your spouse agrees to the divorce and will cooperate in signing the necessary documents and following the required procedures.

3. You and your spouse do not have any minor or dependent children. (A minor child is one who is under the age of eighteen. A dependent child may be over the age of eighteen, but is still dependent upon you for support due to mental or physical illness, disease, or disability. You may still use the procedure if you have children from a prior marriage, as long as your current spouse has not adopted them.)

4. The wife is not pregnant.

5. You and your spouse have agreed on how your property and debts will be divided.

6. Neither you nor your spouse want alimony.

7. You are both willing to give up your right to a trial and to appeal.

8. You both agree that you do not need to give each other any financial information, except what is given in the **Family Law Financial Affidavit** each of you will file (these will be explained later).

9. You are both willing to go to the court clerk's office to sign the **Petition** (you do not need to go at the same time).

10. You and your spouse will both attend the court hearing.

If you do not meet all ten of these conditions, you may **NOT** use the simplified procedure. However, you may still want to read this section, as it may help you understand the standard procedure better. If the only requirement you do not meet is that you cannot agree on the division of your property, you may want to reconsider your position on the property. Read this chapter, and have your spouse read it. Then compare the simplified procedure to the standard procedures in Chapter 7 and Chapter 9 of this book. Once you see how much easier the simplified procedure is, you may want to try harder to resolve your differences over the property. The simplified procedure can take as little as three weeks to complete.

Basically, the procedure is as follows.

- You and your spouse complete the necessary forms.
- You file the appropriate forms with the court clerk.
- You and your spouse appear for a brief hearing with the judge.

The following is a list of the forms you will need to complete and file in order to use the simplified procedure.

- ❑ **Civil Cover Sheet** (form 50).
- ❑ **Petition for Simplified Dissolution of Marriage** (form 3).

- ❏ **Family Law Financial Affidavit** (form 8 or 9). (You and your spouse will each need to complete and file one of these forms.)

- ❏ **Marital Settlement Agreement for Simplified Dissolution of Marriage** (form 13).

- ❏ **Notice of Social Security Number** (form 17). (You and your spouse will each need to complete and file one of these forms.)

- ❏ **Notice of Current Address** (form 26). (Although your addresses are listed on the **Petition**, some counties may also require you and your spouse to each complete and file one of these forms. The purpose of this form is simply to inform the court and your spouse of your current address and telephone number. This form will need to be filed again in the event your address changes. To complete the form, fill in your name, address, and telephone information on the lines indicated; fill in the certificate of service section to indicate how and when you provided a copy to your spouse; and, date and sign the form before a notary public or court clerk.)

- ❏ *Verification of residency*. (See the section on "Verification of Residency" in Chapter 5 for information on how to do this.)

- ❏ **Final Judgment of Simplified Dissolution of Marriage** (form 44).

- ❏ **Final Disposition Form** (form 51).

The remainder of this chapter discusses these forms and the simplified procedure.

CIVIL COVER SHEET

You will need to prepare a **Civil Cover Sheet.** (see form 50, p.336.) File it along with your **Petition for Simplified Dissolution of Marriage**. (see form 3, p.180.)

To complete form 50, you must do the following.

- In "Section I. Case Style," cross out the word "Petitioner," and type in the word "Husband" just before it. Cross out the word "Respondent," and type in the word "Wife" just before it.

  NOTE: *Instead of using the terms "Petitioner" and "Respondent," the simplified procedure uses "Husband" and "Wife"—in that order, regardless of who is preparing and filing the papers. Unfortunately, the drafters of the Supreme Court forms apparently have not thought of this when preparing the forms, so many still use the wrong terms when applied to the simplified procedure.*

  Type the husband's name on the first line and the wife's name on the second line. The clerk will fill in the case number and the division designation at the time you file your **PETITION**.

- Under the heading "II. Type of Case," check the box marked "Simplified dissolution."

- Under the heading "III. Is Jury Trial Demanded in Complaint?", the box marked "No" is already checked. (Jury trials are not available in divorce cases.)

- Fill in the date on the line indicated, and sign your name on the line above the words "Signature of Attorney or Party Initiating Action." Type in your address and phone number on the lines where indicated.

CIVIL COVER SHEET forms are available from the court clerk, so in the event the clerk finds a major error in the form you have brought, you can always get another form and fill it out at the clerk's office.

PETITION FOR SIMPLIFIED DISSOLUTION OF MARRIAGE

The **PETITION FOR SIMPLIFIED DISSOLUTION OF MARRIAGE** is used to open your case and ask for a divorce. (see form 3, p.180.)

Use the following instructions to complete form 3.

- Complete the top portion of the form according to the instructions at the beginning of Chapter 5, page 56.

NOTE: *This form uses the designations of "Husband" and "Wife," rather than "Petitioner" and "Respondent." This is because you are both considered petitioners since you are signing and filing the Petition together.*

- In the first (unnumbered) paragraph, fill in your name and your spouse's name on the appropriate lines. Again, note that the first line is for the husband's name and the second line is for the wife.

- Fill in the blanks in items 2, 3, and 9. Item 9 asks whether the wife wants her former name restored. Check the appropriate line for "yes" or "no." If you check "yes," type the wife's former name on the line.

- Below the signature lines on the second page, type in the name, address, and phone information for the husband and wife.

- The following forms must be completed and stapled to the **PETITION**.

  - ❑ Your **FAMILY LAW FINANCIAL AFFIDAVIT** (form 8 or form 9).

  - ❑ Your spouse's **FAMILY LAW FINANCIAL AFFIDAVIT** (form 8 or form 9).

  - ❑ **MARITAL SETTLEMENT AGREEMENT FOR SIMPLIFIED DISSOLUTION OF MARRIAGE** (form 13).

- You and your spouse must go to the court clerk's office and sign on the appropriate signature lines before the clerk. You will also each need to have a completed **NOTICE OF SOCIAL SECURITY NUMBER** (form 17). This form must be filed at the same time as your **PETITION** (but not stapled to it).

FAMILY LAW FINANCIAL AFFIDAVIT

Both parties must complete and file a **FAMILY LAW FINANCIAL AFFIDAVIT** (form 8 or form 9). (Florida Family Law Rules, Rule 12.105(c).) Be sure to make an extra copy of the appropriate **FAMILY LAW FINANCIAL AFFIDAVIT** (form 8 or form 9) for your spouse to complete.

If you (or your spouse) have annual income and expenses of less than $50,000, you will use the **FAMILY LAW FINANCIAL AFFIDAVIT (SHORT FORM)**. (see form 8, p.195.) If annual income or expenses are $50,000 or more, you will use the

Family Law Financial Affidavit (Long Form). (see form 9, p.200.) The form to be used is determined by each of you separately.

Example: If your income is less than $50,000 and your spouse's is more than $50,000, you will file form 8 and your spouse will file form 9.

Form 9 is more detailed than form 8, but both require the same type of information about the following four areas: your income, expenses, assets, and debts.

The child support guidelines use monthly income figures, so the **Family Law Financial Affidavit** is monthly. Therefore, you may need to convert non-monthly income and expense items to monthly figures. To convert weekly amounts to monthly amounts, just take the weekly figure and multiply it by 4.3 (there are roughly 4.3 weeks to a month). To convert from every two weeks, divide by 2 and then multiply by 4.3.

Fill in all of the blank spaces on the **Family Law Financial Affidavit** forms, then take them to a notary public before you sign them. You will sign them before the notary, then file them along with your **Petition** (after you have made three copies). Most of the blanks in the **Family Law Financial Affidavit** clearly indicate what information is to be filled in. However, the following may answer some questions.

Family Law Financial Affidavit (Short Form)

Use the following instructions to complete the **Family Law Financial Affidavit (Short Form)** (form 8).

- Complete the top portion of the form according to the instructions at the beginning of Chapter 5, page 56.

- Type your name in the blank in the first paragraph.

- Fill in the information about your employment and income. If you are unemployed, you will need to check the box in the last line of that paragraph and attach a sheet explaining what efforts you are making to seek employment.

- For each item listed in "Section I. Present Monthly Gross Income," fill in the monthly amount (before taxes) that you receive. Total the amounts you listed and fill in the total on line 17.

- Complete section marked "Present Monthly Deductions." Total the deductions and fill in the total on line 26.

- Subtract the amount on line 26 from the amount on line 17, and fill in the answer on line 27.

- For "Section II. Average Monthly Expenses," simply refer to each item listed and estimate as best you can the amount you spend on that item in a month. If a particular item is an annual expense, such as auto insurance, convert it to a monthly amount.

- To complete the sections marked "Section III: Assets and Liabilities":

  - In the subsection marked "A. Assets," fill in a description of each item of property, and fill in the value for each item listed. Refer to the **PROPERTY INVENTORY** (form 1) to be sure you list everything. Check the box before each item you believe you should keep. If you believe any item should be considered nonmarital property, check one of the columns at the right to indicate if it is the husband's or wife's nonmarital property. For more information on what constitutes nonmarital property, see page 30.

    NOTE: *If you and your spouse are signing a* **MARITAL SETTLEMENT AGREEMENT**, *the items checked as being kept by you should agree with what is stated in the* **MARITAL SETTLEMENT AGREEMENT**. (see form 13, p.224.)

    Use extra sheets if necessary. Add up the value of all listed assets and fill in the total on the line marked "Total Assets."

  - In the subsection marked "B. Liabilities," fill in a description of each debt and fill in the amount owed for each debt listed. Refer to the **DEBT INVENTORY** (form 2) to be sure you list everything. Check the appropriate spaces to indicate debts that will continue to be your responsibility, and any that are nonmarital debts.

    NOTE: *If you and your spouse are signing a* **MARITAL SETTLEMENT AGREEMENT**, *the items checked as being your continued responsibility by you should agree with what is stated in the* **MARITAL SETTLEMENT AGREEMENT**. (see form 13, p.224.)

Use extra sheets if necessary. Add up the value of all listed debts and fill in the total on the line marked "Total Debts."

- For the subsection marked "C. Contingent Assets and Liabilities," read the instructions for that subsection on the form and fill in any information that applies.

- Regarding "Section IV: Child Support Guidelines Worksheet," check the line for "A Child Support Guidelines Worksheet IS NOT being filed in this case."

- Fill in the appropriate information to indicate how and when you sent or delivered a copy of the form to your spouse (or his or her attorney); and fill in your spouse's (or his or her attorney's) name, address, and telephone information.

- Do not sign this form yet. Fill in your name, address, and telephone information on the lines below the signature line.

- Take this form to a notary public, and sign before the notary on the line marked "Signature of Party."

- This form will be stapled to your **PETITION**.

Family Law Financial Affidavit (Long Form)

Use the following instructions to complete the **FAMILY LAW FINANCIAL AFFIDAVIT (LONG FORM)** (form 9).

- Complete the top portion of the form according to the instructions at the beginning of Chapter 5, page 56.

- Type in your name in the blank in the first paragraph.

- In "Section I. Income," fill in the information about yourself, and your employment and income. If you are unemployed, you will need to check item 4.a., and explain what efforts you are making to seek employment.

- Under the subsection marked "Last Year's Gross Income," fill in the gross income amount from your W-2 or 1099 forms.

- For each item listed under "Present Monthly Gross Income," fill in the monthly amount (before taxes) that you receive.

- Total the amounts you listed and fill in the total on line 17.

- Complete section marked "Present Monthly Deductions." Total the deductions and fill in the total on line 26.

- Subtract the amount on line 26 from the amount on line 17 and fill in the answer on line 27.

- For the section marked "Section II. Average Monthly Expenses," simply refer to each item listed and estimate as best you can the amount you spend on that item in a month. If a particular item is an annual expense, such as auto insurance, convert it to a monthly amount. Add up amounts and fill in subtotals and totals where indicated.

- Complete the subsection marked "Summary" after item 105.

- To complete the sections marked "Section III: Assets and Liabilities":

  - In the subsection marked "A. Assets," list and fill in the value for each item listed. Check the box before each item you believe you should keep. If you believe any item should be considered nonmarital property, check one of the columns at the right to indicate if it is the husband's or wife's nonmarital property. For more information on what constitutes nonmarital property, see page 30.

    NOTE: *If you and your spouse are signing a* **MARITAL SETTLEMENT AGREEMENT***, the items checked as being kept by you should agree with what is stated in the* **MARITAL SETTLEMENT AGREEMENT**. (see form 13, p224.)

    Use extra sheets if necessary. Add up the value of all listed assets and fill in the total on the line marked "Total Assets."

  - In the subsection marked "B. Liabilities/Debts," fill in the amount owed for each type of debt listed. Check the appropriate spaces to indicate debts that will continue to be your responsibility, and any that are nonmarital debts. Use extra sheets if necessary. Add up the value of all listed debts and fill in the total on the line marked "Total Debts."

- For the subsection marked "C. Net Worth," fill in the total assets figure and the total liabilities figure; subtract liabilities from assets; and, fill in the answer on the line marked "Total Net Worth."

- For the subsection marked "D. Contingent Assets and Liabilities," read the instructions for that subsection on the form and fill in any information that applies.

- Regarding "E. Child Support Guidelines Worksheet," and the heading "Attachments," check the line for "A Child Support Guidelines Worksheet IS NOT being filed in this case."

- Fill in the certificate of service section (beginning with "I certify…") to indicate how and when you sent or delivered a copy of the form to your spouse (or his or her attorney); and fill in your spouse's (or his or her attorney's) name, address, and telephone information.

- Do not sign this form yet. Fill in your name, address, and telephone information on the lines below the signature line.

- Take this form to a notary public, and sign before the notary on the line marked "Signature of Party."

- Staple this form to your **Petition** before filing it with the clerk.

MARITAL SETTLEMENT AGREEMENT FOR SIMPLIFIED DISSOLUTION OF MARRIAGE

The **Marital Settlement Agreement for Simplified Dissolution of Marriage** spells out how your property and debts will be divided. (see form 13, p.224.)

To complete the **Marital Settlement Agreement for Simplified Dissolution of Marriage** (form 13), follow these instructions.

- Complete the top portion of the form according to the instructions at the beginning of Chapter 5, on page 56.

- Type your name and your spouse's name in the appropriate spaces in the first (unnumbered) paragraph. (Be sure to put the husband's name in the first space in this paragraph.)

- Type the date you were married on the line in paragraph 1.

- Under the heading "Section I. Marital Assets and Liabilities," on the chart below paragraph 1, under the heading "A. Division of Assets," list the items the wife will keep (refer to your **PROPERTY INVENTORY** (form 1)). Be as specific as possible in describing the items. If you need more space, attach another sheet of paper and type in "see attached sheet" under "Other assets." Add up the value of all of the assets you listed and write the total in on the line marked "Total Assets to Wife."

- In Paragraph 2 under the same heading (beginning on the third page of this form), list all of the items the husband will keep. Add up the value of all of the assets you listed and write the total in on the line marked "Total Assets to Husband."

- In paragraph 1 under the heading "B. Division of Liabilities/Debts," list all of the debts the wife will be responsible for paying (refer to your **DEBT INVENTORY** (form 2)). Add up the value of all of the debts you listed and write the total in on the line marked "Total debts to be paid by Wife." In Paragraph 2, list all of the debts the husband will pay. Add up the value of all of the debts you listed and write the total in on the line marked "Total debts to be paid by Husband."

- Under the heading "C. Contingent Assets and Liabilities," indicate how you will divide any items that you listed in Section III of your **FINANCIAL AFFIDAVITS**.

- Under "Section III. Other," type in any agreements you and your spouse have that are not covered elsewhere in the form.

- Type in the date, and each of your names, addresses, and phone numbers where indicated below the signature lines.

- On the last two pages of the form, you and your spouse need to sign before a deputy court clerk. The clerk will ask to see a photo identification card, such as a Florida driver's license or Florida state identification card.

- Staple this form to your **PETITION**.

VERIFYING RESIDENCY

As stated earlier, either you or your spouse must be a resident of Florida for at least six months immediately before the **PETITION** is filed. At the final hearing, you will need to provide proof that the residency requirement has been met. For more information about what is required, see the section on "Verifying Residency" in Chapter 5 on page 61.

FINAL JUDGMENT OF SIMPLIFIED DISSOLUTION OF MARRIAGE

The **FINAL JUDGMENT OF SIMPLIFIED DISSOLUTION OF MARRIAGE** is the paper the judge will sign at the final hearing to formally grant your divorce. (see form 44, p.311.)

To complete form 44 you will need to do the following.

- Complete the top portion of the form according to the instructions at the beginning of Chapter 5, page 56.

- Check one of the lines in paragraph 5. Check subparagraph "a" if you and your spouse filed a **MARITAL SETTLEMENT AGREEMENT** that divided all of your property. Check "b" if you and your spouse divided all of your property previously, and each of you will keep what is now in your possession.

- If the wife is to have her former name restored, check the space for "yes" in paragraph 6, then type in her former name on the line. If not, check the line for "no."

- Leave the date and judge's signature spaces blank, as the judge will fill these in at the final hearing.

FINAL DISPOSITION FORM

Like the **Civil Cover Sheet** (form 50), the **Final Disposition Form** is another form required by the courts for their administrative purposes. (see form 51, p.337.)

- Part I of the form should be completed exactly the same as the **Civil Cover Sheet** (see the second section of this chapter, page 75), but be sure to fill in the case number, judge, and division.
- Under the heading "II. Means of Final Disposition," check the box marked "Disposed by Judge."
- This form also needs to be dated and signed by you, but be sure to use the date of the final hearing.
- Also, type in your address and phone number below the signature line.

Take this form with you to the final hearing. You will need to give it to the judge at the hearing so that it can be included in your file when it is sent to the court clerk.

Uncontested Divorce Procedure

chapter 7

This chapter explains the forms and procedures for the situation in which you and your spouse will be signing a **MARITAL SETTLEMENT AGREEMENT**, but for some reason do not qualify for the simplified procedure. In order to use the forms and procedures described in this chapter, you and your spouse must be in agreement on the following points:

- that you want a divorce;
- how your property will be divided;
- how your debts will be divided; and,
- whether any alimony is to be paid; and if so, how much and for how long a period of time.

If you have any minor children, you will also need to be in agreement on the following:

- which of you will have custody of the child or children;
- the visitation arrangement for the parent without custody; and,
- how much child support is to be paid by the parent not having custody.

NOTE: *Although a case is also uncontested when your spouse does not respond to your* **PETITION**, *different forms must be used in this situation, including the judgment forms that are used in contested cases. Therefore, the situation in which your spouse does not respond will be covered in the next chapter. If you cannot find your spouse, you will need to file several other forms. Those forms will be explained in Chapter 11. If your spouse actively opposes you, then you will need to see Chapter 9 on the contested case.*

Most lawyers have had the following experience: A new client comes in, saying she wants to file for divorce. She has discussed it with her husband and it will be a *simple, uncontested* divorce. Once the papers are filed, the husband and wife begin arguing over a few items of property. The lawyer then spends a lot of time negotiating with the husband. After much arguing, an agreement is finally reached. The case will proceed in the court as uncontested, but only after a lot of contesting out of court.

For the purposes of this book, a contested case is one in which you and your spouse will be doing your arguing in court and leaving the decision up to the judge. An uncontested case is one in which you will do your arguing and deciding before court. The judge will only be approving your **MARITAL SETTLEMENT AGREEMENT**. You may start off believing that your case will be uncontested, but later find out that your spouse is not going to be cooperative. You will not know for certain until your spouse has actually signed the **MARITAL SETTLEMENT AGREEMENT**. (see forms 13, 14, and 15.)

To begin your divorce case, the following forms should be filed with the court clerk in all cases (see Chapter 5, page 56 for filing instructions):

- ❑ **CIVIL COVER SHEET** (form 50);
- ❑ **PETITION FOR DISSOLUTION OF MARRIAGE** (form 4, 5, or 6);
- ❑ **FAMILY LAW FINANCIAL AFFIDAVIT** (form 8 or form 9);
- ❑ **NOTICE OF SOCIAL SECURITY NUMBER** (form 17) (you and your spouse will each need to complete and file one of these forms);

- ❑ **NOTICE OF CURRENT ADDRESS** (form 26) (Although your addresses are listed on the **PETITION**, some counties may also require you and your spouse to each complete and file one of these forms. The purpose of this form is simply to inform the court and your spouse of your current address and telephone number. This form will need to be filed again in the event your address changes. To complete the form, fill in your name, address, and telephone information on the lines indicated; fill in the certificate of service section to indicate how and when you provided a copy to your spouse; and, date and sign the form before a notary public or court clerk.); and,

- ❑ **MARITAL SETTLEMENT AGREEMENT** (form 14 or 15).

Other forms that you determine to be necessary in your situation will also be filed, either with your petition or at some time before the final hearing. These may include such forms as the **SUMMONS** (form 19), **MARITAL SETTLEMENT AGREEMENT** (comprised of several forms), **MOTION FOR DEFAULT** (form 28), **NONMILITARY AFFIDAVIT** (form 22), and some type of residency verification. All of these forms will be discussed later in this chapter and the next.

The following forms will be prepared in advance in all cases, but will not be filed until the final hearing:

- ❑ **FINAL JUDGMENT OF DISSOLUTION OF MARRIAGE** (form 45, 48, or 49) and

- ❑ **FINAL DISPOSITION FORM** (form 51).

Once the necessary forms have been filed, you will need to call the judge's secretary to arrange for a hearing date for the **FINAL JUDGMENT**. (See Chapter 5 regarding setting a hearing.) You should tell the secretary that you need to schedule a *final hearing for an uncontested divorce*. Such a hearing should not usually take more than ten minutes. See Chapter 10 for information on how to handle the final hearing.

The following sections explain when you need each form and give instructions for completing them.

CIVIL COVER SHEET

You will need to prepare a **Civil Cover Sheet** (form 50) and file it along with your **Petition for Dissolution of Marriage** (form 4, 5, or 6).

To complete form 50:

- In "Section I. Case Style," type in your name on the line marked "Petitioner," and your spouse's name on the line marked "Respondent." The clerk will fill in the case number and the division designation at the time you file your **Petition**.

- Under the heading "II. Type of Case," check the box marked "Dissolution."

- Under the heading "III. Is Jury Trial Demanded in Complaint?", the box marked "No" is already checked. (Jury trials are not available in divorce cases.)

- Fill in the date on the line indicated, and sign your name on the line above the words "Signature of Attorney or Party Initiating Action." Type in your address and phone number on the lines where indicated.

Civil Cover Sheet forms are available from the court clerk, so in the event the clerk finds a major error in the form you have brought, you can always get another form and fill it out at the clerk's office.

PETITION FOR DISSOLUTION OF MARRIAGE

The **Petition for Dissolution of Marriage** is simply the paper you file with the court to begin your case and to ask the judge to give you a divorce. (see form 3, 4, 5, or 6.) You will need to select the proper form for your situation. In Appendix B, you will find the following four **Petition** forms:

1. Form 3: **Petition for Simplified Dissolution of Marriage** (See Chapter 6 to find out if you qualify for this procedure.)

2. Form 4: **Petition for Dissolution of Marriage with Dependent or Minor Child(ren)** (Use form 4 if you have children and have property to be divided.)

3. Form 5: **PETITION FOR DISSOLUTION OF MARRIAGE WITH PROPERTY BUT NO DEPENDENT OR MINOR CHILD(REN)** (Use form 5 if you have property to be divided, but do not have children.)

4. Form 6: **PETITION FOR DISSOLUTION OF MARRIAGE WITH NO DEPENDENT OR MINOR CHILD(REN) OR PROPERTY**. (Use form 6 if you do not have property to be divided and do not have children, but are unable to use the simplified procedure described in Chapter 6 (most likely because your spouse cannot be located or will not cooperate as required by the simplified procedure).)

Each **PETITION** form will be explained in the following sections. The **PETITION** should be accompanied by your **FAMILY LAW FINANCIAL AFFIDAVIT** (form 8 or form 9), which gives the judge financial information, and a **NOTICE OF SOCIAL SECURITY NUMBER** (form 17). The **PETITION** may also be accompanied by other forms, depending upon your situation. For example, if you have a minor child, you will need to file a **UNIFORM CHILD CUSTODY JURISDICTION AND ENFORCEMENT ACT (UCCJEA) AFFIDAVIT**. (see form 10, p.211.) Later sections of this chapter will discuss these other forms and explain when you need to file them. Together, these papers give the judge information about your situation and states what you want him or her to do.

Petition for Dissolution of Marriage—with Children

Use the following instructions to complete the **PETITION FOR DISSOLUTION OF MARRIAGE WITH DEPENDENT OR MINOR CHILD(REN)** (form 4, p.183).

- Complete the top portion of the form according to the instructions at the beginning of Chapter 5, page 56.

- In the first (unnumbered) paragraph, type in your name, and check the appropriate space to indicate whether you are the "Husband" or the "Wife."

- In paragraph 1, check the space before "Husband," "Wife," or "Both," depending upon which of you has lived in Florida for at least six months, or whether you have both lived in Florida that long.

- In paragraph 2, check the appropriate spaces to indicate whether either you or your spouse are in the military service.

- In paragraph 3, on the appropriate lines, type in the date you were married; the city, state, and country where you were married; and, the date you and your spouse were separated. (Check the box at the end of this line if the separation date is approximate. Leave this line blank if you and your spouse are still living together.)

- In paragraph 4, under the heading "Dependent or Minor Child(ren)," check the line or lines that describe your situation.

  Item a. If you (or your spouse) are pregnant, type in the expected delivery date.

  Item b. If you and your spouse have minor children together, fill in their names, places of birth, birth dates, and sexes.

  Item c. If you or your spouse (whichever of you is the wife) have minor children who were born or conceived during your marriage, but are ***not*** the husband's children, fill in the name, place of birth, birth date, and sex for each child; and the name and address of the child's birth father.

  Item d. If you have any children together who are eighteen years of age or older and are dependent upon you because of a mental or physical disability, fill in the name, place of birth, birth date, and sex for each child.

- As indicated in paragraph 5, if you have minor children, you will also need to complete the **UNIFORM CHILD CUSTODY JURISDICTION AND ENFORCEMENT ACT (UCCJEA) AFFIDAVIT** (form 10).

- In paragraph 7, check the line for "a. The marriage is irretrievably broken."

- The following instructions relate to the portion of the form marked "Section I. Marital Assets and Liabilities."

  - Check the line for paragraph 1 if there are no marital assets or liabilities. (Refer back to page 30 for an explanation of what constitutes marital assets and liabilities.) Check the line for paragraph 2 if there are marital assets or liabilities.

- If you checked paragraph 2, you will then need to read items "a," "b," and "c"; and check any of these items that apply. Check item "a" if you and your spouse are signing a **MARITAL SETTLEMENT AGREEMENT** that divides all of your property. Check item "b" if the judge will need to divide your property. Check item "c" if you are claiming an interest in what might otherwise be considered to be your spouse's nonmarital property. If you check item "c," you will need to type in a statement as to what property you claim an interest in, and why you claim an interest. (Refer back to page 30 for a discussion of marital and nonmarital assets, and when a special equity may be claimed in a nonmarital asset.)

- The following instructions relate to the portion of the form marked "Section II. Spousal Support (Alimony)."

  - If you are not requesting alimony from your spouse, check the line for paragraph 1. If you are requesting alimony, check paragraph 2.

  - If you checked paragraph 2, you will need to read paragraph 2 and fill in the required information relating to the amount of alimony you are requesting and the reason you believe you should be awarded alimony. Refer back to Chapter 4 for information about the types of situations in which alimony is likely to be awarded. Also, check the space at the end of the lines for your explanation if you want the alimony award to be secured by a life insurance policy.

- The following instructions relate to the portion of the form marked "Section III. Child Custody, Parental Responsibility, and Visitation."

  - In paragraph 1, check the appropriate space to indicate whether the children currently live with the mother or father if they currently live with just one of you. Check the box for "Other" if any other situation exists, and describe that situation.

    Example 1: *John, Jr., resides with father; Mary resides with mother.*

    Example 2: *The minor child, mother, and father all reside together.*

    Example 3: *The minor children reside with their maternal aunt, Mary Smith.*

- Paragraph 2 relates to "Parental Responsibility." This refers to who will make major decisions regarding the children. Check the appropriate space to indicate what you are requesting. Remember that Florida law favors this responsibility to be shared by both parents. If you want the sole responsibility for these decisions, you will need to show that shared responsibility would be harmful to the children. Therefore, if you check item "b," you will need to type in a brief explanation of why shared responsibility would be detrimental to your child.

- Paragraph 3 relates to "Primary Residential Parent (Custody)." This refers to where the children will have their primary residence. Check the appropriate space to indicate your wishes regarding custody, and type in a short statement of why you think this would be in the best interest of the children. If you and your spouse have reached agreement on these matters, you can simply type in "it is the agreement of the parties." (Refer to Chapter 4 for more information.)

- Paragraph 4, titled "Visitation or Time Sharing," relates to the time allotted to the parent who is not the primary residential parent. For items "a" through "f," check all items that apply. Where indicated, type in an explanation of the visitation schedule you desire. Where indicated, type in an explanation of why the proposed arrangement is in the best interest of the children. If you and your spouse have reached agreement on these matters, you can simply type in "it is pursuant to agreement of the parties." Check the appropriate space to indicate whether your spouse has agreed to the visitation arrangement. (Refer to Chapter 4 for more information.)

- In the portion of the form marked "Section IV. Child Support," read paragraphs 1 through 6 and check all that apply. Follow the directions on the form to complete any of the paragraphs you check. If you and your spouse have agreed to child support that is above or below what the guidelines call for, you will need to check paragraph 3, and file a **MOTION TO DEVIATE FROM CHILD SUPPORT GUIDELINES**. (see form 12, p.220.) (Form 12 is discussed in detail in Chapter 5.)

- The following instructions relate to the portion of the form marked "Section V. Other."

- If you are the wife, and you would like to have your former name restored, in paragraph 1 check the space for "yes," and fill in your former name. If not, check the space for "no."

- If there are any other things you want the judge to order that are not covered elsewhere on the form, type them in paragraph 2.

- In "Section VI. Petitioner's Request," check all of the items that indicate what you want the judge to order.

- Below the line marked "Signature of Petitioner," type in your name, address, and telephone numbers.

- Take this form to a notary public, and sign it before the notary on the line marked "Signature of Petitioner."

Petition for Dissolution of Marriage—with Property; No Children

If you have property to be divided, but do not have any children, you will use the **PETITION FOR DISSOLUTION OF MARRIAGE WITH PROPERTY BUT NO DEPENDENT OR MINOR CHILD(REN)**. (see form 5, p.189.) This form is basically the same as form 4, except it does not have the paragraphs relating to child custody, visitation, and support. Therefore, for each paragraph in form 5, refer to the instructions for the similar paragraph in form 4 (the paragraph numbers will not be the same in both forms).

NOTE: *Although form 5 is specifically designed for the situation in which there is property, it has a provision in "Section I. Marital Assets and Liabilities" stating "There are no marital assets or liabilities." If there are no marital assets or liabilities (and no children), you would use form 6 instead of form 5. (This appears to be an error in drafting form 5, which was not corrected when it was revised.)*

Petition for Dissolution of Marriage—No Property; No Children

If you do not have property to be divided and do not have any children, you will use the **PETITION FOR DISSOLUTION OF MARRIAGE WITH NO DEPENDENT OR MINOR CHILD(REN) OR PROPERTY**. (see form 6, p.192.)

Use the following instructions to complete form 6.

- Complete the top portion of the form according to the instructions at the beginning of Chapter 5, page 56.

- In the first (unnumbered) paragraph, type in your name, and check the appropriate box to indicate whether you are the "Husband" or the "Wife."

- In paragraph 1, check the space before "Husband," "Wife," or "Both," depending upon which of you has lived in Florida for at least six months, or whether you have both lived in Florida that long.

- In paragraph 2, check the appropriate spaces to indicate whether either you or your spouse are in the military service.

- In paragraph 3, on the appropriate lines, type in the date you were married; the city, state, and country where you were married; and, the date you and your spouse were separated. (Check the box at the end of this line if the separation date is approximate. Leave this line blank if you and your spouse are still living together.)

- In paragraph 6, check the line for "a. The marriage is irretrievably broken."

- In paragraph 9, if you are the wife, and you would like to have your former name restored, check the space for "yes," and fill in your former name. If not, check the space for "no."

- If there are any other things you want the judge to order that are not covered elsewhere on the form, type them in paragraph 10.

- Under the heading "Petitioner's Request," check the items that indicate what you want the judge to order.

- Below the line marked "Signature of Petitioner," type in your name, address, and telephone numbers.

- Take this form to a notary public, and sign it before the notary on the line marked "Signature of Petitioner."

Filing and Serving the Petition

Your **PETITION** is now ready for filing. If you need to have your spouse served by the sheriff, be sure to prepare the **SUMMONS** (form 19) to go along with your **PETITION**. (See the section on the **SUMMONS** in Chapter 5.)

FAMILY LAW FINANCIAL AFFIDAVIT

A **FAMILY LAW FINANCIAL AFFIDAVIT** (form 8 or form 9) must be filed by each party in all cases (except, of course, where your spouse does not respond or cannot be found). See Chapter 6 for instructions on how to complete these forms.

CERTIFICATE OF COMPLIANCE WITH MANDATORY DISCLOSURE

The **CERTIFICATE OF COMPLIANCE WITH MANDATORY DISCLOSURE** must be filed in all cases. (see form 27, p.272.) It is used to satisfy the judge that you have provided your spouse with the required documents and a **FAMILY LAW FINANCIAL AFFIDAVIT**. (A copy of this form should also be given to your spouse, so that he or she can complete it to certify that he or she has provided the required information to you.)

To complete the **CERTIFICATE OF COMPLIANCE WITH MANDATORY DISCLOSURE** (form 27), use the following instructions.

- Complete the top portion of the form according to the instructions at the beginning of Chapter 5, page 56.

- In the first (unnumbered) paragraph, type in your name.

- You will only fill in the section marked "1. For Temporary Financial Relief, Only," if you are filing a **MOTION FOR TEMPORARY SUPPORT** (form 52 or form 54). (See Chapter 12 for more information about temporary support.)

- In paragraph marked "2. For Initial, Supplemental, and Permanent Financial Relief," type in the date the documents were mailed or personally delivered to your spouse. For items "a" through "q," check all that apply.

- Fill in the certificate of service section after item "q," to indicate how and where you provided a copy of this form to your spouse or your spouse's attorney.

- In the paragraph below item "q," check the appropriate space to indicate how you provided a copy of this form to your spouse (or his or her attorney); fill in the date it was mailed, faxed, or delivered; and, fill in the name, address, etc., of where it was sent on the lines indicated.

- Do not sign this form yet, but below the signature line fill in your name, address, phone number, and fax number (if any).
- Take this form to a notary public, sign it before the notary, and have the notary complete the notary provisions.
- Mail a copy of this form to your spouse in the manner indicated in the certificate of service section.
- File the original of this form with the court clerk.

INTERROGATORIES

Interrogatories are written questions that one party submits to the other. The party receiving the interrogatories must provide written answers that are certified under oath. This means they are the same as testifying in court, and the person answering can be charged with perjury or contempt of court for not answering or for not answering truthfully. The Family Law Rules of Procedure contain a set of standard **INTERROGATORIES**. These are reproduced as form 31 in Appendix B of this book. (see form 31, p.278.) The Family Law Rules of Procedure require that answers to these standard interrogatories be provided by any party with annual income or expenses of $50,000 or more. Therefore, if you have annual income or expenses of $50,000 or more, you will need to provide your spouse with the answers to the **STANDARD FAMILY LAW INTERROGATORIES** (form 31), even if the answers are not requested by your spouse.

Standard Family Law Interrogatories

Use the following instructions to complete the **STANDARD FAMILY LAW INTERROGATORIES FOR ORIGINAL OR ENFORCEMENT PROCEEDINGS** (form 31).

- Complete the top portion of the form according to the instructions at the beginning of Chapter 5, page 56.
- Type in the answer to each question. If you need more space, type in "see attached sheet" and attach additional sheets of paper with your answers. Be sure to indicate the number of the question you are answering on the additional sheets.

- On the first page, add the words "Answers to" just above the title "Standard Family Law Interrogatories."

- Send a copy of your answers to your spouse.

To prove to the court that you have answered the interrogatories, check the appropriate box on the **Certificate of Compliance with Mandatory Disclosure** (form 27). (See the instructions for form 27 on page 272.) If your spouse has annual income or expenses of $50,000 or more, he or she will need to provide you with the answers even if you do not request them.

Notice of Service of Standard Family Law Interrogatories

If your spouse has annual income and expenses of less than $50,000, you may still require him or her to submit answers to the standard interrogatories. To do so, send your spouse a copy of form 31 and file a **Notice of Service of Standard Family Law Interrogatories** (form 30, p.277) with the clerk.

To complete form 30, use the following instructions.

- Fill in the top portion of the form according to the instructions at the beginning of Chapter 5, page 56.

- On the lines in the main paragraph, type your name, the date the **Standard Family Law Interrogatories** (form 31) was served on your spouse, and your spouse's name (or his or her attorney's name).

- Check the space for "Original or Enforcement Proceedings."

- Below the sentence beginning "I am requesting," check the line for each type of questions you want your spouse to answer. This will require you to read the **Standard Family Law Interrogatories** to see what questions are asked. If there are questions you would like answered that are not in form 31, you may type out your additional questions and attach them to form 30. If you do this, you will need to fill in the number of new questions you are asking on the line where indicated.

- Complete the certificate of service section to indicate how you will provide your spouse with a copy of form 30. Fill in your spouse's or his or her attorney's information.

- Sign your name on the line marked "Signature of Party." Type in your name, address, and telephone number information below the signature line.

- Send or deliver a copy of the form to your spouse in the manner you indicated in the certificate of service section.

- File the original with the court clerk.

Your spouse has thirty days from the date he or she receives the interrogatories to send you answers and file a copy of his or her answers with the clerk.

MARITAL SETTLEMENT AGREEMENT

Whether you and your spouse agreed on everything from the start or have gone through extensive negotiations to reach an agreement, you need to put your agreement in writing. Even if you do not agree on everything, put what you do agree on into a written settlement agreement. The exact **MARITAL SETTLEMENT AGREEMENT** will depend upon the type of **PETITION** you filed.

- If you filed a **PETITION FOR DISSOLUTION OF MARRIAGE WITH DEPENDENT OR MINOR CHILD(REN)** (form 4), you will use form 14.

- If you filed a **PETITION FOR DISSOLUTION OF MARRIAGE WITH PROPERTY BUT NO DEPENDENT OR MINOR CHILD(REN)** (form 5) or if you filed a **PETITION FOR DISSOLUTION OF MARRIAGE BUT NO DEPENDENT OR MINOR CHILD(REN) OR PROPERTY** (form 6), you will use form 15.

Marital Settlement Agreement—with Children

Use the following instructions to complete the **MARITAL SETTLEMENT AGREEMENT FOR DISSOLUTION OF MARRIAGE WITH DEPENDENT OR MINOR CHILD(REN)**. (see form 14, p.231.)

- Complete the top portion of the form according to the instructions at the beginning of Chapter 5, page 56.

- Type your name and your spouse's name in the appropriate spaces in the first (unnumbered) paragraph. (Be sure to put the husband's name in the first space in this paragraph.)

- Type the date you were married on the line in paragraph 1.

- Regarding "Section I. Marital Assets and Liabilities:"

  - Under the heading "A. Division of Assets," on the chart below paragraph 1, list the items the wife will keep (refer to your **PROPERTY INVENTORY** (form 1)). Be as specific as possible in describing the items. If you need more space, attach another sheet of paper and type in "see attached sheet" under "Other assets." Add up the value of all of the assets you listed and write the total on the line marked "Total Assets to Wife."

    On the chart below paragraph 2 (beginning on the third page), list all of the items the husband will keep. Add up the value of all of the assets you listed and write the total on the line marked "Total Assets to Husband."

  - Under the heading "B. Division of Liabilities/Debts," list all of the debts the wife will be responsible for paying (refer to your **DEBT INVENTORY** (form 2)). Add up the value of all of the debts you listed and write the total on the line marked "Total debts to be paid by Wife."

    On the chart below paragraph 2 under the same heading, list all of the debts the husband will pay. Add up the value of all of the debts you listed and write the total on the line marked "Total debts to be paid by Husband."

  - Under the heading "C. Contingent Assets and Liabilities," indicate how you will divide any items that you listed in Section III of your Family Law Financial Affidavits.

- Under "Section II. Spousal Support (Alimony)," check paragraph 1 if both of you are giving up all rights to alimony. If you have agreed that one of you will pay alimony, check paragraph 2, then fill in the information required about who will pay alimony, the amount, how often payments will be made, etc. If the exact nature and extent of alimony is not clear from what you fill in, or if there are any other agreements regarding alimony, type in a further explanation on the lines provided. If alimony will be secured by a life insurance policy, check the appropriate space and fill in the amount of life insurance to be obtained or maintained.

- The following information relates to "Section III. Child Custody, Parental Responsibility, and Visitation":
  - In paragraph 1, type in your children's names and birth dates.
  - In paragraph 2, fill in the necessary information to indicate your agreement regarding parental responsibility. This relates to who will have the responsibility for major decisions regarding your children. (See Chapter 4 for more information.)
  - In paragraph 3, check the spaces to reflect your agreement regarding the primary residence of your children. This relates to who your children will live with a majority of the time. (See Chapter 4 for more information.)
  - In paragraph 4, fill in the visitation schedule you and your spouse have agreed upon, as well as your agreement on the other matters mentioned in paragraph 4. (See Chapter 4 for more information.)
- Under "Section IV. Child Support," read carefully through each paragraph and fill in the required spaces and blanks to reflect your agreement regarding child support. Florida law requires that provisions for health insurance be in every divorce judgment. Paragraph 7 may be used to set forth any agreements regarding child support that are not covered elsewhere.
- Under "Section V. Other," type in any agreements you and your spouse have that are not covered elsewhere in the form.
- Under "Section VI.," list any issues that you and your spouse have not agreed upon. If you have agreed on everything, type in the word "none."
- Type in the date and each of your names, addresses, and phone numbers where indicated below the signature lines. Then, both you and your spouse need to sign the last two pages of the form before a notary public.

Marital Settlement Agreement—No Children

Use the following instructions to complete the **MARITAL SETTLEMENT AGREEMENT FOR DISSOLUTION OF MARRIAGE WITH PROPERTY BUT NO DEPENDENT OR MINOR CHILD(REN)**. (see form 15, p.242.)

- Complete the top portion of the form according to the instructions at the beginning of Chapter 5, page 56.

- Type your name and your spouse's name in the appropriate spaces in the first (unnumbered) paragraph. (Be sure to put the husband's name in the first space in this paragraph.)

- Type the date you were married on the line in paragraph 1.

- The following information relates to "Section I. Marital Assets and Liabilities":

  - Under the heading "A. Division of Assets," on the chart below paragraph 1, list the items the wife will keep (refer to your **Property Inventory** (form 1)). Be as specific as possible in describing the items. If you need more space, attach another sheet of paper and type in "see attached sheet" under "Other assets." Add up the value of all of the assets you listed and write the total in on the line marked "Total Assets to Wife." On the chart below paragraph 2 (beginning on the third page), list all of the items the husband will keep. Add up the value of all of the assets you listed and write the total in on the line marked "Total Assets to Husband."

  - Under the heading "B. Division of Liabilities/Debts," on the chart below paragraph 1, list all of the debts the wife will be responsible for paying (refer to your **Debt Inventory** (form 2)). Add up the value of all of the debts you listed and write the total in on the line marked "Total debts to be paid by Wife." On the chart below paragraph 2 under the same heading, list all of the debts the husband will pay. Add up the value of all of the debts you listed and write the total in on the line marked "Total debts to be paid by Husband."

  - Under the heading "C. Contingent Assets and Liabilities," indicate how you will divide any items that you listed in Section III of your Family Law Financial Affidavits.

- Under "Section II. Spousal Support (Alimony)," check paragraph 1 if both of you are giving up all rights to alimony. If you have agreed that one of you will pay alimony, check paragraph 2, fill in the information required about who will pay alimony, the amount, how often payments will be made, etc. If the exact nature and extent of alimony is not clear from what you fill in or if there are any other agreements regarding alimony, type in a further explanation on the lines provided. If alimony will be secured by a life insurance policy, check the appropriate space and fill in the amount of life insurance to be obtained or maintained.

- Under "Section III. Other," type in any agreements you and your spouse have that are not covered elsewhere in the form.
- In "Section IV.," list any issues that you and your spouse have not agreed upon. If you've agreed on everything, type in "none."
- On the last two pages, you and your spouse must sign before a notary public. Type in the date, and each of your names, addresses, and phone numbers where indicated below the signature lines.

VERIFYING RESIDENCY

As stated earlier, either you or your spouse must be a resident of Florida for at least six months immediately before the **Petition** is filed. At the final hearing, you will need to provide proof that the residency requirement has been met. For more information about what is required, see the section on "Verifying Residency" in Chapter 5 on page 61.

UNIFORM CHILD CUSTODY JURISDICTION AND ENFORCEMENT ACT (UCCJEA) AFFIDAVIT

The **Uniform Child Custody Jurisdiction and Enforcement Act (UCCJEA) Affidavit** must be completed if you have minor children. (see form 10, p.211.) To complete this form you need to do the following.

- Complete the top portion of the form according to the instructions at the beginning of Chapter 5, page 56.
- On the line in the first (unnumbered) paragraph, fill in your name.
- On the line in paragraph 1, fill in the number of children you and your spouse have.

- In paragraph 1, below the heading "The Following Information Is True About Child #1," fill in all blanks with the required information. If the child is not yet 5 years old, go back to the child's birth. If the child has only lived with you and your spouse, type in: "With the Husband and Wife for past five years at," then type in the addresses where you have lived during this period. If you have lived in Florida during this entire time, you can just type in: "With the Husband and Wife for the past five years in the State of Florida."

- On the second page of the form are spaces for two additional children, if needed. If you have more than three children, make as many additional copies of the second page as you need to include all of your children.

- Read paragraphs 2 through 5, and check the appropriate lines and fill in any required information that relates to your situation.

- In the certificate of service section below paragraph 6, fill in the appropriate spaces to indicate how you provided a copy of this form to your spouse (or your spouse's attorney).

- Take this form to a notary public, and sign it before the notary. This form should be filed with the court clerk along with your **Petition**.

CHILD SUPPORT GUIDELINES WORKSHEET

Fill in the **Child Support Guidelines Worksheet** (form 11) according to the instructions in the "Child Support" section of Chapter 4, page 41. Be sure to complete all sections of the form.

FINAL JUDGMENT OF DISSOLUTION OF MARRIAGE

In all uncontested cases, you will complete one of the following forms:

- Form 45: **Final Judgment of Dissolution of Marriage with Minor Child(ren) (Uncontested)**;

- Form 48: **FINAL JUDGMENT OF DISSOLUTION OF MARRIAGE WITH PROPERTY BUT NO DEPENDENT OR MINOR CHILD(REN) (UNCONTESTED)**; or,

- Form 49: **FINAL JUDGMENT OF DISSOLUTION OF MARRIAGE WITH NO PROPERTY OR DEPENDENT OR MINOR CHILD(REN) (UNCONTESTED)**.

These forms will be referred to generally as the **FINAL JUDGMENT**. You should complete as much of the **FINAL JUDGMENT** as possible before the hearing. Other portions of the **FINAL JUDGMENT** forms may need to be completed at the hearing (or shortly thereafter) according to what the judge decides on each issue.

If you have any questions about how to complete the **FINAL JUDGMENT**, ask the judge at the hearing. After all, it is the judge's order, so you want to be sure it accurately reflects his or her decision. You can complete ahead of time any items that you and your spouse have agreed upon. You should give your spouse a copy of the **FINAL JUDGMENT** before the hearing, so that he or she can tell the judge that he or she is aware of what it says, and agrees with it.

Although these forms contain different titles and some different provisions, all three have the same items to be completed. The previous versions of these forms required you to restate the terms of your **MARITAL SETTLEMENT AGREEMENT**. These new forms simply refer to the **MARITAL SETTLEMENT AGREEMENT**, which is attached to the **FINAL JUDGMENT** as *Exhibit A*.

Use the following instructions to complete either form 45, form 48, or form 49.

- Complete the top portion of the form according to the instructions at the beginning of Chapter 5, on page 56.

- In paragraph 6 on forms 45 and 49, and paragraph 7 on form 48, check the appropriate space to indicate whether the wife will resume her former name. If you check "yes," fill in the full name the wife will resume.

- At the bottom of the first page of your **MARITAL SETTLEMENT AGREEMENT**, type in the words *Exhibit A*. Make at least four copies of the **FINAL JUDGMENT** and **MARITAL SETTLEMENT AGREEMENT** marked *Exhibit A*. (You will need one copy for the judge, one for you, and one for your spouse. You may need other copies for the court clerk, the child support enforcement office, and for your spouse's attorney if he or she has one.) Then, staple the **MARITAL SETTLEMENT AGREEMENT** to the **FINAL JUDGMENT**.

◈ Take all of the copies with you to the final hearing. The judge will fill in the date in the paragraph beginning "Ordered on," and will sign the **FINAL JUDGMENT**. The judge will probably only sign one copy. For the others, you can usually go to the judge's secretary or judicial assistant, who will stamp the date and the judge's name on the other copies.

Preparing and Submitting the Final Judgment

Since you and your spouse agree to everything, you can prepare the **FINAL JUDGMENT** before the hearing and give it to the judge to sign at the end of the hearing. If the judge tells you to change something major in the **FINAL JUDGMENT**, you will need to redo the **FINAL JUDGMENT** the way the judge instructed; then take it back to the judge for signature.

If you submit the **FINAL JUDGMENT** after the hearing, you will also complete and submit a **CERTIFICATE OF SERVICE**. (see form 25, p.269.) Provide two extra copies and two stamped envelopes: one addressed to yourself and one addressed to your spouse. Sometimes the judge's secretary will handle mailing the judgment after the judge signs it, in which case the secretary may sign the **CERTIFICATE OF SERVICE**; otherwise you will do this.

NOTE: *You will also have to file a* **FINAL DISPOSITION FORM**. *See Chapter 6 for instructions on completing the* **FINAL DISPOSITION FORM**. *(see form 51, p.337.)*

Default Procedures

chapter 8

The forms and procedures in this chapter cover the situation wherein your spouse will not be signing a **Marital Settlement Agreement**, but is not actively opposing you. If you do not know where your spouse is, you will also need to read Chapter 11.

To begin your divorce case, the following forms should be filed with the court clerk in all cases:

- ❑ **Civil Cover Sheet** (form 50);
- ❑ **Petition for Dissolution of Marriage** (form 4, 5, or 6);
- ❑ **Family Law Financial Affidavit** (form 8 or form 9); and,
- ❑ **Notice of Social Security Number** (form 17).

Depending upon your situation, you may also have to file one or more of the various other forms that are discussed in this chapter.

For the final hearing, you will need to prepare the following forms:

- ❑ **Final Judgment** (form 46 or form 47) and
- ❑ **Final Disposition Form** (form 51).

Once the necessary forms are filed, and your spouse has had the required opportunity to respond, you will need to call the judge's secretary or judicial assistant to arrange for a hearing date for the **FINAL JUDGMENT**. (See Chapter 5 regarding setting a hearing.) See Chapter 10 for more information about how to handle the final hearing. The following sections explain when you need each form, and give instructions for completing them.

CIVIL COVER SHEET

See Chapter 7 for instructions on how to complete the **CIVIL COVER SHEET**.

PETITION FOR DISSOLUTION OF MARRIAGE

See Chapter 7 for instructions on how to complete the various Petitions. Please note that in "Section I. Marital Assets and Liabilities," under paragraph 2, you will not check item "a," as you and your spouse will not be signing a **MARITAL SETTLEMENT AGREEMENT**.

FAMILY LAW FINANCIAL AFFIDAVIT

A **FAMILY LAW FINANCIAL AFFIDAVIT** must be filed by each party in all cases. (see form 8 or form 9.) The only exception is where your spouse does not respond or cannot be found. See Chapter 6 for instructions on determining which form to use, and how to complete it.

CERTIFICATE OF COMPLIANCE WITH MANDATORY DISCLOSURE

See Chapter 7 for instructions on how to complete the **CERTIFICATE OF COMPLIANCE WITH MANDATORY DISCLOSURE**. (see form 27, p.272.)

INTERROGATORIES

See Chapter 7 for instructions on how to complete the **STANDARD FAMILY LAW INTERROGATORIES FOR ORIGINAL OR ENFORCEMENT PROCEEDINGS** (form 31) and the **NOTICE OF SERVICE OF STANDARD FAMILY LAW INTERROGATORIES** (form 30).

VERIFYING RESIDENCY

As stated earlier, either you or your spouse must be a resident of Florida for at least six months immediately before the **PETITION** is filed. At the final hearing, you will need to provide proof that the residency requirement has been met. See Chapter 5 for more information about what is required to prove residency.

UNIFORM CHILD CUSTODY JURISDICTION AND ENFORCEMENT ACT (UCCJEA) AFFIDAVIT

If you have any minor children, you must complete a **UNIFORM CHILD CUSTODY JURISDICTION AND ENFORCEMENT ACT (UCCJEA) AFFIDAVIT**. (see form 10, p.211.) See Chapter 7 for how to complete this form.

ANSWER, WAIVER, AND REQUEST FOR COPY OF FINAL JUDGMENT OF DISSOLUTION OF MARRIAGE

If you and your spouse agree on everything, and both of you sign a **MARITAL SETTLEMENT AGREEMENT**, you do not need to complete an **ANSWER, WAIVER, AND REQUEST FOR COPY OF FINAL JUDGMENT OF DISSOLUTION OF MARRIAGE**. (see form 18, p.253.) If you and your spouse are in full agreement, but for some reason your spouse will not sign a **MARITAL SETTLEMENT AGREEMENT**, you can have your spouse sign form 18 before a notary public. If this form is used, you will not need to go through the procedure in Chapter 5 on notifying your spouse by having the sheriff personally serve your spouse, and you will not need to complete the **NONMILITARY AFFIDAVIT**. (see form 22, p.262.) (See the last section in Chapter 11 for information about other types of responses to the **PETITION**.)

To complete the **ANSWER, WAIVER, AND REQUEST FOR COPY OF JUDGMENT OF DISSOLUTION OF MARRIAGE** (form 18), use the following instructions.

- Complete the top portion of the form according to the instructions at the beginning of Chapter 5, page 56.

- In the first (unnumbered) paragraph, type in your spouse's name.

- In the unnumbered paragraph after paragraph 6, indicate how your spouse provides you with a copy of this form. Your name, address, and telephone numbers should be filled in below the words "Other party or his/her attorney."

- Type your spouse's name, address, and telephone numbers on the lines below the line marked "Signature of Respondent."

- Have your spouse fill in the date and sign before a notary public.

- File this form with the court clerk, and be sure your spouse also completes and files a **UNIFORM CHILD CUSTODY JURISDICTION AND ENFORCEMENT ACT (UCCJEA) AFFIDAVIT** (form 10), if you have any children; a **FAMILY LAW FINANCIAL AFFIDAVIT** (form 8 or 9); and, a **NOTICE OF SOCIAL SECURITY NUMBER** (form 17).

NONMILITARY AFFIDAVIT

If your spouse is not in the military service and will not sign either a **MARITAL SETTLEMENT AGREEMENT** or the **ANSWER, WAIVER, AND REQUEST FOR COPY OF JUDGMENT OF DISSOLUTION OF MARRIAGE** (form 18) (or file his or her own answer), you will need to complete the **NONMILITARY AFFIDAVIT**. (see form 22, p.262.)

Use the following instructions to complete form 22.

- Complete the top portion of the form according to the instructions at the beginning of Chapter 5, page 56.

- Type your name in the blank space in the first (unnumbered) paragraph.

- Check paragraph 1, paragraph 2, or both, whichever applies.

- Do not date or sign the form yet, but type in your name, address, and telephone information on the lines below the line marked "Signature of Petitioner."

- Take this form to a notary public and date and sign it before the notary on the line marked "Signature of Petitioner."

Call the court clerk to ask when the **NONMILITARY AFFIDAVIT** needs to be filed. Some courts require that it not be signed too far in advance, because they want the information to be reasonably current. Some courts require that the notary public's date on the **NONMILITARY AFFIDAVIT** be within a certain number of days before filing a **MOTION FOR DEFAULT** (form 28) or before the final hearing.

If your spouse is not willing to file an **ANSWER, WAIVER, AND REQUEST FOR COPY OF FINAL JUDGMENT OF DISSOLUTION OF MARRIAGE** (form 18), a **MARITAL SETTLEMENT AGREEMENT**, or a **FAMILY LAW FINANCIAL AFFIDAVIT** (form 8 or form 9), and ***is*** in the military service, you do not need to complete this form and should consult a lawyer. Federal laws designed to protect service personnel while overseas can create special problems in these situations and you will need a lawyer to help you. If you do not know whether your spouse is in the military service, see the next section.

MEMORANDUM FOR CERTIFICATE OF MILITARY SERVICE

If you do not know whether your spouse is in the military service, you will need to complete the **MEMORANDUM FOR CERTIFICATE OF MILITARY SERVICE**. (see form 21, p.260.)

Use the following instructions to complete form 21.

- Complete the top portion of the form according to the instructions at the beginning of Chapter 5, page 56.

- Type your spouse's name on the line marked "Name of Respondent" and Social Security number on the line marked "Respondent's Social Security Number."

- Make six copies of the form, one for each branch of the service listed on the form after the word "To." On each copy, check a different space for each service branch.

- Make a call to each branch at the telephone numbers listed below, and ask how much is the search fee and how the check should be written.

Coast Guard:	202-267-1340	**Marine Corps:**	703-784-3941
Air Force:	210-652-5775	**Surgeon Gen.:**	301-594-2963
Navy:	703-614-5011	**Army:**	703-325-3732
or	703-614-9221		

- Fill in the amount of the search fee on the line in the main paragraph of the form. Be sure that the amount you fill in is the correct amount for the branch of service checked on the particular copy of the form.

- Fill in the date, sign your name, and fill in your name, address, and telephone information on the designated lines.

- Mail one copy of the form to each branch of the service, along with a check for the required amount and a self-addressed, stamped envelope.

Each service branch will check its records and mail you a notice as to whether your spouse is in that branch (these notices may be filed with the court clerk). If your spouse is in one of the service branches, his or her address will be provided. You can then send your spouse notice of the divorce and see if some agreement can be reached so you can use the uncontested procedure. If your spouse is in the military, but cannot be contacted or will not cooperate (by either filing an **ANSWER, WAIVER, AND REQUEST FOR COPY OF FINAL JUDGMENT OF DISSOLUTION OF MARRIAGE** (form 18); a **FAMILY LAW FINANCIAL AFFIDAVIT** (form 8 or form 9); or a **MARITAL SETTLEMENT AGREEMENT**), you should contact an attorney.

CHILD SUPPORT GUIDELINES WORKSHEET

If you have any minor children, you will need to complete the **CHILD SUPPORT GUIDELINES WORKSHEET**. (see form 11, p.216.) See Chapter 4 for instructions on how to complete this form.

MOTION FOR DEFAULT

If your spouse does not file an **ANSWER, WAIVER, AND REQUEST FOR COPY OF FINAL JUDGMENT OF DISSOLUTION OF MARRIAGE** (form 18); or his or her own answer; or a **FAMILY LAW FINANCIAL AFFIDAVIT** (form 8 or form 9); or sign a **MARITAL SETTLEMENT AGREEMENT** within twenty days after the sheriff delivers the **PETITION**, your spouse is in *default*. You will need to ask the clerk to enter the default in your court file. To do this, you need to complete a **MOTION FOR DEFAULT** and deliver it to the clerk. (see form 28, p.275.)

Use the following instructions to complete the **MOTION FOR DEFAULT** (form 28).

- Complete the top portion of the form according to the instructions at the beginning of Chapter 5, page 56.
- Fill in the certificate of service section to show how, and to whom, you sent a copy of the form. (This should be to your spouse's last known address, which will probably be the address where he or she was served by the sheriff with the **PETITION**.)
- Fill in the date; sign your name on the line marked "Signature of Petitioner"; and type in your name, address, and phone numbers on the lines below your signature.
- Send or deliver a copy of this form to your spouse as you indicated in the certificate of service section.

DEFAULT

The **DEFAULT** is the form the court clerk will sign to officially declare your spouse to be in default. (see form 29, p.276.)

Use the following instructions to complete form 29.

- Complete the top portion of the form according to the instructions at the beginning of Chapter 5, page 56.
- Leave the first line marked "Dated" and the clerk's signature line blank.
- Below the clerk's signature line, fill in the certificate of service section to indicate how, and to whom, you will send a copy of the form. (This should be to your spouse's last known address, which will probably be the address where he or she was served by the sheriff with the **PETITION**; but leave the date blank for now.)
- Below the line marked "Signature of Petitioner," type in your name, address, and telephone number information.

- Take this form to the clerk along with the **MOTION FOR DEFAULT** (form 28). If you will be mailing your spouse a copy of the **DEFAULT**, also take a stamped envelope, addressed to your spouse, so that you can mail the **DEFAULT** immediately. The clerk will review these forms, check the court file to be sure that the required time has expired and that no response has been filed by you spouse, and will date and sign the **DEFAULT** (form 29). In front of the clerk, you will fill in the date in the certificate of service section, fill in the date on the second line marked "Dated," and sign your name on the line marked "Signature of Petitioner."

- Send or deliver a copy of this form to your spouse as you indicated in the certificate of service section.

FINAL JUDGMENT OF DISSOLUTION OF MARRIAGE

In all cases in which you do not have a **MARITAL SETTLEMENT AGREEMENT**, you will need to complete one of the following forms:

- ❑ **FINAL JUDGMENT OF DISSOLUTION OF MARRIAGE WITH DEPENDENT OR MINOR CHILD(REN)** (form 46) or

- ❑ **FINAL JUDGMENT OF DISSOLUTION OF MARRIAGE WITH PROPERTY BUT NO DEPENDENT OR MINOR CHILD(REN)** (form 47).

Unless there is a significant difference between these forms, they will be referred to generally as the **FINAL JUDGMENT**. You should complete as much of the **FINAL JUDGMENT** as possible before the hearing. Other portions of the **FINAL JUDGMENT** form will need to be completed at the hearing (or shortly thereafter) according to what the judge decides on each issue.

If you have any questions about how to complete the **FINAL JUDGMENT**, ask the judge at the hearing. After all, it is the judge's order, so you want to be sure it accurately reflects his or her decision. You can complete ahead of time any items that you and your spouse have agreed upon, if any. You should give your spouse a copy of the **FINAL JUDGMENT** before the hearing, so that he or she can tell the judge that he or she is aware of what it says, and indicate whether he or she is in agreement with the terms (or explain why he or she disagrees). Of course, if your spouse does not attend the hearing you will not be able to give your spouse a copy and he or she will not be able to argue anything.

As you can see from the different titles of these two **FINAL JUDGMENT** forms, they vary depending upon whether there are any children involved. The instructions that follow are for the **FINAL JUDGMENT OF DISSOLUTION OF MARRIAGE WITH DEPENDENT OR MINOR CHILD(REN)**. (see form 46, p.314.) However, they are also the instructions for completing the **FINAL JUDGMENT OF DISSOLUTION OF MARRIAGE WITH PROPERTY BUT NO DEPENDENT OR MINOR CHILD(REN)** (form 47, p.326), with the following exception: form 47 does not have the provisions for child custody, visitation, or support that are in form 46; and the sections have been renumbered accordingly. Therefore, if you do not have any minor children, just skip over the items in the following instructions that relate to child custody, visitation, and support.

- Complete the top portion of the form according to the instructions at the beginning of Chapter 5, page 56.
- The following instructions relate to "Section I. Marital Assets and Liabilities":
  - In subsection "A. Date of Valuation of Property," check item "a," and fill in the date you filed your Petition (unless the judge orders something else).
  - In subsection "B. Division of Assets," in the chart under paragraph 1, list all nonmarital assets. In the three columns at the right, fill in the current value of each item and carry that value over to either the wife's or the husband's column, depending upon which owns each item of nonmarital property. Add up each of the three columns and write in the totals.

    In the chart below paragraph 2, list the marital assets. In the three columns at the right, fill in the current value of each item, and carry that value over to either the wife's or the husband's column, depending upon which will keep that item. Add up each of the three columns and write in the totals.
  - In subsection "C. Division of Liabilities/Debts," in the chart under paragraph 1, list all nonmarital debts. In the three columns at the right, fill in the current amount owed for each debt, and carry that amount over to either the wife's or the husband's column, depending upon which is responsible for the debt. Add

up each of the three columns and write in the totals. In the chart below paragraph 2, list the marital debts. In the three columns at the right, fill in the current amount owed on each debt, and carry that amount over to either the wife's or the husband's column, depending upon which will be responsible for that debt. Add up each of the three columns and write in the totals.

- In subsection D, type in an explanation of how the assets and debts you listed in your **FAMILY LAW FINANCIAL AFFIDAVIT** (form 8 or 9), Section III., paragraph "D. Contingent Assets and Liabilities," will be divided. If there are no contingent assets and debts, type in the word "none."

- Florida law requires the judge to divide property equally or give a reason for an unequal division. If the division of assets and debts is not close to equal, you will need to state a reason in subsection E. In this situation, Florida law requires the judge to state a reason, and the judge should do so at the hearing. If you are in doubt, ask the judge what reason he or she wants stated in the final judgment.

- Regarding "Section II. Exclusive Use and Possession of Home," check any items that reflect the judge's order. Leave this section blank if none of these provisions apply (such as if you and your spouse are already living in separate rental units). When there is a home owned by the parties, it is fairly common for the custodial parent to be awarded the use of the marital home until the last child reaches the age of majority.

- The following instructions relate to "Section III. Custody of and Visitation with Dependent or Minor Child(ren)."

  - In paragraph 2, type in the name and birth date of each child.

  - In paragraphs 3 through 9, check the appropriate spaces and fill in the necessary information to reflect what the judge ordered regarding custody and visitation. These provisions are designed to prevent common visitation problems.

- Under "Section IV. Alimony" (this is Section III in form 47), check the appropriate spaces and fill in the necessary information to reflect what the judge ordered regarding these matters. By reading the paragraphs in this section, it will be obvious how to complete any paragraphs that apply. Leave any items blank that do not apply. If the judge denies a request for alimony, you will check the first space in paragraph 1 and leave the rest of this section blank. Again, you are completing this form to reflect what the judge ordered. If you are not sure how to fill out a particular provision, ask the judge how he or she wants it completed.

- Under "Section V. Child Support," check the spaces and fill in the information to reflect what the judge ordered regarding these matters. By reading the paragraphs in this section, it will be obvious how to complete any paragraphs that apply. Leave any items blank that do not apply. Again, you are completing this form to reflect what the judge ordered. If you are not sure how to fill out a particular provision, ask the judge how he or she wants it completed.

- In "Section VI. Method of Payment" (Section IV in form 47), and "Section VII. Attorney Fees, Costs, and Suit Money" (Section V in form 47), check the appropriate spaces and fill in the necessary information to reflect what the judge ordered regarding these matters. Leave any items blank that do not apply.

- Under "Section VIII. Other" (Section VI in form 47), complete paragraph 1 if the wife's former name is to be restored. Paragraph 2 is for any other orders not covered elsewhere in this form.

- The judge will fill in the date in the last paragraph beginning "Ordered on," and will sign the **FINAL JUDGMENT**.

If you can fill in all of the spaces in the **FINAL JUDGMENT** as the judge goes through them at the hearing, you can submit the **FINAL JUDGMENT** to the judge at the end of the hearing. However, you may not be able to fully prepare the **FINAL JUDGMENT** at the hearing. You may need to use one copy of the **FINAL JUDGMENT** form for making notes on at the hearing, according to what the judge orders. You can then prepare a copy to submit for the judge's signature. If you submit the **FINAL JUDGMENT** after the hearing, you will also need to complete and submit a **CERTIFICATE OF SERVICE**. (see form 25, p.269.) Provide two extra copies and two stamped envelopes, one addressed to yourself and one addressed to your spouse. Sometimes the judge's secretary or judicial assistant will handle mailing the **FINAL JUDGMENT** after the judge signs it, in which case, the secretary or judicial assistant may sign the **CERTIFICATE OF SERVICE**; otherwise, you will sign it.

FINAL DISPOSITION FORM

See Chapter 6 for instructions on how to complete the **FINAL DISPOSITION FORM**. (see form 51, p.337.) If your spouse did not respond or appear at the hearing and a **DEFAULT** was issued, you will check the box in Part II for "Disposed by Default."

chapter 9

Contested Divorce Procedure

This book cannot turn you into a trial lawyer. It can be very risky to try to handle a contested case yourself, although it has been done. There are several differences between a contested and an uncontested case. First, in an uncontested case, the judge will usually go along with whatever you and your spouse have composed. In a contested case, you need to prove that you are entitled to what you are requesting. This means you will need a longer time for the hearing; you will need to present papers as evidence; and, you may need to have witnesses testify for you.

Second, you may have to do some extra work to get the evidence you need, such as by sending out subpoenas (which are discussed in the next section of this chapter), or even hiring a private investigator. Also, you will need to pay extra attention to ensure that your spouse is properly notified of any court hearings, and that he or she is sent copies of any papers you file with the court clerk.

When it becomes apparent that you have a contested divorce, it is probably time to consider hiring an attorney, especially if the issue of child custody is involved. If you are truly ready to go to war over custody, it shows that this is an extremely important matter for you—you may want to get professional assistance. You can predict a contested case when your spouse is seriously threatening to fight you every inch of the way, or when he or she hires an attorney.

On the other hand, you should not assume that you need an attorney just because your spouse has hired one. Sometimes it will be easier to deal with the attorney than with your spouse. The attorney is not as emotionally involved and may see your settlement proposal as reasonable. So, discuss things with your spouse's attorney first and see if things can be settled. You can always hire your own lawyer if your spouse's is not reasonable. Just be very cautious about signing any papers until you are certain you understand what they mean. You may want to have an attorney review any papers prepared by your spouse's lawyer before you sign them.

Aside from deciding if you want a lawyer, there are two main procedure differences between the uncontested and the contested divorce. First, you will need to be more prepared for the hearing. Second, you will not prepare the **FINAL JUDGMENT** until after the hearing with the judge. This is because you will not know what to put in the **FINAL JUDGMENT** until the judge decides the various matters in dispute.

Chapter 10 discusses how to prepare for the issues to be argued at the hearing, and provides more information about how to prepare the **FINAL JUDGMENT**.

COLLECTING INFORMATION

The court rules require each party to file a **FAMILY LAW FINANCIAL AFFIDAVIT** (form 8 or form 9). If your spouse has indicated that he or she will not cooperate at all and will not provide a **FAMILY LAW FINANCIAL AFFIDAVIT**, you may have to try to get the information yourself. You can go to the hearing and tell the judge that your spouse will not cooperate, but the judge may just issue an order requiring your spouse to provide information (or be held in contempt of court) and continue the hearing to another date. It may help to speed things up if you are able to get the information yourself and have it available at the hearing. This will require you to get subpoenas issued.

Before you send a **SUBPOENA FOR PRODUCTION OF DOCUMENTS FROM NONPARTY (SUBPOENA)** (form 33) to your spouse's employer, bank, or accountant, you need to let your spouse know what you are about to do. The thought that you are about to get these other people involved in your divorce may be enough to get your spouse to cooperate. If your spouse calls and says, "I'll give you the information," give him or her a few days to follow through. Ask when you can expect to receive his or her completed **FAMILY LAW FINANCIAL AFFIDAVIT** and offer to send your spouse another blank copy if he or she needs one. If your spouse sends a completed **FAMILY LAW FINANCIAL AFFIDAVIT** as promised, do not send the **SUBPOENA**. If your spouse does not follow through, go ahead with the **SUBPOENA**. You can send out subpoenas to as many people or organizations as you need, but you will need to use the following procedure for each **SUBPOENA**.

Notice of Production from Nonparty

The advance notice to your spouse is called a **NOTICE OF PRODUCTION FROM NONPARTY**. (see form 32, p.290.)

To complete form 32 you need to do the following.

- Complete the top portion of the form according to the instructions at the beginning of Chapter 5, page 56.
- Type your spouse's name after the word "To."
- In the main paragraph, type in the name of the person, company, bank, etc., where the subpoena will be sent.
- Complete the certificate of service section (beginning with "I certify"), indicating how and when you send or deliver a copy of the form to your spouse. Fill in the spaces under the heading "Other party or his/her attorney (if represented)."
- On the labeled lines, fill in the date; sign your name; and, fill in your name, address, and telephone information.
- Make a copy of the completed form 32, and two copies of the **SUBPOENA FOR PRODUCTION OF DOCUMENTS FROM NONPARTY** (form 33).
- Staple a copy of form 33 to the original form 32 and file them with the court clerk.
- Staple a copy of form 33 to a copy of form 32 and send or deliver them to your spouse in the manner you indicated in the certificate of service section.

Subpoena for Production of Documents from Nonparty

Next, you will complete the **SUBPOENA FOR PRODUCTION OF DOCUMENTS FROM NONPARTY**. (see form 33, p.292.) This form will eventually be sent to whomever you want to get information from. Look at the **FAMILY LAW FINANCIAL AFFIDAVIT** (form 8 or form 9) and Florida Family Law Rule 12.285(c) and (d) in Appendix A. See what type of information is needed.

If you were able to do a good job making copies of important papers while preparing to file for divorce, you should have the information you need to figure out where you need to send subpoenas. Your spouse's income information can be obtained from his or her employer. Stock and bond information can be obtained from his or her stock broker, bank account balances from the bank, auto loan balances from the lender, etc.

You can have subpoenas issued to any or all of these places, but do not overdo it. Concentrate on income information (especially if you are asking for child support or expect to pay child support) and information on the major property items. It may not be necessary to send out subpoenas if you already have recent copies of the papers relating to these items. You can always show the judge the copies of your spouse's paystubs, W-2 tax statements, or other papers at the hearing.

Use the following instructions to complete the **SUBPOENA FOR PRODUCTION OF DOCUMENTS FROM NONPARTY** (form 33).

- Complete the top portion of the form according to the instructions at the beginning of Chapter 5, page 56.

- After the word "To," type in the name and address of the person, business, organization, or other entity from whom you are seeking documents (e.g., your spouse's employer, broker, bank).

- In the paragraph beginning "YOU MUST go to," type in where and when you want the documents produced, and what documents or types of documents you want. The location can be your home, your office, the office of the person who has the documents, or anywhere else. However, you will need to make photocopies of the documents produced, so you should choose a place where you will have access to a copy machine. In describing the documents, be sufficiently specific and detailed so that it is clear what you are requesting. (For example: *Payroll records for John*

Smith, Social Security #555-55-9999, for the year 2001 and year-to-date for 2002. Do not just say "John Smith's records.")

NOTE: *The* **SUBPOENA** *gives the person receiving it the option to just make copies and send them to you, instead of appearing on the date specified, and you may be required to pay the reasonable cost of copying the documents.*

- Leave the date and clerk's signature spaces blank. The clerk will fill these in later.
- At the bottom of the first page of the form is a provision relating to persons with disabilities. Call the clerk's office to ask if you need to complete this section, and if so, to get the information you need to fill in the blanks.
- On the labeled lines on the second page, fill in the date; sign your name; and, type in your name, address, and telephone information.

> ***Warning:*** You may not have the **SUBPOENA** served on the employer until your spouse has had at least ten days to file a written objection.

Notifying Your Spouse

Next, mail a copy of the **NOTICE OF PRODUCTION FROM NONPARTY** (form 32), along with a copy of the **SUBPOENA FOR PRODUCTION OF DOCUMENTS FROM NONPARTY** (form 33), to your spouse. Make sure that you actually mail it on the date you filled in on the **NOTICE OF PRODUCTION FROM NONPARTY**. If your spouse does not file a **FAMILY LAW FINANCIAL AFFIDAVIT** or send you a written objection to the **SUBPOENA** within ten days, you will proceed with getting the **SUBPOENA** issued by the clerk. If your spouse does send you a written objection, you will either need to get your spouse to agree to give you the information or you will have to file a **MOTION TO ISSUE SUBPOENA** and get a hearing date from the judge's secretary. The judge will decide if you can send out the **SUBPOENA**.

Serving the Subpoena

Next, have the sheriff personally serve the **SUBPOENA** to the person or place named in the **SUBPOENA**. The sheriff will need at least one extra copy of the **SUBPOENA** and a check for the service fee. The employer, bank, etc., should send you the requested information. If the employer, bank, etc., calls you and says you must pay for copies, ask how much the copies will cost and send a check or money order (if the amount is not too high and you do not already have some fairly recent income information).

If the employer, bank, etc., does not provide the information, you can try sending a letter to the employer, bank, etc., saying: "unless you provide the information requested in the subpoena within seven days, a motion for contempt will be filed with the circuit court." This may scare the employer, bank, etc., into sending you the information.

The sheriff will have also filed an affidavit verifying when the **SUBPOENA** was served. There are more procedures you could go through to force the employer, bank, etc., to give the information, but it probably is not worth the hassle and you would probably need an attorney to help you with it. You can tell the judge at the final hearing that your spouse refused to provide income information and that the **SUBPOENA** was not honored by the employer. The judge may do something to help you out, or he or she may advise you to see a lawyer.

Once you collect the information needed, you can prepare for the hearing.

PROPERTY AND DEBTS

Generally, the judge will look at your property and debts and will try to divide them up *fairly*. This does not necessarily mean they will be divided fifty-fifty. What you want to do is offer the judge a reasonable solution that looks fair. Adultery or other misconduct on the part of one party may be used to justify an unequal division of property and debts.

It is time to review the **PROPERTY INVENTORY** (form 1) and the **DEBT INVENTORY** (form 2) you prepared earlier. For each item or property, note which of the following categories it fits into (it may fit into more than one):

- you really want;
- you would like to have;
- you do not care either way;
- your spouse really wants;
- your spouse would like to have; and,
- your spouse does not care either way.

Now using these categories, start a list of what each of you should own in the end. You will eventually end up with a list of things you can probably get with little difficulty (you really want and your spouse does not care), those that you will fight over (you both really want), and those that need to be divided but can probably be easily divided equally (you both do not really care).

The judge will probably try to get you to work out your disagreements at the hearing, but will not tolerate arguing for very long. In the end, the judge will arbitrarily divide up the items you cannot agree upon, or he or she may order you to sell those items and divide the money you get equally.

On the few items that are really important to you, it may be necessary for you to try to prove why you should get them. It will help if you can convince the judge of one or more of the following.

- You paid for the item out of your own earnings or funds.
- You are the one who primarily uses that item.
- You use the item in your employment, business, or hobby.
- You are willing to give up something else you really want in exchange for that item. (Of course, you will try to give up something from your *don't care* or your *like to have* list.)
- The item is needed for your children (assuming you will have custody).

The best thing you can do is make up a list of how you think the property should be divided. Make it a reasonably fair and equal list, regardless of how angry you are at your spouse. Even if the judge changes some of it to appear fair to your spouse, you will most likely get more of what you want than if you do not offer a suggestion. (No, this is not an exception to the negotiating rule of letting your spouse make the first offer because you are no longer just negotiating with your spouse. You are now negotiating with the judge. At this point, you are trying to impress the judge with your fairness—not trying to convince your spouse.)

Nonmarital Property

Special problems arise if a claim of nonmarital property becomes an issue. This may be in terms of your spouse trying to get your nonmarital property or in terms of you trying to get property you feel your spouse is wrongly claiming to be nonmarital. Basically, nonmarital property is property either of you had before you were married and kept separate. (Refer to page 30 and to Florida Statutes, Section 61.075 in Appendix A if you need to review exactly what is marital and nonmarital property.)

It is also a good idea to have any papers that prove that the property you claim to be nonmarital property is actually nonmarital property. These would be papers showing that:

- you bought the item before you were married (such as dated sales receipts);
- you inherited the item as your own property (such as certified copies of wills and probate court papers); or,
- you got the property in exchange for property you had before you got married, or for property received as a gift or through an inheritance (such as a statement from the person you made the exchange with, or some kind of receipt showing what was exchanged).

If you want to get at assets your spouse is claiming are nonmarital assets, you will need to collect the following types of evidence:

- papers showing that you helped pay for the asset (such as a check that you wrote or bank statements showing that your money went into the same account that was used to make payments on the asset);

  Example: Suppose your spouse purchased a house before you got married. During your marriage you made some of the mortgage payments with your own checking account (you will have cancelled checks, hopefully with the mortgage account number on them, to prove this). At other times, you deposited some of your paychecks into your spouse's checking account and your spouse wrote checks from that account to pay the mortgage (again, there should be some bank records and cancelled checks that can show that this was done). Since you contributed to the purchase of the house, you can claim some of the value of the house as a marital asset.

- papers showing that you paid for repairs of the asset (if you paid for repairs on the home or a car your spouse had before you were married, you can claim part of the value); or,

- papers showing that the asset was improved or increased in value during your marriage.

Example 1: Your spouse owned the house before you were married. During your marriage you and your spouse added a family room to the house. This will enable you to make a claim for some of the value of the house.

Example 2: Your spouse owned the house before you were married. The day before you got married, the house was worth $85,000. Now the house is appraised at $115,000. You can claim part of the $30,000 of the increased value.

In order to make a claim on what would otherwise appear to be your spouse's nonmarital property, you need to ask for it in your **PETITION**. If you have a contested case with property, you will use either the **PETITION FOR DISSOLUTION OF MARRIAGE WITH DEPENDENT OR MINOR CHILD(REN)** (form 4) or the **PETITION FOR DISSOLUTION OF MARRIAGE WITH PROPERTY BUT NO DEPENDENT OR MINOR CHILD(REN)** (form 5). With either form 4 or form 5, under "Section I. Marital Assets and Liabilities," you will need to check the line for item 2.c. On the lines after item 2.c., fill in a brief explanation of what property you are claiming and why. You may attach additional sheets of paper if needed and type in "see attached exhibit" on these lines. Generally, you will be claiming an interest in what would otherwise be nonmarital property because (1) you have contributed to the purchase, repair, or improvement of the property or (2) the property has increased in value during the marriage. The judge will look at whatever papers you show him or her, listen to what you and any witnesses say about the situation, and decide if you are entitled to any of the value of the property.

Judge's Decision

The judge will announce who gets which items at the hearing. Make a list of this as the judge tells you, and complete the **FINAL JUDGMENT** accordingly. Once you have completed the **FINAL JUDGMENT**, make a copy and send it to your spouse. Send the original to the judge (not the court clerk), along with a completed **CERTIFICATE OF SERVICE** (form 25) stapled to it showing the date you sent a copy to your spouse. If your spouse does not object to how you have prepared the **FINAL JUDGMENT**, the judge will sign it and return a copy to you. Send the judge the original and two copies of the **FINAL JUDGMENT**, along with two stamped envelopes (one addressed to yourself, and one to your spouse).

CHILD CUSTODY AND VISITATION

Generally, if you are the wife, the odds start out in favor of you getting custody. However, do not depend upon the odds. Start out by reviewing the guidelines the judge will use to decide the custody question. These can be found in Chapter 4. For each item listed in that section, write down an explanation of how that item applies to you. This will be your argument when you have your hearing with the judge.

Many custody battles revolve around the moral fitness of one or both of the parents. If you become involved in this type of a custody fight, you should consult a lawyer. Charges of moral unfitness (such as illegal drug use, child abuse, or immoral sexual conduct) can require long court hearings involving the testimony of many witnesses, as well as possibly the employment of private investigators. For such a hearing, you will require the help of an attorney who knows the law, what questions to ask witnesses, and the rules of evidence.

However, if the only question is whether you or your spouse have been the main caretaker of the child, you can always have friends, neighbors, and relatives come into the hearing (if they are willing to help you out) to testify on your behalf. It may not be necessary for you to have an attorney. However, if you need to subpoena unwilling witnesses to testify, you should have an attorney.

The judge's decision regarding custody will have to be put into the **FINAL JUDGMENT**. Read Chapter 7 for instructions on preparing the **FINAL JUDGMENT**.

CHILD SUPPORT

In Florida, as in most states, the question of child support is mostly a matter of a mathematical calculation. Getting a fair child support amount depends upon the accuracy of the income information presented to the judge. If you feel fairly sure that the information your spouse presents is accurate or that you have obtained accurate information about his or her income, there is not much to dispute. The judge will simply take the income information provided, use the formula to calculate the amount to be paid, and order that amount to be paid.

In most cases, there will not be much room to argue about the amount of child support, so there usually is not a need to get an attorney. If you claim your spouse has not provided accurate income information, it will be up to you to prove this to the judge by showing the income information you have obtained from your spouse's employer or other source of income.

The only areas open for argument are whatever special needs are claimed by the party asking for child support. Once again, it will be necessary for that party to provide proof of the cost of these special needs by producing billing statements, receipts, or other papers to show the amount of these needs.

The judge's decision regarding child support will have to be put into the **FINAL JUDGMENT**. Read Chapter 7 for instructions on preparing the **FINAL JUDGMENT**.

ALIMONY

A dispute over alimony may require a lawyer, especially if there is a request for permanent alimony because of a disability. Such a claim may require the testimony of expert witnesses (such as doctors, accountants, and actuaries) and requires the special knowledge of an attorney. A charge of adultery may also require a lawyer and possibly a private investigator as well.

If alimony has been requested, take a look at the section of the **PETITION** asking for alimony, and review the reasons alimony was requested. These reasons will be the subject of the court hearing on this question. You should determine what information (including papers and the testimony of witnesses) you will need to present to the judge to either support or refute the reasons alimony was requested.

For temporary (also called *rehabilitative*) alimony, the most common reason is that the person needs help until he or she can get training to enter the work force. The following questions need to be answered.

- What has the person been trained for in the past?
- What type of training is needed before the person can again be employable in that field?
- How long will this training take?
- What amount of income can be expected upon employment?
- How much money is required for the training?

Questions that may be asked in either a temporary or a permanent alimony situation include an examination of the situation of the parties during their marriage that led to the person not working; what contribution to the marriage that person made; and, what improper conduct on the part of the other party makes an award of alimony appropriate. You should be prepared to present evidence regarding these questions.

FORMS

In a contested case, your **PETITION** will have been prepared in the same manner as for an uncontested case without a **MARITAL SETTLEMENT AGREEMENT** (that is, you will prepare your **PETITION** based upon what you want the judge to order, rather than based upon an agreement with your spouse). Often, you will not know you have a contested case until your spouse files an answer to your **PETITION** that indicates he or she is disputing something. See Chapter 7 for instructions about preparing your **PETITION**. Other necessary forms include the following.

Notice for Trial

In some counties, before you can schedule a final hearing you will need to notify the court that certain things have been done, and all necessary papers have been filed. This involves such things as completing the mandatory disclosure requirements; having your spouse properly served with all necessary papers; and, (in some counties) completing any required mediation or parenting course. Notifying the court that everything is in order is accomplished by filing a **NOTICE FOR TRIAL**. (see form 39, p.304.)

This is a simple form that merely requires you to fill in the number of hours you think the trial will take and to fill in the certificate of service section to indicate how and when a copy of the form is provided to your spouse. Once this form is filed, you can then contact the clerk's office, family law intake staff, or the judge's judicial assistant to find out what you need to do to schedule the trial. Once you have a trial date, you can prepare the **ORDER SETTING MATTER FOR FINAL HEARING OR FOR STATUS CONFERENCE** (form 41) or **NOTICE OF HEARING** (form 34) as directed in Chapter 5.

Final Judgment

Your **FINAL JUDGMENT** will need to be prepared after your final hearing, to reflect what the judge orders. You will use either form 46 (if you have children) or form 47 (if you have property, but no children). You will not be able to prepare it in advance because you will not know what is ordered until the judge announces his or her decision. See Chapter 8 for instructions about preparing the **FINAL JUDGMENT**.

Final Disposition Form

See Chapter 6 for instructions for completing the **FINAL DISPOSITION FORM** (form 51). In Part II, you will check the box for "Disposed by Non-Jury Trial."

The Court Hearing

chapter 10

This chapter will help you to prepare for, and get through, the hearing with the judge to complete your divorce case. In addition to this chapter, be sure to review the information in Chapter 5 on setting a court hearing and courtroom manners. Other information may also be obtained in the chapter on your particular type of case (i.e., simplified, uncontested, or contested), as well as in Chapter 8 if you have a default situation.

PREPARATION

You will need to schedule a date for your final hearing. See Chapter 5 for instructions on setting a hearing date. Once you obtain a hearing date, you will need to notify your spouse of when the hearing will be. Even if you can call your spouse on the phone, it is a good idea to send a formal **NOTICE OF HEARING**. (see form 34 or form 35.) Fill in the **NOTICE OF HEARING** according to the instructions in Chapter 5. Then make three copies of the **NOTICE OF HEARING**. Mail one copy to your spouse, file the original with the court clerk, and keep two copies for yourself.

What Papers to Bring

You should bring copies of all papers to the hearing, including the following documents:

- ❑ all documents filed in your case (these should also be in the court clerk's file);
- ❑ your most recent paystub, federal income tax return, and W-2 forms, and any other papers showing your or your spouse's financial situation;
- ❑ any papers showing your spouse's income or property;
- ❑ the **MARITAL SETTLEMENT AGREEMENT** (form 13, 14, or 15) if you have one that has not yet been filed with the court;
- ❑ the **FINAL JUDGMENT**; and,
- ❑ the **FINAL DISPOSITION FORM** (form 51).

TESTIMONY OF CHILDREN

If you intend to have your minor child testify at the hearing, you first need to get the judge's permission. It is generally a bad idea to have your minor children testify. This can cause the child great emotional stress, due to being placed in the middle of an argument between his or her parents and due to the stress of appearing in court and testifying. Therefore, a minor child should only be brought to testify as a last resort. However, there may be situations (such as in abuse cases) in which it will help to have a child testify, or the child may want to testify (such as where the child strongly wants you to have custody). In rare cases, a child may be the only witness who can testify that a parent who claims to have no income is actually employed.

Motion for Testimony and Attendance of Minor Child(ren)

If you decide your minor child should testify, you will need to prepare and file a **MOTION FOR TESTIMONY AND ATTENDANCE OF MINOR CHILD(REN)**. (see form 42, p.307.) This form asks the judge's permission for a minor child to be subpoenaed to appear at a hearing or deposition. The form is self-explanatory and requires you to state why the court should issue the order. This is where you need to state what the child will testify about, and why the child's testimony is necessary (such as stating that there are no others with the knowledge the child has).

Example: The child will testify about incidents of physical abuse by the Respondent on January 3, 2007, and January 17, 2007, when only the child and the Respondent were present.

You will need to notify your spouse of your motion by properly serving him or her with a copy of form 42. You will also need to contact the judge's secretary or judicial assistant to find out if a hearing will be required. If so, you will need to schedule a hearing and send the proper **NOTICE OF HEARING** to your spouse. See the section on "Notifying Your Spouse" in Chapter 5.

Order for Testimony and Attendance of Minor Child(ren)

If the judge grants your request, you will need to prepare an **ORDER FOR TESTIMONY AND ATTENDANCE OF MINOR CHILD(REN)** (form 43). This form is very similar to form 42 and is also self-explanatory.

THE HEARING

The hearing will probably not take place in a large courtroom like you see on TV or in the movies. It will most likely be in what looks more like a conference room. The judge will be at the head of a table with you and your spouse on either side. The judge may start the hearing by summarizing what you are there for, asking you and your spouse if you have any additional evidence to present, and asking each of you any questions he or she may have. The judge will review the papers you filed and will probably ask you whether you understand and agree with what is in the papers. He will also ask you to explain why your marriage is *irretrievably broken*. Just tell him why you are getting divorced.

Example 1: We just don't have any interests in common anymore, and have drifted apart.

Example 2: My husband has had several affairs.

If you have any information that is different and more current than what is in the **FAMILY LAW FINANCIAL AFFIDAVITS**, you should mention to the judge that you have more current information. You will give a copy of whatever papers you have to show the changed situation (such as current paystub showing an increase in pay, or a current bank statement showing a new balance). The judge may ask to see any papers you have to prove what you have put in your **FAMILY LAW FINANCIAL AFFIDAVIT**. Your basic job at the hearing is to answer the judge's questions and provide the information needed to get your divorce.

If there are any items that you and your spouse have not yet agreed upon, tell the judge what these items are. Refer to Chapter 9 relating to the contested divorce for more information about how to handle these unresolved issues. Be prepared to make a suggestion as to how these matters should be settled and to explain to the judge why your suggestion is the best solution. If the judge asks for any information that you have not brought with you, tell the judge that you do not have it with you but you will be happy to provide him or her with the information by the end of the following day. Just be sure you get the papers to him or her.

At the end of the hearing, the judge will tell you if he or she is going to grant you a divorce and accept your settlement agreement. It would be very unusual for a judge not to grant the divorce and accept your agreement. You will tell the judge that you have prepared a proposed **FINAL JUDGMENT** and hand him or her the original. Refer to Chapter 7 regarding how to prepare the **FINAL JUDGMENT**.

You should have two extra copies of the **FINAL JUDGMENT** with you, one for yourself and one for your spouse. You should also bring two envelopes, one addressed to yourself and one addressed to your spouse, and two stamps. This is in case the judge wants to review the **FINAL JUDGMENT** and mail it to you later, instead of signing it at the hearing. If the judge wants you to make any changes in the **FINAL JUDGMENT**, make a careful note of exactly what the judge wants (ask him or her to explain it again if you did not understand the first time), and tell the judge that you will make the correction and deliver the **FINAL JUDGMENT** the following day. If the change requested is a small one, you might even be able to write in the change by hand at the hearing.

If child support or alimony is to be paid, bring a third copy of the **FINAL JUDGMENT** that can then be forwarded to the Central Governmental Depository.

When the hearing is over, thank the judge and leave. The original **FINAL JUDGMENT** and **FINAL DISPOSITION FORM** will be sent to the court clerk's office to be entered in the court's file. Take the copies of the **FINAL JUDGMENT** to the judge's secretary or judicial assistant, who will write in the date and use a stamp with the judge's name on each copy to authenticate them.

If any serious problems develop at the hearing (such as your spouse's attorney starts making a lot of technical objections or the judge gives you a hard time), just tell the judge you would like to continue the hearing so you can retain an attorney. Then go get one.

CHILD SUPPORT AGENCIES

There are two agencies you need to be aware of—the Central Governmental Depository and the Child Support Enforcement Office.

Central Governmental Depository

The *Central Governmental Depository* is the agency that processes child support and alimony payments. This is frequently a division of the court clerk's office. The spouse responsible to pay the support (or his or her employer) will make payments to the Depository. The Depository cashes that check and issues a check to the spouse entitled to receive support or alimony. Sometimes the judge's secretary or the court clerk will take an extra copy of the **FINAL JUDGMENT** and send it to the Central Depository. The Central Depository keeps the official records of what has and has not been paid.

Child Support Enforcement Office

The *Child Support Enforcement Office* is responsible for enforcing the payment of child support to parents receiving welfare (Aid to Families with Dependent Children), and others who request their services. If you are to receive support and you would like to use the enforcement services of this office, you will need to contact your local Child Support Enforcement Office. This may not be necessary if your spouse goes on an income deduction order immediately and keeps his or her job. However, if some payments are missed, you may call the Child Support Enforcement Office at any time and ask for their assistance. Visit **http://dor.myflorida.com/dor/childsupport** or call 800-622-KIDS (5437) for more information.

When You Cannot Find Your Spouse

chapter 11

Your spouse has run off and you have no idea of where he or she might be. You therefore cannot use the sheriff to deliver (personally serve) a copy of your **Petition for Dissolution of Marriage** to your spouse. Instead, you will use a method of giving notice called *service by publication*. This is one of the more complicated procedures in the legal system. You will need to follow the steps listed in this chapter very carefully.

THE DILIGENT SEARCH

The court will only permit publication when you cannot locate your spouse. This also includes the situation in which the sheriff has tried several times to personally serve your spouse, but it appears that your spouse is hiding to avoid being served. First, you will have to show that you cannot locate your spouse by letting the court know what you have done to try to find him or her.

To get an idea of what is expected of such a search, read the items in paragraph 1 of the **Affidavit of Diligent Search and Inquiry** in Appendix B. (see form 24, p.266.) You should try all of the items listed in form 24 that you believe might lead you to find your spouse. Some of these will apply to everyone, while others will only be used if they would apply to your spouse.

Example: If you know that your spouse has never been engaged in a job that might be under a union, or that is subject to any kind of professional or occupational licensing, you would not be expected to make that kind of search.

If you do come up with a current address in Florida, go back to personal service by the sheriff or service by mail. If not, continue with this procedure.

PREPARING AND FILING COURT PAPERS

Once you have completed your search, you need to notify the court. This is done by filing the **AFFIDAVIT OF DILIGENT SEARCH AND INQUIRY**. (see form 24, p.266.) This form tells the court what you have done to try to locate your spouse and asks for permission to publish your notice. (If your spouse lives in another state and you have his or her address, you may use this procedure. Since this is fairly complicated, you may want to call the sheriff in the county and state where your spouse lives and arrange for personal service by the sheriff.)

Affidavit of Diligent Search and Inquiry

Use the following instructions to complete the **AFFIDAVIT OF DILIGENT SEARCH AND INQUIRY** (form 24).

- Complete the top portion according to the instructions in the first section of Chapter 5, page 56.
- Type your name in the blank in the first (unnumbered) paragraph.
- In paragraph 1, check the line before all of the items that you used in your search for your spouse. If you cannot locate your spouse by other means, you will need to check with the various branches of the armed forces to find out if your spouse is in the military service. This will require you to use the **MEMORANDUM FOR CERTIFICATE OF MILITARY SERVICE** (form 21). It is explained in more detail on page 113. The last item is for you to add anything that was not covered by the other items.
- In paragraph 2, check the appropriate space to indicate if you know your spouse's age. (If you do know, fill in his or her age on the line indicated.)
- In paragraph 3, you will need to select one of the three optional paragraphs. If you have located your spouse and he or she lives outside of Florida, you will need to fill in his or her address on the line in paragraph "b."

- Fill in your name, address, and telephone information on the lines below the line marked "Signature of Petitioner."

- Take the form to a notary public and sign your name before the notary on the line marked "Signature of Petitioner."

Notice for Action for Dissolution of Marriage

You will also prepare a **NOTICE OF ACTION FOR DISSOLUTION OF MARRIAGE**. (see form 23, p.264.)

To complete form 23, you must do the following.

- Complete the top portion according to the instructions in the first section of Chapter 5, page 56.

- Type your spouse's name and last known address where indicated after the words "TO: {name of Respondent}."

- Type your name and address in the blanks in the first paragraph. Leave the other spaces blank, as they are for the clerk to complete.

- Take the original **AFFIDAVIT OF DILIGENT SEARCH AND INQUIRY** (form 24) and the original and two copies of the **NOTICE OF ACTION** (form 23) to the court clerk.

The clerk will fill in the remaining blanks on the **NOTICE OF ACTION FOR DISSOLUTION OF MARRIAGE** (form 23) and return two copies to you. If the clerk finds any errors in your papers, he or she will notify you on what needs to be corrected. You should provide the clerk with a self-addressed, stamped envelope when you deliver these papers.

PUBLISHING

Your next step is to have a newspaper publish your **NOTICE OF ACTION FOR DISSOLUTION OF MARRIAGE** (form 23). Check the Yellow Pages listings under *Newspapers*, and call several of the smaller ones in your county (making sure it is in the same county as the court), and ask if they are approved for legal announcements. If they are, ask how much they charge to publish a **NOTICE OF ACTION FOR DISSOLUTION OF MARRIAGE** that does not involve property. What you are searching for is the cheapest paper. Most areas have a paper that specializes in the publishing of legal announcements at a much cheaper rate than the regular daily newspapers. If you look around the courthouse, you may be able to find a copy or newsstand for this paper.

Once you have found the paper you want, send them a copy of the **Notice of Action for Dissolution of Marriage**, along with a cover letter stating:

> *Please take notice of the return date in the enclosed Notice of Action, and ensure that the dates of publication meet the legal requirement that the return date be not less than twenty-eight nor more than sixty days after the first publication. If you cannot comply with this requirement, please notify me immediately so I can obtain an amended Notice of Action.*

The **Notice of Action for Dissolution of Marriage** will be published once a week for four weeks. Get a copy of the paper the first time it will appear and check to be sure it was printed correctly. If you find an error, notify the newspaper immediately.

Look at the date the clerk put in the blank space in the main paragraph of the **Notice of Action for Dissolution of Marriage**. You must make sure that this date is at least twenty-eight days after the date the newspaper first published the **Notice of Action for Dissolution of Marriage**. Also, make sure it is no more than sixty days after the date of the first publication. If these requirements are not met, notify the newspaper of *their* mistake. Remind them of your cover letter if necessary. You will also need to prepare a new **Notice of Action for Dissolution of Marriage** for the clerk to sign and go through this procedure again. If the newspaper made the mistake, they should not charge you for the second publication.

As indicated in the **Notice of Action for Dissolution of Marriage**, your spouse has until a certain date to respond. If your spouse responds to the notice published in the newspaper, proceed with either the uncontested or contested procedure as necessary. If your spouse does not respond by the date indicated in the **Notice of Action for Dissolution of Marriage**, proceed with the **Motion for Default** (form 28), as discussed in Chapter 8.

Special Circumstances

chapter 12

This chapter covers some of the special situations that are not elsewhere in this book, such as:

- what to do if you cannot afford the court costs (such as filing fees and service fees);
- how to protect yourself and your children from an abusive spouse;
- how to protect your property if you fear your spouse may try to dispose of it or hide it;
- how to obtain temporary support and custody;
- how your divorce will affect your tax situation;
- how pension plans are treated in divorce;
- what to do if your spouse also files for divorce; and,
- how to enforce a temporary court order for support.

WHEN YOU CANNOT AFFORD COURT COSTS

In order to qualify for a waiver of the filing fee, you must be *indigent*. If you are indigent, your income is probably low enough for you to qualify for public assistance (welfare).

Application for Determination of Civil Indigent Status

If you cannot afford to pay the filing fee and other costs associated with the divorce, you will need to file an **APPLICATION FOR DETERMINATION OF CIVIL INDIGENT STATUS**. (see form 7, p.194.)

> ***Warning:*** If you decide to use this form, you will probably be asked for more information to prove that you meet the requirements for being declared indigent and are eligible to have the filing and service fees waived. Before you file this form, you may want to see if the court clerk will give you any information on what is required to be declared indigent. Be aware that you can be held in contempt of court for giving false information on this form.

Use the following instructions to complete the **APPLICATION FOR DETERMINATION OF CIVIL INDIGENT STATUS** (form 7).

- Complete the top portion of the form according to the instructions in Chapter 5, page 56.
- In paragraph 1, fill in the number of dependents you have.
- In paragraph 2, fill in your take-home pay, and check the appropriate space to indicate if the amount is paid weekly, biweekly (every other week), semimonthly (twice a month), monthly, or yearly.
- For paragraph 3, circle either "Yes" or "No" for each item. For any items you check "Yes," fill in the amount. Also check the appropriate space to indicate if the amount is paid weekly, biweekly, semimonthly, monthly, or yearly.
- For paragraph 4, circle either "Yes" or "No" for each category or item of property. For any items you check "Yes," fill in the value of that item of property.
- In paragraph 5, fill in the total amount of your debts. Refer to your **DEBT INVENTORY** (form 2), which lists your debts.

- In paragraph 6, circle either "Yes" or "No" at the far right of the page, to indicate whether you have hired a lawyer.

- Fill in the date you sign this form, your date of birth, and your driver's license or other ID number in the spaces as indicated; sign on the signature line; and, fill in your name, address, and phone number in the spaces as indicated.

- Take this form to the court clerk, along with cash, check, or money order for $25. The clerk will complete the portion of the form below the heading "Clerk's Determination."

The clerk will review the information you have filled in, and will either check "Indigent" or "Not Indigent," and will fill in the date and sign the form. If you are determined to be indigent, you will need to enroll in the clerk's office payment plan, and follow any other instructions given by the clerk. Being determined indigent allows you to special arrangements for the payment of court costs and the sheriff's service fee. However, if you need to publish a **Notice of Action for Dissolution of Marriage** (form 23) in a newspaper, you will still need to pay the newspaper's fee. The determination of indigency only relates to fees charged by certain government agencies, such as the court and the sheriff's office. Private persons or companies are not required to make any special arrangements or provide you with free services.

PROTECTING YOURSELF, YOUR CHILDREN, AND YOUR PROPERTY

Some people have three special concerns when getting prepared to file for a divorce—fear of physical attack by their spouse, fear that their spouse will take the children and leave the state or go into hiding, and fear that their spouse will try to take the marital property and hide it. There are additional legal papers you can file if you feel you are in any of these situations.

Protecting Yourself

If you fear violence from your spouse, go to the court clerk and ask for assistance in filing a *Petition for Protection From Domestic Violence*. The clerk can provide the necessary forms and advise you of the procedure to follow.

Protecting Your Children

If you fear physical violence directed at your children, you can use the same procedures you would use for protecting yourself from violence. If you are worried that your spouse may try to kidnap your children, you should make sure that the day care center, babysitter, relative, or whomever you leave the children with at any time, is aware that you are in the process of a divorce and that the children are only to be released to you personally (not to your spouse or to any other relative, friend, etc.).

To prevent your spouse from taking the children out of the United States, you can apply for a passport for each child. Once a passport is issued, the government will not issue another. So, get their passport and lock it up in a safe-deposit box. (This will prevent them from being taken to Canada, Mexico, and overseas.) You can also file a motion to prevent the removal of the children from the state and to deny passport services. You should be able to obtain forms for this motion from the court clerk of your local law library.

Protecting Your Property

If you genuinely fear that your spouse will try to remove money from bank accounts and try to hide important papers showing what property you own, you may want to take this same action before your spouse can. However, you can make a great deal of trouble for yourself with the judge if you do this to try to get these assets for yourself. So, make a complete list of any property you do take, and be sure to include these items in your **FAMILY LAW FINANCIAL AFFIDAVIT** (form 8 or form 9).

You may need to convince the judge that you only took these items temporarily, in order to preserve them until a **FINAL JUDGMENT** is entered. Also, do not spend any cash you take from a bank account, or sell or give away any items of property you take. Any cash should be placed in a separate bank account, without your spouse's name on it, and kept separate from any other cash you have. Any papers—such as deeds, car titles, stock or bond certificates, etc.—should be placed in a safe-deposit box, without your spouse's name on it. The idea is not to take these things for yourself, but to get them in a safe place so your spouse cannot hide them and deny they ever existed.

If your spouse is determined and resourceful, there is no guaranteed way to prevent the things discussed in this section from happening. All you can do is put as many obstacles in his or her way as possible and prepare him or her to suffer legal consequences for acting improperly.

TEMPORARY SUPPORT AND CUSTODY

If your spouse has left you with the mortgage and the monthly bills and is not helping you out financially, you may want to consider asking the court to order your spouse to make temporary support payments for you (and your children if you have any) during the period of time you are going through the divorce procedure. Of course, if you were the only person bringing in income and have been paying all the bills, do not expect to get any temporary support.

Motion for Temporary Support—with Children

If you have any children, you will need to prepare a **MOTION FOR TEMPORARY SUPPORT WITH DEPENDENT OR MINOR CHILD(REN)**. (see form 52, p.338.) Also, prepare a **TEMPORARY ORDER OF SUPPORT WITH DEPENDENT OR MINOR CHILD(REN)**. (see form 53, p.341.) If you do not have any children, you will prepare a **MOTION FOR TEMPORARY SUPPORT WITH NO DEPENDENT OR MINOR CHILD(REN)** (form 54, p.350) and a **TEMPORARY SUPPORT ORDER WITH NO DEPENDENT OR MINOR CHILD(REN)**. (see form 55, p.352.)

Use the following instructions to complete the **MOTION FOR TEMPORARY SUPPORT WITH DEPENDENT OR MINOR CHILD(REN)** (form 52).

- Complete the top portion of the form according to the instructions at the beginning of Chapter 5, page 56.
- Check the space for "Petitioner" or "Respondent," whichever applies to you.
- In paragraphs 1 through 4, check all of the items that you want the judge to order, and fill in the required information for each item you check. For each item, you need to fill in enough information to clearly explain what you want the judge to order, and why the judge should do what you ask. Paragraph 5 is where you would fill in any requests that are not covered in paragraphs 1 through 4. Read paragraphs 6 through 8 and be sure you have filed any of the forms required, or be sure to file the necessary forms along with form 52.
- Complete the certificate of service section beginning with "I certify."
- Sign your name on the line marked "Signature of Party," and type in your name, address, and telephone information on the lines where indicated.

- If available, attach copies of any of your spouse's paystubs, most recent tax forms, or other information showing your spouse's income. You should have already filed your **FAMILY LAW FINANCIAL AFFIDAVIT** (form 8 or form 9), which will show what your monthly expenses are, as well as your income.

Motion for Temporary Support—No Children

The **MOTION FOR TEMPORARY SUPPORT WITH NO DEPENDENT OR MINOR CHILD(REN)** (form 54) is completed in the same manner as form 52, except that form 54 does not have the provisions for temporary child custody and child support, as there are no dependent or minor children involved.

Temporary Order

If you have a good reason for not notifying your spouse in advance, either form 52 or 54 needs to be presented to the judge, along with the **TEMPORARY ORDER OF SUPPORT WITH DEPENDENT OR MINOR CHILD(REN)** (form 53) or **TEMPORARY SUPPORT ORDER WITH NO DEPENDENT OR MINOR CHILD(REN)** (form 55). Call the judge's secretary and say that you would like to submit a *motion for temporary support* to the judge and ask how you should submit it. The secretary may tell you to come in with your papers at a certain time, to mail them to the judge, or to submit them to the court clerk's office. Just follow the instructions. If possible, you should notify your spouse of your motion just before you go see the judge, either verbally or by mailing and filing a **CERTIFICATE OF SERVICE** (form 25). Otherwise, be prepared to tell the judge why you were unable to notify your spouse.

The **TEMPORARY ORDER OF SUPPORT WITH DEPENDENT OR MINOR CHILD(REN)** (form 53) is very similar to the **FINAL JUDGMENT OF DISSOLUTION OF MARRIAGE WITH DEPENDENT OR MINOR CHILD(REN)** (form 46). To complete form 53, see the instructions in Chapter 8 for completing form 46. The **TEMPORARY SUPPORT ORDER WITH NO DEPENDENT OR MINOR CHILD(REN)** (form 55) is very similar to the **FINAL JUDGMENT OF DISSOLUTION OF MARRIAGE WITH PROPERTY BUT NO DEPENDENT OR MINOR CHILD(REN)** (form 47). To complete form 55, see the instructions in Chapter 8 for completing form 47.

Once you have a copy of the **TEMPORARY ORDER** (form 53 or form 55) that has been signed by the judge, mail or deliver a copy to your spouse. Then complete a **CERTIFICATE OF SERVICE** (form 25) to show that you have notified your spouse. If your spouse has not filed any papers with the court yet, you should have the **TEMPORARY ORDER** served on him or her by the sheriff (see Chapter 5 for information on having papers served by the sheriff). It is important to satisfy the judge that your spouse knew about the **TEMPORARY ORDER** if you need to collect support arrearages or file contempt proceedings for violation of the custody order.

TAXES

As you are no doubt aware, the United States' income tax code is complicated and ever-changing. For this reason, it is impossible to give detailed legal advice with respect to taxes in a book such as this. Any such information could easily be out of date by the time of publication. Therefore, it is strongly recommended that you consult your accountant, lawyer, or whomever prepares your tax return, about the tax consequences of a divorce. A few general concerns are discussed in this chapter, to give you an idea of some of the tax questions that can arise.

Taxes and Property Division

You and your spouse may be exchanging title to property as a result of your divorce. Generally, there will not be any tax to pay as the result of such a transfer. However, whomever gets a piece of property will be responsible to pay any tax that may become due upon sale.

The Internal Revenue Service (IRS) has issued numerous rulings about how property is to be treated in divorce situations. You need to be especially careful if you are transferring any tax shelters or other complicated financial arrangements.

Be sure to read the following section on alimony because fancy property settlements are susceptible to tax problems.

Taxes and Alimony

Alimony can cause the most tax problems of any aspect of divorce. The IRS is always making new rulings on whether an agreement is really alimony or is really property division. The basic rule is that alimony is treated as income to the person receiving it, and as a deduction for the person paying it. Therefore, in order to manipulate the tax consequences, many couples try to show something as part of the property settlement, instead of as alimony; or the reverse.

As the IRS becomes aware of these tax games, it issues rulings on how it will view a certain arrangement. If you are simply talking about the regular, periodic payment of cash, the IRS will probably not question that it is alimony. (However, if you try to call it property settlement, you may run into problems.) The important thing is to consult a tax expert if you are considering any unusual or creative property settlement or alimony arrangements.

Taxes and Child Support

There are simple tax rules regarding child support.

- Whoever has custody gets to claim the children on his or her tax return (unless both parents file a special IRS form agreeing to a different arrangement each year).
- The parent receiving child support does not need to report it as income.
- The parent paying child support cannot deduct it.

If you are sharing physical custody, the parent with whom the child lives for the most time during the year is entitled to claim the child as a dependent.

The IRS form to reverse this must be filed each year. Therefore, if you and your spouse have agreed that you will get to claim the children (even though you do not have custody), you should get your spouse to sign an open-ended form that you can file each year, so that you do not have to worry about it each year. A phone call to the IRS can help you get answers to questions on this point. Visit **www.irs.gov** or call 800-829-1040 for more information.

PENSION PLANS

Pension plans or retirement plans for you and your spouse are marital assets. They may be very valuable assets. If you and your spouse are young, and have not been working very long, your pension plans may not be worth the worry. Also, if you have both worked and have similar pensions plans, it may be best just to include a provision in your settlement agreement that "each party shall keep his or her own pension plan."

However, if you have been married a long time and your spouse worked while you stayed home to raise the children, your spouse's pension plan may be worth a lot of money and may be necessary to see you through retirement. If you and your spouse cannot agree on how to divide a pension plan, you should see an attorney. The valuation of pension plans and how they are to be divided is a complicated matter that you should not attempt alone.

IF YOUR SPOUSE ALSO FILED FOR DIVORCE

If your spouse filed for divorce first, you need to respond in writing within twenty days of receiving the **SUMMONS** (form 19) and **PETITION**. You can use the **ANSWER, WAIVER, AND REQUEST FOR COPY OF FINAL JUDGMENT OF DISSOLUTION OF MARRIAGE**, but this will basically admit what your spouse is asking for in his or her **PETITION**. (see form 18, p.253.) If you want to file a more complete response, go to the court clerk or your local law library and obtain a form called an *Answer/Response to and Counterpetition for Dissolution of Marriage*. This is also known as *Florida Family Law Form 12.902(a)*. This is similar to the **PETITION** forms, so refer to the instructions for those forms if you need further information. File your *Answer/Response to and Counterpetition for Dissolution of Marriage* with the clerk. You will also need to mail a copy to your spouse, and complete and file a **CERTIFICATE OF SERVICE** (form 25) to show the court that copies were mailed. Your spouse has twenty days to respond to your counterpetition.

If you filed for divorce first, but your spouse then filed an *Answer/Response to and Counterpetition for Dissolution of Marriage*, you will need to file an *Answer to Counterpetition*. This is also known as *Form 12.903(d)*, which can also be obtained from the court clerk or your local law library.

ENFORCING TEMPORARY ORDERS

If your spouse is not complying with a temporary order or with the final judgment, you need to ask the court to enforce the existing order. If the problem is nonpayment of support, the easiest way to do this is to contact your local *Child Support Enforcement* (CSE) office, which can tell you what they can do to help you try to collect. There should be a listing for the CSE office in the government section of your telephone directory, or you can call the court clerk's office for the phone number. If the noncompliance is with something the CSE office cannot help you with or for some reason you want to try enforcement on your own, file a **MOTION FOR CIVIL CONTEMPT/ENFORCEMENT**. (see form 56, p.358.)

Use the following instructions to complete form 56.

- Complete the top portion of the form according to the instructions at the beginning of Chapter 5, page 56.

- In the first, unnumbered paragraph, check the spaces for "Petitioner" or "Respondent" to indicate you and your spouse.

- In paragraph 1, fill in the title of the order that your spouse has violated (e.g, **Temporary Order of Support** or **Final Judgment of Dissolution of Marriage**); the date of the order; and, the identity of the court that entered it (e.g., Circuit Court, Tampa, Florida).

- In paragraph 2, fill in what the order required your spouse to do (e.g., *Pay the sum of $200 per month for the support of one minor child*, or *Allow visitation on alternate weekends*).

- In paragraph 3, fill in a statement of how the order has been violated (e.g., *The Respondent has failed to make any child support payments since February 12, 2007*, or *The Petitioner has refused to permit visitation since March 24, 2007*).

- In paragraph 4, indicate what you want the judge to do. If you check item "0," you will need to type in that you want your spouse held in jail until he or she pays a certain amount of the arrearage that is owed, or otherwise agrees to comply with the order (e.g., *That the Respondent be incarcerated until such time as he pays the sum of $500 toward the arrearage owed*). If you do not do this, the judge will decide the period of incarceration and the amount to get out of jail earlier.

- Complete the certificate of service section, including your spouse's name, address, and phone information.

- Take this form to a notary public and sign it before the notary.

You will need to follow the standard procedures indicated in Chapter 5 to file this form with the clerk, obtain a hearing date, and properly notify your spouse. At the hearing, you will need to produce evidence of your spouse's failure to comply with the court order. This can consist of such things as your testimony; the testimony of others; written records of payment or account statements from you, the Central Governmental Depository, or CSE office; and, records subpoenaed from your spouse's employer, bank, stock broker, etc.

The Future

chapter 13

Once the judge signs your divorce judgment, it is an enforceable order of the court. If you have a settlement agreement, this includes all of the terms of the settlement agreement. You or your spouse are legally required to follow it and are subject to penalties for contempt of court if the terms are not followed. If your spouse does not follow some provision of the judgment, that does not mean that you can retaliate by not following another provision.

Example: If the noncustodial parent is not paying child support, this does not give the custodial parent the right to withhold visitation. Conversely, if the custodial parent denies visitation, this does not give the noncustodial parent the right to stop paying child support.

In any such situation, the proper course of action is to go back to court to complain of your ex-spouse's noncompliance.

Although it is extremely difficult, if not impossible, to change your property division, other parts of your divorce judgment are not necessarily forever carved in stone. If circumstances change, it may be possible to change alimony, child support, child custody, or visitation. These matters can be changed if you and your ex-spouse agree to the change. They may also be changed without the agreement of the parties if the circumstances justify a change.

If alimony was not awarded in the divorce judgment, it is very unlikely that you will be able to ask for it later. However, if alimony was awarded, it can be increased, decreased, or eliminated if the circumstances warrant.

Child support may be modified (up or down) if the needs of the children change, if the amount of time they spend with each parent changes, or if the income of you or your spouse change. Child custody can be changed (this is more difficult than changing support), but usually requires proof that the current custodial parent is somehow unfit to have continued custody.

A visitation schedule that becomes unworkable may be changed, although it is more difficult to limit or end a parent's visitation without a showing that the children are likely to suffer harm.

Once your divorce is final, you are legally free to get married again. If you ever find yourself thinking about marriage, be careful before getting married again now that you know and appreciate how difficult it can be to get out of a marriage. If you decide to get married, you would be wise to consider a *premarital agreement*, also called a *prenuptial agreement*. This is an agreement made before marriage, in which both parties disclose all of their property and debts, and agree how things will be handled in the event they separate, or in the event one of them dies. A premarital agreement can avoid a long and costly divorce. You can either see a lawyer for a premarital agreement, or prepare your own with the help of various books.

Glossary

A

acknowledgment. A statement, written or oral, made before a person authorized by law to administer oaths (such as a notary public).

adult. In Florida, a person 18 years of age or older.

affiant. The legal term for the person who signs an affidavit.

affidavit. A person's written statement of facts, signed under oath before a person authorized to administer oaths (such as a notary public or court clerk).

alimony. Money paid by one spouse to help support the other spouse.

annulment. A legal procedure by which a marriage is declared invalid.

answer. The title of a legal pleading that responds to a petition, usually by either admitting or denying the allegations in the petition.

C

counterpetition. A response to a petition, which seeks some relief from the court rather than merely admitting or denying the allegations in the petition.

creditor. A person or institution to whom money is owed.

D

debtor. A person or institution who owes money.

deposition. The posing of verbal questions to one party, who is required to answer verbally under oath, usually before a court reporter.

dissolution of marriage. The legal term for divorce used in Florida (as well as in some other states).

E

equitable distribution. A way to divide marital property, the goal of which is to treat the parties fairly under the circumstances.

execute. To sign a legal document, in the legally required manner (e.g., before witnesses or a notary public), thereby making it effective.

F

final judgment. The order of the court at the end of a trial or pursuant to a settlement agreement.

Florida Statutes. The laws passed by the Florida legislature.

H

homestead. Real estate that is a person's primary place of residence. In Florida, the homestead is given special treatment for property tax purposes and is exempt from the claims of creditors (other than a creditor holding a mortgage on the homestead property).

I

institution. As used in this book, any type of business entity (e.g., corporation, partnership, limited liability company), organization, or other entity other than an individual person.

instrument. A legal term for a document.

interrogatories. Written questions sent by one party to the other that must be answered in writing under oath.

irretrievably broken. A legal way of saying that a marriage is broken and cannot be repaired.

J

joint custody. Where both parents share the responsibility of making decisions regarding their child.

joint tenancy. A way for two or more people to own property, so that when one owner dies, his or her interest in the property passes automatically to the remaining owner or owners.

M

marital assets. Assets that are considered the property of both parties to a marriage.

motion. A party's written or oral request that the judge take certain action.

N

nonmarital assets. Assets that are considered the separate property of only one party to a marriage. Generally these are assets that were acquired before the marriage, or acquired by one party as a separate gift or inheritance.

notary public. A person who is legally authorized by the state to acknowledge signatures on legal documents.

P

pay-on-death account. A financial account, such as a bank account or certificate of deposit, which is payable to a certain person upon the death of the account holder.

personal property. All property other than land and things permanently attached to the land (such as buildings).

petition. The title of the legal pleading that begins a divorce case.

primary residential responsibility. The parent with whom a child will live a majority of the time has the primary residential responsibility.

R

recording. The process of filing a deed, mortgage, or other legal document affecting title to land, with the court clerk's office.

rotating custody. Where custody changes periodically (e.g., the child lives with the mother for three months, then with the father for the next three months).

S

secondary residential responsibility. The parent with whom a child will live less than a majority of the time has secondary residential responsibility.

shared custody. *See joint custody.*

shared parental responsibility. *See joint custody.*

sole parental custody. Where one parent is given the sole legal right to make decisions regarding his or her child.

specified visitation. Visitation with a set schedule, and often detailed terms for how visitation is to be carried out.

subpoena. An order from a court that a person appear before the court, or at a deposition, and give testimony.

subpoena duces tecum. A particular type of subpoena that requires the person to bring certain, specified documents, records, or other items to the court or deposition.

supervised visitation. Visitation that is in the presence of a third party.

T

tenancy by the entirety. This is essentially the same as joint tenancy, but it can only occur between a husband and wife. Upon the death of one spouse, the property automatically passes to the surviving spouse.

tenancy in common. A way for two or more people to own property, whereby if one of the owners dies, his or her interest in the property passes to his or her heirs (not to the other co-owners).

title. A document that proves ownership of property.

Florida Statutes, Child Support Schedule, and Family Law Rules of Procedure

appendix a

The following are excerpts from the Florida Statutes relating to property distribution, alimony, and child support (including the Child Support Schedule) and the Family Law Rules of Procedure regarding mandatory disclosure. These are not the only provisions relating to these subjects. It is strongly recommended that you read Chapter 61 of the Florida Statutes in its entirety, as well as the Family Law Rules of Procedure. Visit **www.leg.state.fl.us/statutes** for the complete statutes.

Florida Statutes

61.075 Equitable distribution of marital assets and liabilities.—

(1) In a proceeding for dissolution of marriage, in addition to all other remedies available to a court to do equity between the parties, or in a proceeding for disposition of assets following a dissolution of marriage by a court which lacked jurisdiction over the absent spouse or lacked jurisdiction to dispose of the assets, the court shall set apart to each spouse that spouse's nonmarital assets and liabilities, and in distributing the marital assets and liabilities between the parties, the court must begin with the premise that the distribution should be equal, unless there is a justification for an unequal distribution based on all relevant factors, including:

(a) The contribution to the marriage by each spouse, including contributions to the care and education of the children and services as homemaker.

(b) The economic circumstances of the parties.

(c) The duration of the marriage.

(d) Any interruption of personal careers or educational opportunities of either party.

(e) The contribution of one spouse to the personal career or educational opportunity of the other spouse.

(f) The desirability of retaining any asset, including an interest in a business, corporation, or professional practice, intact and free from any claim or interference by the other party.

(g) The contribution of each spouse to the acquisition, enhancement, and production of income or the improvement of, or the incurring of liabilities to, both the marital assets and the nonmarital assets of the parties.
(h) The desirability of retaining the marital home as a residence for any dependent child of the marriage, or any other party, when it would be equitable to do so, it is in the best interest of the child or that party, and it is financially feasible for the parties to maintain the residence until the child is emancipated or until exclusive possession is otherwise terminated by a court of competent jurisdiction. In making this determination, the court shall first determine if it would be in the best interest of the dependent child to remain in the marital home; and, if not, whether other equities would be served by giving any other party exclusive use and possession of the marital home.
(i) The intentional dissipation, waste, depletion, or destruction of marital assets after the filing of the petition or within 2 years prior to the filing of the petition.
(j) Any other factors necessary to do equity and justice between the parties.
(2) If the court awards a cash payment for the purpose of equitable distribution of marital assets, to be paid in full or in installments, the full amount ordered shall vest when the judgment is awarded and the award shall not terminate upon remarriage or death of either party, unless otherwise agreed to by the parties, but shall be treated as a debt owed from the obligor or the obligor's estate to the obligee or the obligee's estate, unless otherwise agreed to by the parties.
(3) In any contested dissolution action wherein a stipulation and agreement has not been entered and filed, any distribution of marital assets or marital liabilities shall be supported by factual findings in the judgment or order based on competent substantial evidence with reference to the factors enumerated in subsection (1). The distribution of all marital assets and marital liabilities, whether equal or unequal, shall include specific written findings of fact as to the following:
(a) Clear identification of nonmarital assets and ownership interests;
(b) Identification of marital assets, including the individual valuation of significant assets, and designation of which spouse shall be entitled to each asset;
(c) Identification of the marital liabilities and designation of which spouse shall be responsible for each liability;
(d) Any other findings necessary to advise the parties or the reviewing court of the trial court's rationale for the distribution of marital assets and allocation of liabilities.
(4) The judgment distributing assets shall have the effect of a duly executed instrument of conveyance, transfer, release, or acquisition which is recorded in the county where the property is located when the judgment, or a certified copy of the judgment, is recorded in the official records of the county in which the property is located.
(5) As used in this section:
(a) "Marital assets and liabilities" include:
1. Assets acquired and liabilities incurred during the marriage, individually by either spouse or jointly by them;
2. The enhancement in value and appreciation of nonmarital assets resulting either from the efforts of either party during the marriage or from the contribution to or expenditure thereon of marital funds or other forms of marital assets, or both;
3. Interspousal gifts during the marriage;
4. All vested and nonvested benefits, rights, and funds accrued during the marriage in retirement, pension, profit-sharing, annuity, deferred compensation, and insurance plans and programs; and
5. All real property held by the parties as tenants by the entireties, whether acquired prior to or during the marriage, shall be presumed to be a marital asset. If, in any case, a party makes a claim to the contrary, the burden of proof shall be on the party asserting the claim for a special equity.
(b) "Nonmarital assets and liabilities" include:
1. Assets acquired and liabilities incurred by either party prior to the marriage, and assets acquired and liabilities incurred in exchange for such assets and liabilities;
2. Assets acquired separately by either party by noninterspousal gift, bequest, devise, or descent, and assets acquired in exchange for such assets;
3. All income derived from nonmarital assets during the marriage unless the income was treated, used, or relied upon by the parties as a marital asset;
4. Assets and liabilities excluded from marital assets and liabilities by valid written agreement of the parties, and assets acquired and liabilities incurred in exchange for such assets and liabilities; and
5. Any liability incurred by forgery or unauthorized signature of one spouse signing the name of the other spouse. Any such liability shall be a nonmarital liability only of the party having committed the forgery or having affixed the unauthorized signature. In determining an award of attorney's fees and costs pursuant to s. 61.16, the court may consider forgery or an unauthorized signature by a party and may make a separate award for attorney's fees and costs occasioned by the forgery or unauthorized signature.

This subparagraph does not apply to any forged or unauthorized signature that was subsequently ratified by the other spouse.

(6) The cut-off date for determining assets and liabilities to be identified or classified as marital assets and liabilities is the earliest of the date the parties enter into a valid separation agreement, such other date as may be expressly established by such agreement, or the date of the filing of a petition for dissolution of marriage. The date for determining value of assets and the amount of liabilities identified or classified as marital is the date or dates as the judge determines is just and equitable under the circumstances. Different assets may be valued as of different dates, as, in the judge's discretion, the circumstances require.

(7) All assets acquired and liabilities incurred by either spouse subsequent to the date of the marriage and not specifically established as nonmarital assets or liabilities are presumed to be marital assets and liabilities. Such presumption is overcome by a showing that the assets and liabilities are nonmarital assets and liabilities. The presumption is only for evidentiary purposes in the dissolution proceeding and does not vest title. Title to disputed assets shall vest only by the judgment of a court. This section does not require the joinder of spouses in the conveyance, transfer, or hypothecation of a spouse's individual property; affect the laws of descent and distribution; or establish community property in this state.

(8) The court may provide for equitable distribution of the marital assets and liabilities without regard to alimony for either party. After the determination of an equitable distribution of the marital assets and liabilities, the court shall consider whether a judgment for alimony shall be made.

(9) To do equity between the parties, the court may, in lieu of or to supplement, facilitate, or effectuate the equitable division of marital assets and liabilities, order a monetary payment in a lump sum or in installments paid over a fixed period of time.

61.076 Distribution of retirement plans upon dissolution of marriage.—

(1) All vested and nonvested benefits, rights, and funds accrued during the marriage in retirement, pension, profit-sharing, annuity, deferred compensation, and insurance plans and programs are marital assets subject to equitable distribution.

(2) If the parties were married for at least 10 years, during which at least one of the parties who was a member of the federal uniformed services performed at least 10 years of creditable service, and if the division of marital property includes a division of uniformed services retired or retainer pay, the final judgment shall include the following:

(a) Sufficient information to identify the member of the uniformed services;

(b) Certification that the Soldiers' and Sailors' Civil Relief Act of 1940 was observed if the decree was issued while the member was on active duty and was not represented in court;

(c) A specification of the amount of retired or retainer pay to be distributed pursuant to the order, expressed in dollars or as a percentage of the disposable retired or retainer pay.

(3) An order which provides for distribution of retired or retainer pay from the federal uniformed services shall not provide for payment from this source more frequently than monthly and shall not require the payor to vary normal pay and disbursement cycles for retired or retainer pay in order to comply with the order.

61.08 Alimony.—

(1) In a proceeding for dissolution of marriage, the court may grant alimony to either party, which alimony may be rehabilitative or permanent in nature. In any award of alimony, the court may order periodic payments or payments in lump sum or both. The court may consider the adultery of either spouse and the circumstances thereof in determining the amount of alimony, if any, to be awarded. In all dissolution actions, the court shall include findings of fact relative to the factors enumerated in subsection (2) supporting an award or denial of alimony.

(2) In determining a proper award of alimony or maintenance, the court shall consider all relevant economic factors, including but not limited to:

(a) The standard of living established during the marriage.

(b) The duration of the marriage.

(c) The age and the physical and emotional condition of each party.

(d) The financial resources of each party, the nonmarital and the marital assets and liabilities distributed to each.

(e) When applicable, the time necessary for either party to acquire sufficient education or training to enable such party to find appropriate employment.

(f) The contribution of each party to the marriage, including, but not limited to, services rendered in homemaking, child care, education, and career building of the other party.

(g) All sources of income available to either party.

The court may consider any other factor necessary to do equity and justice between the parties.

(3) To the extent necessary to protect an award of alimony, the court may order any party who is ordered to pay alimony to purchase or maintain a life

insurance policy or a bond, or to otherwise secure such alimony award with any other assets which may be suitable for that purpose.

(4)(a) With respect to any order requiring the payment of alimony entered on or after January 1, 1985, unless the provisions of paragraph (c) or paragraph (d) apply, the court shall direct in the order that the payments of alimony be made through the appropriate depository as provided in s. 61.181.

* * * * *

(c) If there is no minor child, alimony payments need not be directed through the depository.

(d) 1. If there is a minor child of the parties and both parties so request, the court may order that alimony payments need not be directed through the depository. In this case, the order of support shall provide, or be deemed to provide, that either party may subsequently apply to the depository to require that payments be made through the depository. The court shall provide a copy of the order to the depository.

2. If the provisions of subparagraph 1. apply, either party may subsequently file with the depository an affidavit alleging default or arrearages in payment and stating that the party wishes to initiate participation in the depository program. The party shall provide copies of the affidavit to the court and the other party or parties. Fifteen days after receipt of the affidavit, the depository shall notify all parties that future payments shall be directed to the depository.

61.30 Child support guidelines.—

(1)(a) The child support guideline amount as determined by this section presumptively establishes the amount the trier of fact shall order as child support in an initial proceeding for such support or in a proceeding for modification of an existing order for such support, whether the proceeding arises under this or another chapter. The trier of fact may order payment of child support which varies, plus or minus 5 percent, from the guideline amount, after considering all relevant factors, including the needs of the child or children, age, station in life, standard of living, and the financial status and ability of each parent. The trier of fact may order payment of child support in an amount which varies more than 5 percent from such guideline amount only upon a written finding explaining why ordering payment of such guideline amount would be unjust or inappropriate. Notwithstanding the variance limitations of this section, the trier of fact shall order payment of child support which varies from the guideline amount as provided in paragraph (11)(b) whenever any of the children are required by court order or mediation agreement to spend a substantial amount of time with the primary and secondary residential parents. This requirement applies to any living arrangement, whether temporary or permanent.

(b) The guidelines may provide the basis for proving a substantial change in circumstances upon which a modification of an existing order may be granted. However, the difference between the existing monthly obligation and the amount provided for under the guidelines shall be at least 15 percent or $50, whichever amount is greater, before the court may find that the guidelines provide a substantial change in circumstances.

(c) For each support order reviewed by the department as required by s. 409.2564(12), if the amount of the child support award under the order differs by at least 10 percent but not less than $25 from the amount that would be awarded under s. 61.30, the department shall seek to have the order modified and any modification shall be made without a requirement for proof or showing of a change in circumstances.

(2) Income shall be determined on a monthly basis for the obligor and for the obligee as follows:

(a) Gross income shall include, but is not limited to, the following items:

1. Salary or wages.
2. Bonuses, commissions, allowances, overtime, tips, and other similar payments.
3. Business income from sources such as self-employment, partnership, close corporations, and independent contracts. “Business income” means gross receipts minus ordinary and necessary expenses required to produce income.
4. Disability benefits.
5. All workers' compensation benefits and settlements.
6. Unemployment compensation.
7. Pension, retirement, or annuity payments.
8. Social security benefits.
9. Spousal support received from a previous marriage or court ordered in the marriage before the court.
10. Interest and dividends.
11. Rental income, which is gross receipts minus ordinary and necessary expenses required to produce the income.
12. Income from royalties, trusts, or estates.
13. Reimbursed expenses or in kind payments to the extent that they reduce living expenses.
14. Gains derived from dealings in property, unless the gain is nonrecurring.

(b) Income on a monthly basis shall be imputed to an unemployed or underemployed parent when such employment or underemployment is found to be voluntary on that parent's part, absent physical or mental incapacity or other circumstances over which the parent has no control. In the event of such voluntary unemployment or underemployment, the employment potential and probable earnings level of the parent shall be determined based upon his or her recent work history, occupational qualifications, and prevailing earnings level in the community; however, the court may refuse to impute income to a primary residential parent if the court finds it necessary for the parent to stay home with the child.

(c) Public assistance as defined in s. 409.2554 shall be excluded from gross income.

(3) Allowable deductions from gross income shall include:

(a) Federal, state, and local income tax deductions, adjusted for actual filing status and allowable dependents and income tax liabilities.

(b) Federal insurance contributions or self-employment tax.

(c) Mandatory union dues.

(d) Mandatory retirement payments.

(e) Health insurance payments, excluding payments for coverage of the minor child.

(f) Court-ordered support for other children which is actually paid.

(g) Spousal support paid pursuant to a court order from a previous marriage or the marriage before the court.

(4) Net income for the obligor and net income for the obligee shall be computed by subtracting allowable deductions from gross income.

(5) Net income for the obligor and net income for the obligee shall be added together for a combined net income.

(6) The following schedules shall be applied to the combined net income to determine the minimum child support need:

For combined monthly available income less than the amount set out on the above schedules, the parent should be ordered to pay a child support amount, determined on a case-by-case basis, to establish the principle of payment and lay the basis for increased orders should the parent's income increase in the future. For combined monthly available income greater than the amount set out in the above schedules, the obligation shall be the minimum amount of support provided by the guidelines plus the following percentages multiplied by the amount of income over $10,000:

Child or Children					
One	Two	Three	Four	Five	Six
5.0%	7.5%	9.5%	11.0%	12.0%	12.5%

(7) Child care costs incurred on behalf of the children due to employment, job search, or education calculated to result in employment or to enhance income of current employment of either parent shall be reduced by 25 percent and then shall be added to the basic obligation. After the adjusted child care costs are added to the basic obligation, any moneys prepaid by the noncustodial parent for child care costs for the child or children of this action shall be deducted from that noncustodial parent's child support obligation for that child or those children. Child care costs shall not exceed the level required to provide quality care from a licensed source for the children.

(8) Health insurance costs resulting from coverage ordered pursuant to s. 61.13(1)(b), and any noncovered medical, dental, and prescription medication expenses of the child, shall be added to the basic obligation unless these expenses have been ordered to be separately paid on a percentage basis. After the health insurance costs are added to the basic obligation, any moneys prepaid by the noncustodial parent for health-related costs for the child or children of this action shall be deducted from that noncustodial parent's child support obligation for that child or those children.

(9) Each parent's percentage share of the child support need shall be determined by dividing each parent's net income by the combined net income.

(10) Each parent's actual dollar share of the child support need shall be determined by multiplying the minimum child support need by each parent's percentage share.

(11)(a) The court may adjust the minimum child support award, or either or both parents' share of the minimum child support award, based upon the following considerations:

1. Extraordinary medical, psychological, educational, or dental expenses.
2. Independent income of the child, not to include moneys received by a child from supplemental security income.
3. The payment of support for a parent which regularly has been paid and for which there is a demonstrated need.
4. Seasonal variations in one or both parents' incomes or expenses.
5. The age of the child, taking into account the greater needs of older children.
6. Special needs, such as costs that may be associated with the disability of a child, that have traditionally been met within the family budget even though the fulfilling of those needs will cause the support to exceed the proposed guidelines.
7. Total available assets of the obligee, obligor, and the child.

8. The impact of the Internal Revenue Service dependency exemption and waiver of that exemption. The court may order the primary residential parent to execute a waiver of the Internal Revenue Service dependency exemption if the noncustodial parent is current in support payments.
9. When application of the child support guidelines requires a person to pay another person more than 55 percent of his or her gross income for a child support obligation for current support resulting from a single support order.
10. The particular shared parental arrangement, such as where the child spends a significant amount of time, but less than 40 percent of the overnights, with the noncustodial parent, thereby reducing the financial expenditures incurred by the primary residential parent; or the refusal of the noncustodial parent to become involved in the activities of the child.
11. Any other adjustment which is needed to achieve an equitable result which may include, but not be limited to, a reasonable and necessary existing expense or debt. Such expense or debt may include, but is not limited to, a reasonable and necessary expense or debt which the parties jointly incurred during the marriage.
(b) Whenever a particular shared parental arrangement provides that each child spend a substantial amount of time with each parent, the court shall adjust any award of child support, as follows:
1. In accordance with subsections (9) and (10), calculate the amount of support obligation apportioned to the noncustodial parent without including day care and health insurance costs in the calculation and multiply the amount by 1.5.
2. In accordance with subsections (9) and (10), calculate the amount of support obligation apportioned to the custodial parent without including day care and health insurance costs in the calculation and multiply the amount by 1.5.
3. Calculate the percentage of overnight stays the child spends with each parent.
4. Multiply the noncustodial parent's support obligation as calculated in subparagraph 1. by the percentage of the custodial parent's overnight stays with the child as calculated in subparagraph 3.
5. Multiply the custodial parent's support obligation as calculated in subparagraph 2. by the percentage of the noncustodial parent's overnight stays with the child as calculated in subparagraph 3.
6. The difference between the amounts calculated in subparagraphs 4. and 5. shall be the monetary transfer necessary between the custodial and noncustodial parents for the care of the child, subject to an adjustment for day care and health insurance expenses.
7. Pursuant to subsections (7) and (8), calculate the net amounts owed by the custodial and noncustodial parents for the expenses incurred for day care and health insurance coverage for the child. Day care shall be calculated without regard to the 25-percent reduction applied by subsection (7).
8. Adjust the support obligation owed by the custodial or noncustodial parent pursuant to subparagraph 6. by crediting or debiting the amount calculated in subparagraph 7. This amount represents the child support which must be exchanged between the custodial and noncustodial parents.
9. The court may deviate from the child support amount calculated pursuant to subparagraph 8. based upon the considerations set forth in paragraph (a), as well as the custodial parent's low income and ability to maintain the basic necessities of the home for the child, the likelihood that the noncustodial parent will actually exercise the visitation granted by the court, and whether all of the children are exercising the same shared parental arrangement.
10. For purposes of adjusting any award of child support under this paragraph, "substantial amount of time" means that the noncustodial parent exercises visitation at least 40 percent of the overnights of the year.
(c) A noncustodial parent's failure to regularly exercise court-ordered or agreed visitation not caused by the custodial parent which resulted in the adjustment of the amount of child support pursuant to subparagraph (a)10. or paragraph (b) shall be deemed a substantial change of circumstances for purposes of modifying the child support award. A modification pursuant to this paragraph shall be retroactive to the date the noncustodial parent first failed to regularly exercise court-ordered or agreed visitation.
(12)(a) A parent with a support obligation may have other children living with him or her who were born or adopted after the support obligation arose. If such subsequent children exist, the court, when considering an upward modification of an existing award, may disregard the income from secondary employment obtained in addition to the parent's primary employment if the court determines that the employment was obtained primarily to support the subsequent children.
(b) Except as provided in paragraph (a), the existence of such subsequent children should not as a general rule be considered by the court as a basis for disregarding the amount provided in the guidelines. The parent with a support obligation for subsequent children may raise the existence of such subsequent children as a justification for deviation from the guidelines. However, if the existence of such subsequent children is raised, the income of the other

parent of the subsequent children shall be considered by the court in determining whether or not there is a basis for deviation from the guideline amount.

(c) The issue of subsequent children under paragraph (a) or paragraph (b) may only be raised in a proceeding for an upward modification of an existing award and may not be applied to justify a decrease in an existing award.

(13) If the recurring income is not sufficient to meet the needs of the child, the court may order child support to be paid from nonrecurring income or assets.

(14) Every petition for child support or for modification of child support shall be accompanied by an affidavit which shows the party's income, allowable deductions, and net income computed in accordance with this section. The affidavit shall be served at the same time that the petition is served. The respondent, whether or not a stipulation is entered, shall make an affidavit which shows the party's income, allowable deductions, and net income computed in accordance with this section. The respondent shall include his or her affidavit with the answer to the petition or as soon thereafter as is practicable, but in any case at least 72 hours prior to any hearing on the finances of either party.

(15) For purposes of establishing an obligation for support in accordance with this section, if a person who is receiving public assistance is found to be noncooperative as defined in s. 409.2572, the IV-D agency is authorized to submit to the court an affidavit attesting to the income of the custodial parent based upon information available to the IV-D agency.

(16) The Legislature shall review the guidelines established in this section at least every 4 years beginning in 1997.

(17) In an initial determination of child support, whether in a paternity action, dissolution of marriage action, or petition for support during the marriage, the court has discretion to award child support retroactive to the date when the parents did not reside together in the same household with the child, not to exceed a period of 24 months preceding the filing of the petition, regardless of whether that date precedes the filing of the petition. In determining the retroactive award in such cases, the court shall consider the following:

(a) The court shall apply the guidelines in effect at the time of the hearing subject to the obligor's demonstration of his or her actual income, as defined by subsection (2), during the retroactive period. Failure of the obligor to so demonstrate shall result in the court using the obligor's income at the time of the hearing in computing child support for the retroactive period.

(b) All actual payments made by the noncustodial parent to the custodial parent or the child or third parties for the benefit of the child throughout the proposed retroactive period.

(c) The court should consider an installment payment plan for the payment of retroactive child support.

CHILD SUPPORT SCHEDULE

[from Section 61.30(6), Florida Statutes]

Combined Monthly Available Income	Number of Children: One	Two	Three	Four	Five	Six
$650	74	75	75	76	77	78
700	119	120	121	123	124	125
750	164	166	167	169	171	173
800	190	211	213	218	218	220
850	202	257	259	262	265	268
900	213	302	305	309	312	315
950	224	347	351	355	359	363
1000	235	365	397	402	406	410
1050	246	382	443	448	453	458
1100	258	400	489	495	500	505
1150	269	417	522	541	547	553
1200	280	435	544	588	594	600
1250	290	451	565	634	641	648
1300	300	467	584	659	688	695
1350	310	482	603	681	735	743
1400	320	498	623	702	765	790
1450	330	513	642	724	789	838
1500	340	529	662	746	813	869
1550	350	544	681	768	836	895
1600	360	560	701	790	860	920
1650	370	575	720	812	884	945
1700	380	591	740	833	907	971
1750	390	606	759	855	931	996
1800	400	622	779	877	955	1022
1850	410	638	798	900	979	1048
1900	421	654	818	923	1004	1074
1950	431	670	839	946	1029	1101
2000	442	686	859	968	1054	1128
2050	452	702	879	991	1079	1154
2100	463	718	899	1014	1104	1181
2150	473	734	919	1037	1129	1207
2200	484	751	940	1060	1154	1234
2250	494	767	960	1082	1179	1261
2300	505	783	980	1105	1204	1287
2350	515	799	1000	1128	1229	1314
2400	526	815	1020	1151	1254	1340
2450	536	831	1041	1174	1279	1367
2500	547	847	1061	1196	1304	1394
2550	557	864	1081	1219	1329	1420
2600	568	880	1101	1242	1354	1447
2650	578	896	1121	1265	1379	1473
2700	588	912	1141	1287	1403	1500
2750	597	927	1160	1308	1426	1524
2800	607	941	1178	1328	1448	1549
2850	616	956	1197	1349	1471	1573
2900	626	971	1215	1370	1494	1598
2950	635	986	1234	1391	1517	1622
3000	644	1001	1252	1412	1540	1647
3050	654	1016	1271	1433	1563	1671
3100	663	1031	1289	1453	1586	1695
3150	673	1045	1308	1474	1608	1720
3200	682	1060	1327	1495	1631	1744
3250	691	1075	1345	1516	1654	1769
3300	701	1090	1364	1537	1677	1793
3350	710	1105	1382	1558	1700	1818
3400	720	1120	1401	1579	1723	1842
3450	729	1135	1419	1599	1745	1867
3500	738	1149	1438	1620	1768	1891
3550	748	1164	1456	1641	1791	1915
3600	757	1179	1475	1662	1814	1940
3650	767	1194	1493	1683	1837	1964
3700	776	1208	1503	1702	1857	1987
3750	784	1221	1520	1721	1878	2009
3800	793	1234	1536	1740	1899	2031
3850	802	1248	1759	1920	1920	2053
3900	811	1261	1570	1778	1940	2075
3950	819	1275	1587	1797	1961	2097
4000	828	1288	1603	1816	1982	2119
4050	837	1302	1620	1835	2002	2141
4100	846	1315	1637	1854	2023	2163
4150	854	1329	1654	1873	2044	2185
4200	863	1342	1670	1892	2064	2207
4250	872	1355	1687	1911	2085	2229
4300	881	1369	1704	1930	2106	2251
4350	889	1382	1721	1949	2127	2273
4400	898	1396	1737	1968	2147	2295
4450	907	1409	1754	1987	2168	2317
4500	916	1423	1771	2006	2189	2339
4550	924	1436	1788	2024	2209	2361
4600	933	1450	1804	2043	2230	2384
4650	942	1463	1821	2062	2251	2406
4700	951	1477	1838	2081	2271	2428
4750	959	1490	1855	2100	2292	2450
4800	968	1503	1871	2119	2313	2472
4850	977	1517	1888	2138	2334	2494
4900	986	1530	1905	2157	2354	2516
4950	993	1542	1927	2174	2372	2535
5000	1000	1551	1939	2188	2387	2551
5050	1006	1561	1952	2202	2402	2567
5100	1013	1571	1964	2215	2417	2583
5150	1019	1580	1976	2229	2432	2599
5200	1025	1590	1988	2243	2447	2615
5250	1032	1599	2000	2256	2462	2631
5300	1038	1609	2012	2270	2477	2647
5350	1045	1619	2024	2283	2492	2663
5400	1051	1628	2037	2297	2507	2679

Combined Monthly Available Income	Number of Children					
	One	Two	Three	Four	Five	Six
5450	1057	1638	2049	2311	2522	2695
5500	1064	1647	2061	2324	2537	2711
5550	1070	1657	2073	2338	2552	2727
5600	1077	1667	2085	2352	2567	2743
5650	1083	1676	2097	2365	2582	2759
5700	1089	1686	2109	2379	2597	2775
5750	1096	1695	2122	2393	2612	2791
5800	1102	1705	2134	2406	2627	2807
5850	1107	1713	2144	2418	2639	2820
5900	1111	1721	2155	2429	2651	2833
5950	1116	1729	2165	2440	2663	2847
6000	1121	1737	2175	2451	2676	2860
6050	1126	1746	2185	2462	2688	2874
6100	1131	1754	2196	2473	2700	2887
6150	1136	1762	2206	2484	2712	2900
6200	1141	1770	2216	2495	7243	2914
6250	1145	1778	2227	2506	2737	2927
6300	1150	1786	2237	2517	2749	2941
6350	1155	1795	2247	2529	2761	2954
6400	1160	1803	2258	2540	2773	2967
6450	1165	1811	2268	2551	2785	2981
6500	1170	1819	2278	2562	2798	2994
6550	1175	1827	2288	2573	2810	3008
6600	1179	1835	2299	2584	2822	3021
6650	1184	1843	2309	2595	2834	3034
6700	1189	1850	2317	2604	2845	3045
6750	1193	1856	2325	2613	2854	3055
6800	1196	1862	2332	2621	2863	3064
6850	1200	1868	2340	2630	2872	3074
6900	1204	1873	2347	2639	2882	3084
6950	1208	1879	2355	2647	2891	3094
7000	1212	1885	2362	2656	2900	3103
7050	1216	1891	2370	2664	2909	3113
7100	1220	1897	2378	2673	2919	3123
7150	1224	1903	2385	2681	2928	3133
7200	1228	1909	2393	2690	2937	3142
7250	1232	1915	2400	2698	2946	3152
7300	1235	1921	2408	2707	2956	3162
7350	1239	1927	2415	2716	2965	3172
7400	1243	1933	2423	2724	2974	3181
7450	1247	1939	2430	2733	2983	3191
7500	1251	1945	2438	2741	2993	3201
7550	1255	1951	2446	2750	3002	3211
7600	1259	1957	2453	2758	3011	3220
7650	1263	1963	2461	2767	3020	3230
7700	1267	1969	2468	2775	3030	3240
7750	1271	1975	2476	2784	3039	3250
7800	1274	1981	2483	2792	3048	3259
7850	1278	1987	2491	2801	3057	3269
7900	1282	1992	2498	2810	3067	3279
7950	1286	1998	2506	2818	3076	3289
8000	1290	2004	2513	2827	3085	3298
8050	1294	2010	2521	2835	3094	3308
8100	1298	2016	2529	2844	3104	3318
8150	1302	2022	2536	2852	3113	3328
8200	1306	2028	2544	2861	3122	3337
8250	1310	2034	2551	2869	3131	3347
8300	1313	2040	2559	2878	3141	3357
8350	1317	2046	2566	2887	3150	3367
8400	1321	2052	2574	2895	3159	3376
8450	1325	2058	2581	2904	3168	3386
8500	1329	2064	2589	2912	3178	3396
8550	1333	2070	2597	2921	3187	3406
8600	1337	2076	2604	2929	3196	3415
8650	1341	2082	2612	2938	3205	3425
8700	1345	2088	2619	2946	3215	3435
8750	1349	2094	2627	2955	3224	3445
8800	1352	2100	2634	2963	3233	3454
8850	1356	2106	2642	2972	3242	3464
8900	1360	2111	2649	2981	3252	3474
8950	1364	2117	2657	2989	3261	3484
9000	1368	2123	2664	2998	3270	3493
9050	1372	2129	2672	3006	3279	3503
9100	1376	2135	2680	3015	3289	3513
9150	1380	2141	2687	3023	3298	3523
9200	1384	2147	2695	3032	3307	3532
9250	1388	2153	2702	3040	3316	3542
9300	1391	2159	2710	3049	3326	3552
9350	1395	2165	2717	3058	3335	3562
9400	1399	2171	2725	3066	3344	3571
9450	1403	2177	2732	3075	3353	3581
9500	1407	2183	2740	3083	3363	3591
9550	1411	2189	2748	3092	3372	3601
9600	1415	2195	2755	3100	3381	3610
9650	1419	2201	2763	3109	3390	3620
9700	1422	2206	2767	3115	3396	3628
9750	1425	2210	2772	3121	3402	3634
9800	1427	2213	2776	3126	3408	3641
9850	1430	2217	2781	3132	3414	3647
9900	1432	2221	2786	3137	3420	3653
9950	1435	2225	2791	3143	3426	3659
10000	1437	2228	2795	3148	3432	3666

Family Law Rules of Procedure

The following is one of the more significant rules of the new Family Law Rules of Procedure. You would be well advised to review both the Florida Rules of Civil Procedure and the full Family Law Rules of Procedure.

RULE 12.285. MANDATORY DISCLOSURE

(a) Application.

(1) Scope. This rule shall apply to all proceedings within the scope of these rules except proceedings involving adoption, simplified dissolution, enforcement, contempt, injunctions for domestic or repeat violence, and uncontested dissolutions when the respondent is served by publication and does not file an answer. Additionally, no financial affidavit or other documents shall be required under this rule from a party seeking attorneys' fees, suit money, or costs, if the basis for the request is solely under section 57.105, Florida Statutes, or any successor statute. Except for the provisions as to financial affidavits and child support guidelines worksheets, any portion of this rule may be modified by order of the court or agreement of the parties.

(2) Original and Duplicate Copies. Unless otherwise agreed by the parties or ordered by the court, copies of documents required under this rule may be produced in lieu of originals. Originals, when available, shall be produced for inspection upon request. Parties shall not be required to serve duplicates of documents previously served.

(b) Time for Production of Documents.

(1) Temporary Financial Hearings. Any document required under this rule in any temporary financial relief proceeding shall be served on the other party for inspection and copying as follows.

(A) The party seeking relief shall serve the required documents on the other party with the notice of temporary financial hearing, unless the documents have been served under subdivision (b)(2) of this rule.

(B) The responding party shall serve the required documents on the party seeking relief on or before 5:00 p.m., 2 business days before the day of the temporary financial hearing if served by delivery or 7 days before the day of the temporary financial hearing if served by mail, unless the documents have been received previously by the party seeking relief under subdivision (b)(2) of this rule. A responding party shall be given no less than 12 days to serve the documents required under this rule, unless otherwise ordered by the court. If the 45-day period for exchange of documents provided for in subdivision (b)(2) of this rule will occur before the expiration of the 12 days, the provisions of subdivision (b)(2) control.

(2) Initial and Supplemental Proceedings. Any document required under this rule for any initial or supplemental proceeding shall be served on the other party for inspection and copying within 45 days of service of the initial pleading on the respondent.

(c) Disclosure Requirements for Temporary Financial Relief. In any proceeding for temporary financial relief heard within 45 days of the service of the initial pleading or within any extension of the time for complying with mandatory disclosure granted by the court or agreed to by the parties, the following documents shall be served on the other party:

(1) A financial affidavit in substantial conformity with Florida Family Law Rules of Procedure Form 12.902(b) if the party's gross annual income is less than $ 50,000, or Florida Family Law Rules of Procedure Form 12.902(c) if the party's gross annual income is equal to or more than $ 50,000. This requirement cannot be waived by the parties. The affidavit also must be filed with the court.

(2) All federal and state income tax returns, gift tax returns, and intangible personal property tax returns filed by the party or on the party's behalf for the past year. A party may file a transcript of the tax return as provided by Internal Revenue Service Form 4506 in lieu of his or her individual federal income tax return for purposes of a temporary hearing.

(3) IRS forms W-2, 1099, and K-1 for the past year, if the income tax return for that year has not been prepared.

(4) Pay stubs or other evidence of earned income for the 3 months prior to service of the financial affidavit.

(d) Parties' Disclosure Requirements for Initial or Supplemental Proceedings. A party shall serve the following documents in any proceeding for an initial or supplemental request for permanent financial relief, including, but not limited to, a request for child support, alimony, equitable distribution of assets or debts, or attorneys' fees, suit money, or costs:

(1) A financial affidavit in substantial conformity with Florida Family Law Rules of Procedure Form 12.902(b) if the party's gross annual income is less than $ 50,000, or Florida Family Law Rules of Procedure Form 12.902(c) if the party's gross annual income is equal to or more than $ 50,000, which requirement cannot be waived by the parties. The financial affidavits also must be filed with the court. A party may request, by using the Standard Family

Law Interrogatories, or the court on its own motion may order, a party whose gross annual income is less than $ 50,000 to complete Florida Family Law Rules of Procedure Form 12.902(c).
(2) All federal and state income tax returns, gift tax returns, and intangible personal property tax returns filed by the party or on the party's behalf for the past 3 years.
(3) IRS forms W-2, 1099, and K-1 for the past year, if the income tax return for that year has not been prepared.
(4) Pay stubs or other evidence of earned income for the 3 months prior to service of the financial affidavit.
(5) A statement by the producing party identifying the amount and source of all income received from any source during the 3 months preceding the service of the financial affidavit required by this rule if not reflected on the pay stubs produced.
(6) All loan applications and financial statements prepared or used within the 12 months preceding service of that party's financial affidavit required by this rule, whether for the purpose of obtaining or attempting to obtain credit or for any other purpose.
(7) All deeds within the last 3 years, all promissory notes within the last 12 months, and all present leases, in which the party owns or owned an interest, whether held in the party's name individually, in the party's name jointly with any other person or entity, in the party's name as trustee or guardian for any other person, or in someone else's name on the party's behalf.
(8) All periodic statements from the last 3 months for all checking accounts, and from the last 12 months for all other accounts (for example, savings accounts, money market funds, certificates of deposit, etc.), regardless of whether or not the account has been closed, including those held in the party's name individually, in the party's name jointly with any other person or entity, in the party's name as trustee or guardian for any other person, or in someone else's name on the party's behalf.
(9) All brokerage account statements in which either party to this action held within the last 12 months or holds an interest including those held in the party's name individually, in the party's name jointly with any person or entity, in the party's name as trustee or guardian for any other person, or in someone else's name on the party's behalf.
(10) The most recent statement for any profit sharing, retirement, deferred compensation, or pension plan (for example, IRA, 401(k), 403(b), SEP, KEOGH, or other similar account) in which the party is a participant or alternate payee and the summary plan description for any retirement, profit sharing, or pension plan in which the party is a participant or an alternate payee. (The summary plan description must be furnished to the party on request by the plan administrator as required by 29 U.S.C. § 1024(b)(4).)
(11) The declarations page, the last periodic statement, and the certificate for all life insurance policies insuring the party's life or the life of the party's spouse, whether group insurance or otherwise, and all current health and dental insurance cards covering either of the parties and/or their dependent children.
(12) Corporate, partnership, and trust tax returns for the last 3 tax years if the party has an ownership or interest in a corporation, partnership, or trust greater than or equal to 30%.
(13) All promissory notes for the last 12 months, all credit card and charge account statements and other records showing the party's indebtedness as of the date of the filing of this action and for the last 3 months, and all present lease agreements, whether owed in the party's name individually, in the party's name jointly with any other person or entity, in the party's name as trustee or guardian for any other person, or in someone else's name on the party's behalf.
(14) All written premarital or marital agreements entered into at any time between the parties to this marriage, whether before or during the marriage. Additionally, in any modification proceeding, each party shall serve on the opposing party all written agreements entered into between them at any time since the order to be modified was entered.
(15) All documents and tangible evidence supporting the producing party's claim of special equity or nonmarital status of an asset or debt for the time period from the date of acquisition of the asset or debt to the date of production or from the date of marriage, if based on premarital acquisition.
(16) Any court orders directing a party to pay or receive spousal or child support.
(c) Duty to Supplement Disclosure; Amended Financial Affidavit.
(1) Parties have a continuing duty to supplement documents described in this rule, including financial affidavits, whenever a material change in their financial status occurs.
(2) If an amended financial affidavit or an amendment to a financial affidavit is filed, the amending party also shall serve any subsequently discovered or acquired documents supporting the amendments to the financial affidavit.
(f) Sanctions. Any document to be produced under this rule that is served on the opposing party fewer than 24 hours before a nonfinal hearing or in violation of the court's pretrial order shall not be admis-

sible in evidence at that hearing unless the court finds good cause for the delay. In addition, the court may impose other sanctions authorized by rule 12.380 as may be equitable under the circumstances. The court may also impose sanctions upon the offending lawyer in lieu of imposing sanctions on a party.

(g) Extensions of Time for Complying with Mandatory Disclosure. By agreement of the parties, the time for complying with mandatory disclosure may be extended. Either party also may file, at least 5 days before the due date, a motion to enlarge the time for complying with mandatory disclosure. The court shall grant the request for good cause shown.

(h) Objections to Mandatory Automatic Disclosure. Objections to the mandatory automatic disclosure required by this rule shall be served in writing at least 5 days prior to the due date for the disclosure or the objections shall be deemed waived. The filing of a timely objection, with a notice of hearing on the objection, automatically stays mandatory disclosure for those matters within the scope of the objection. For good cause shown, the court may extend the time for the filing of an objection or permit the filing of an otherwise untimely objection. The court shall impose sanctions for the filing of meritless or frivolous objections.

(i) Certificate of Compliance. All parties subject to automatic mandatory disclosure shall file with the court a certificate of compliance, Florida Family Law Rules of Procedure Form 12.932, identifying with particularity the documents which have been delivered and certifying the date of service of the financial affidavit and documents by that party.

(j) Child Support Guidelines Worksheet. If the case involves child support, the parties shall file with the court at or prior to a hearing to establish or modify child support a Child Support Guidelines Worksheet in substantial conformity with Florida Family Law Rules of Procedure Form 12.902(e). This requirement cannot be waived by the parties.

(k) Place of Production.

(1) Unless otherwise agreed by the parties or ordered by the court, all production required by this rule shall take place in the county where the action is pending and in the office of the attorney for the party receiving production. Unless otherwise agreed by the parties or ordered by the court, if a party does not have an attorney or if the attorney does not have an office in the county where the action is pending, production shall take place in the county where the action is pending at a place designated in writing by the party receiving production, served at least 5 days before the due date for production.

(2) If venue is contested, on motion by a party the court shall designate the place where production will occur pending determination of the venue issue.

(l) Failure of Defaulted Party to Comply. Nothing in this rule shall be deemed to preclude the entry of a final judgment when a party in default has failed to comply with this rule.

Blank Forms

appendix b

Many of the forms in this appendix are Florida Supreme Court approved forms, which are found in the Family Law Rules of Procedure. You will find an instructive word or phrase in brackets, such as *{name}* or *{address}*, just before the blank to tell you what information to insert. For this reason, line-by-line instructions are not always provided.

Be sure to read the section "Introduction to Legal Forms" in Chapter 5 before you begin using the forms in this appendix.

NOTE: *There are some counties that have their own forms and will not accept the Supreme Court forms. If you find that any of the forms in this book are not acceptable in your county, ask the court clerk to provide you with the acceptable forms. There is likely to be a fee for the forms.*

Additionally, the forms may appear to have mistakes or a word in the wrong place. This is the way the forms appeared in the Rules of Procedure at the time of publication.

You should make photocopies to use for both practice worksheets and the forms you will file with the court. The blank forms can then be used to make more copies in the event you make mistakes, need to amend your forms, or need additional copies.

Some of the forms have similar titles, so check both the exact title of the form and the form number to be sure you are using the correct form.

The following forms are included in this appendix.

PROPERTY INVENTORY

(1) N-M	(2) DESCRIPTION	(3) ID#	(4) VALUE	(5) BALANCE OWED	(6) EQUITY	(7) OWNER H-W-J	(8) H	(9) W

DEBT INVENTORY

(1) N-M	(2) CREDITOR	(3) ACCOUNT NO.	(4) NOTES	(5) MONTHLY PAYMENT	(6) BALANCE OWED	(7) DATE	(8) OWNER H-W-J	(9) H	(10) W

IN THE CIRCUIT COURT OF THE ________________________ JUDICIAL CIRCUIT,
IN AND FOR ________________________ COUNTY, FLORIDA

Case No.: ______________________________
Division: ______________________________

______________________________,
Husband,

and

______________________________,
Wife.

PETITION FOR SIMPLIFIED DISSOLUTION OF MARRIAGE

We, *{full legal name}*____, Husband,

and *{full legal name}* ____, Wife,
being sworn, certify that the following information is true:
[fill in **all** blanks]

1. We are both asking the Court for a dissolution of our marriage.
2. Husband lives in *{name}* __________________ County, *{state}* __________________, and has lived there since *{date}* _____________. Wife lives in *{name}* ____________________County, *{state}* ______________, and has lived there since *{date}* _________________________.
3. We were married to each other on *{date}*__________________ in the city of *{city}* __________ in state of *{state}* _________________, or country of *{country}* _________________________.
4. Our marriage is irretrievably broken.
5. Together, we have no minor (under 18) or dependent children **and** the wife is not pregnant.
6. We have made a marital settlement agreement dividing our assets (what we own) and our liabilities (what we owe). We are satisfied with this agreement. Our marital settlement agreement, Florida Family Law Rules of Procedure Form 12.902(f)(3), is attached. This agreement was signed freely an voluntarily by each of us and we intend to be bound by it.
7. We have each completed and signed financial affidavits, Florida Family Law Rules of Procedure For 12.902(b) or (c), which are attached to this petition.
8. Completed Notice of Social Security Number forms, Florida Supreme Court Approved Family Law Form12.902(j), are filed with this petition.
9. [√ **one** only] ( ) yes ( ) no Wife wants to be known by her former name, which was *{full legal name}* ____.
10. We each certify that we have not been threatened or pressured into signing this petition. We each understand that the result of signing this petition may be a final judgment ending our marriage and allowing no further relief.
11. We each understand that **we both must come to the hearing** to testify about the things we are asking for in this petition.

12. We understand that we each may have legal rights as a result of our marriage and that by signing this petition we may be giving up those rights.

13. We ask the Court to end our marriage and approve our marital settlement agreement.

I understand that I am swearing or affirming under oath to the truthfulness of the claims made in this petition and that the punishment for knowingly making a false statement includes fines and/or imprisonment.

Dated: ______________

____
Signature of HUSBAND
Printed Name: ______________________
Address: ______________________
City, State, Zip: ______________________
Telephone Number: ______________________
Fax Number: ______________________

STATE OF FLORIDA
COUNTY OF ______________

Sworn to or affirmed and signed before me on ____________________ by ______________________.

____
NOTARY PUBLIC or DEPUTY CLERK

[Print, type, or stamp commissioned name of notary or deputy clerk.]

___ Personally known
___ Produced identification
Type of identification produced

I understand that I am swearing or affirming under oath to the truthfulness of the claims made in this petition and that the punishment for knowingly making a false statement includes fines and/or imprisonment.

Dated: ______________

____
Signature of WIFE
Printed Name: ______________________
Address: ______________________
City, State, Zip: ______________________
Telephone Number: ______________________
Fax Number: ______________________

STATE OF FLORIDA
COUNTY OF

Sworn to or affirmed and signed before me on ____________________ by ______________________.

____
NOTARY PUBLIC or DEPUTY CLERK

[Print, type, or stamp commissioned name of notary or deputy clerk.]

____ Personally known
____ Produced identification
Type of identification produced

IF A NONLAWYER HELPED YOU FILL OUT THIS FORM, HE/SHE MUST FILL IN THE BLANKS BELOW: [fill in **all** blanks]
I, *{full legal name and trade name of nonlawyer}* ______________________________,
a nonlawyer, located at *{street}* ______________________, *{city}* ____________,
*{state}*__________, *{phone}* ________, helped *{name}* ______________________,
[√ **one** only] ( ) Husband ( ) Wife **or** ( ) both, fill out this form.
√

IN THE CIRCUIT COURT OF THE ________________________ JUDICIAL CIRCUIT,
IN AND FOR ________________________ COUNTY, FLORIDA

Case No.: ____________________________
Division: ____________________________

________________________________,
Petitioner,

and

________________________________,
Respondent.

PETITION FOR DISSOLUTION OF MARRIAGE WITH DEPENDENT OR MINOR CHILD(REN)

I, *{full legal name}* ____, the [√ **one** only] ( ) Husband ( ) Wife, being sworn, certify that the following statements are true:

1. JURISDICTION/RESIDENCE
   ( ) Husband ( ) Wife ( ) Both has (have) lived in Florida for at least 6 months before the filing of this Petition for Dissolution of Marriage.

2. The husband [√ **one** only] ( ) is ( ) is not a member of the military service.
   The wife [√ **one** only] ( ) is ( ) is not a member of the military service.

3. MARRIAGE HISTORY
   Date of marriage: *{month, day, year}* ____
   Place of marriage: *{city, state, country}* ____________________________________
   Date of separation: *{month, day, year}* ____________________________ (√ **if** approximate)

4. DEPENDENT OR MINOR CHILD(REN)

[√ **all** that apply]

___ a. The wife is pregnant. Baby is due on: *{date}* __________________

___ b. The minor (under 18) child(ren) common to both parties are:

Name	Place of Birth	Birth date	Sex
______________	__________	__________	________
______________	__________	__________	________
______________	__________	__________	________
______________	__________	__________	________
______________	__________	__________	________
______________	__________	__________	________

___ c. The minor child(ren) born or conceived during the marriage who are **not** common to both parties are:

Name	Place of Birth	Birth date	Sex
______________	__________	__________	________
______________	__________	__________	________

The birth father(s) of the above minor child(ren) is (are) *{name and address}* ________________
____

___ d. The child(ren) common to both parties who are 18 or older but who are dependent upon the parties due to a mental or physical disability are:

Name	**Place of Birth**	**Birth date**	**Sex**
______________	______________	______________	__________
______________	______________	______________	__________

5. A completed Uniform Child Custody Jurisdiction and Enforcement Act (UCCJEA) Affidavit, Florida Supreme Court Approved Family Law Form 12.902(d), is filed with this petition. (You **must** complete and attach this form in a dissolution of marriage with minor child(ren)).

6. A completed Notice of Social Security Number, Florida Supreme Court Approved Family Law Form 12.902(j), is filed with this petition.

7. This petition for dissolution of marriage should be granted because:
[√ **one** only]
___ a. The marriage is irretrievably broken.
___ b. One of the parties has been adjudged mentally incapacitated for a period of 3 years prior to the filing of this petition. A copy of the Judgment of Incapacity is attached.

SECTION I. MARITAL ASSETS AND LIABILITIES
[√ **one** only]
___ 1. There are no marital assets or liabilities.

___ 2. There are marital assets or liabilities. All marital and nonmarital assets and liabilities are (or will be) listed in the financial affidavits, Florida Family Law Rules of Procedure Form 12.902(b) or (c), to be filed in this case.
[√ **all** that apply]
___ a. All marital assets and liabilities have been divided by a written agreement between the parties, which is attached, to be incorporated into the final judgment of dissolution of marriage. (The parties may use Marital Settlement Agreement for Dissolution of Marriage with Dependent or Minor Child(ren), Florida Supreme Court Approved Family Law Form 12.902(f)(1).
___ b. The Court should determine how the assets and liabilities of this marriage are to be distributed, under section 61.075, Florida Statutes.
___ c. Petitioner should be awarded an interest in Respondent's property because:
____
____
____
____

SECTION II. SPOUSAL SUPPORT (ALIMONY)
[√ **one** only]
___ 1. **Petitioner forever gives up his/her right to spousal support (alimony) from Respondent.**

___ 2. Petitioner requests that the Court order Respondent to pay the following spousal support (alimony) and claims that he or she has a need for the support that he or she is requesting **and Respondent has the ability to pay that support**. Spousal support (alimony) is requested in the amount of $_____ every ( ) week ( ) other week ( ) month, beginning *{date}* ____________ and continuing until *{date or event}* ______________________________________.

Explain why the Court should order Respondent to pay and any specific request(s) for type of alimony (temporary, permanent, rehabilitative, and/or lump sum): ______________________

____
____
____
____
____
____

[√ **if** applies] (   ) Petitioner requests life insurance on Respondent's life, provided by Respondent, to secure such support.

SECTION III. CHILD CUSTODY, PARENTAL RESPONSIBILITY, AND VISITATION

1. The minor child(ren) currently reside(s) with (   ) Mother (   ) Father (   ) Other: *{explain}* _____

____

2. **Parental Responsibility.** It is in the child(ren)'s best interests that parental responsibility be:
[√ **one** only]
____ a. shared by both Father and Mother.
____ b. awarded solely to (   ) Father (   ) Mother. Shared parental responsibility would be detrimental to the child(ren) because: ______________________________

____
____
____

3. **Primary Residential Parent (Custody).** It is in the best interests of the child(ren) that the primary residential parent be (   ) Father (   ) Mother (   ) undesignated (   ) rotating because: ___

____
____
____

4. **Visitation or Time Sharing.** Petitioner requests that the court order
[√ **all** that apply]
____ a. no visitation.
____ b. limited visitation.
____ c. supervised visitation.
____ d. supervised or third-person exchange of child(ren).
____ e. visitation or time sharing as determined by the Court.
____ f. a visitation or time sharing schedule as follows:
Explain the requested visitation or time sharing schedule: ______________________

____
____
____
____
____
____

Explain why this request is in the best interests of the child(ren): ________________

____
____
____
____

Has the above visitation or time sharing schedule been agreed to by the parties? (   ) yes (   ) no

SECTION IV. CHILD SUPPORT
[√ **all** that apply]

____ 1. Petitioner requests that the Court award child support as determined by Florida's child support guidelines, section 61.30, Florida Statutes. A completed Child Support Guidelines Worksheet, Florida Family Law Rules of Procedure Form 12.902(e), is, or will be filed. Such support should be ordered retroactive to:

____ a. the date of separation *{date}* _______.
____ b. the date of the filing of this petition.
____ c. other *{date}*_______ *{explain}* ______________________________

____ 2. Petitioner requests that the Court award child support to be paid beyond the age of 18 years because:

____ a. the following child(ren) *{name(s)}* ______________________________ is (are) dependent because of a mental or physical incapacity which began before the age of 18. *{explain}* ______________________________
____

____ b. the following child(ren) *{name(s)}* ______________________ is (are) dependent in fact and is (are) in high school while he/she (they) are between the ages of 18 and 19; said child(ren) is (are) performing in good faith with reasonable expectation of graduation before the age of 19.

____ 3. Petitioner requests that the Court award a child support amount that is more than or less than Florida's child support guidelines. Petitioner understands that Motion to Deviate from Child Support Guidelines, Florida Supreme Court Approved Family Law Form 12.943, **must** be filed before the court will consider this request.

____ 4. Petitioner requests that medical/dental insurance coverage for the minor child(ren) be provided by:
[√ **one** only]

____ a. Father.
____ b. Mother.

____ 5. Petitioner requests that uninsured medical/dental expenses for the child(ren) be paid:
[√ **one** only]

____ a. by Father.
____ b. by Mother.
____ c. by Father and Mother [each pay one-half].
____ d. according to the percentages in the Child Support Guidelines Worksheet, Florida Family Law Rules of Procedure Form 12.902(e).
____ e. Other *{explain}*: ______________________________
____
____

____ 6. Petitioner requests that life insurance to secure child support be provided by:

____ a. Father.
____ b. Mother.
____ c. Both.

SECTION V. OTHER

1. [If Petitioner is also the Wife, √ **one** only] ( ) yes ( ) no Petitioner/Wife wants to be known by her former name, which was *{full legal name}* ______________________________.

2. Other relief *{specify}*: ______________________________
____

____
____
____
____

SECTION VI. PETITIONER'S REQUEST (This section summarizes what you are asking the Court to include in the final judgment of dissolution of marriage.)

Petitioner requests that the Court enter an order dissolving the marriage **and**:
[√ **all** that apply]

____ 1. distributing marital assets and liabilities as requested in Section I of this petition;

____ 2. awarding spousal support (alimony) as requested in Section II of this petition;

____ 3. establishing the primary residential parent (custody), parental responsibility, and visitation for the dependent or minor child(ren) common to both parties, as requested in Section III of this petition;

____ 4. establishing child support for the dependent or minor child(ren) common to both parties, as requested in Section IV of this petition;

____ 5. restoring Wife's former name as requested in Section V of this petition;

____ 6. awarding other relief as requested in Section V of this petition; and any other terms the Court deems necessary.

I understand that I am swearing or affirming under oath to the truthfulness of the claims made in this petition and that the punishment for knowingly making a false statement includes fines and/or imprisonment.

Dated: ____________________________ ______________________________________

Signature of Petitioner
Printed Name: ______________________________
Address: ______________________________
City, State, Zip: ______________________________
Telephone Number: ______________________________
Fax Number: ______________________________

STATE OF FLORIDA
COUNTY OF ______________

Sworn to or affirmed and signed before me on ________ by_____________________________________.

____
NOTARY PUBLIC or DEPUTY CLERK

____
[Print, type, or stamp commissioned name of notary or deputy clerk.]

____ Personally known
____ Produced identification
Type of identification produced ___________________________

IF A NONLAWYER HELPED YOU FILL OUT THIS FORM, HE/SHE MUST FILL IN THE BLANKS BELOW: [fill in **all** blanks]
I, *{full legal name and trade name of nonlawyer}* ______________________________________,
a nonlawyer, located at *{street}* ____________________________, *{city}* ________________,
{state} ____________, *{phone}* __________, helped *{name}* ______________________________,
who is the petitioner, fill out this form.

IN THE CIRCUIT COURT OF THE ________________________ JUDICIAL CIRCUIT,
IN AND FOR ________________________ COUNTY, FLORIDA

Case No.: ________________________
Division: ________________________

________________________,
Petitioner,

and

________________________,
Respondent.

PETITION FOR DISSOLUTION OF MARRIAGE
WITH PROPERTY BUT NO DEPENDENT OR MINOR CHILD(REN)

I, *{full legal name}* ____, the [√ **one** only] ( ) Husband ( ) Wife, being sworn, certify that the following statements are true:

1. JURISDICTION/RESIDENCE
( ) Husband ( ) Wife ( ) Both has (have) lived in Florida for at least 6 months before the filing of this Petition for Dissolution of Marriage.

2. The husband [√ **one** only] ( ) is ( ) is not a member of the military service.
The wife [√ **one** only] ( ) is ( ) is not a member of the military service.

3. MARRIAGE HISTORY
Date of marriage: *{month, day, year}* ________________________
Place of marriage: *{city, state, country}* ________________________
Date of separation: *{month, day, year}* ________________________ (√ **if** approximate)

4. THERE ARE NO MINOR (under 18) OR DEPENDENT CHILD(REN) COMMON TO BOTH PARTIES AND THE WIFE IS NOT PREGNANT.

5. A completed Notice of Social Security Number, Florida Supreme Court Approved Family Law Form 12.902(j), is filed with this petition.

6. THIS PETITION FOR DISSOLUTION OF MARRIAGE SHOULD BE GRANTED BECAUSE:
[√ **one** only]
___ a. The marriage is irretrievably broken.
___ b. One of the parties has been adjudged mentally incapacitated for a period of 3 years before the filing of this petition. A copy of the Judgment of Incapacity is attached.

SECTION I. MARITAL ASSETS AND LIABILITIES
[√ **one** only]
___ 1. There are no marital assets or liabilities.

___ 2. There are marital assets or liabilities. All marital and nonmarital assets and liabilities are (or will be) listed in the financial affidavits, Florida Family Law Rules of Procedure Form 12.902(b) or (c), to be filed in this case.

[√ **all** that apply]

____ a. All marital assets and debts have been divided by a written agreement between the parties, which is attached to be incorporated into the final judgment of dissolution of marriage. (The parties may use Marital Settlement Agreement for Simplified Dissolution of Marriage, Florida Family Law Rules of Procedure Form 12.902(f)(3) or Marital Settlement Agreement for Dissolution of Marriage with No Dependent or Minor Child(ren), Florida Supreme Court Approved Family Law Form 12.902(f)(2).

____ b. The Court should determine how the assets and liabilities of this marriage are to be distributed, under section 61.075, Florida Statutes.

____ c. Petitioner should be awarded an interest in Respondent's property because:

SECTION II. SPOUSAL SUPPORT (ALIMONY)

[√ **one** only]

____ 1. **Petitioner forever gives up his/her right to spousal support (alimony) from Respondent.**

____ 2. Petitioner requests that the Court order Respondent to pay the following spousal support (alimony) and claims that he or she has a need for the support that he or she is requesting **and Respondent has the ability to pay that support**. Spousal support (alimony) is requested in the amount of $ _____ every ( ) week ( ) other week ( ) month, beginning *{date}* and continuing until *{date or event}* ____.
Explain why the Court should order Respondent to pay and any specific request(s) for type of alimony (temporary, permanent, rehabilitative, and/or lump sum): ____________________
____
____
____
____
____
____
____

[√ **if** applies] ( ) Petitioner requests life insurance on Respondent's life, provided by Respondent, to secure such support.

SECTION III. OTHER

1. [If Petitioner is also the Wife, √ **one** only] ( ) yes ( ) no Petitioner/Wife wants to be known by her former name, which was *{full legal name}* ____________________________________.

2. Other relief *{specify}*: ____
____
____
____
____
____
____

SECTION IV. PETITIONER'S REQUEST (This section summarizes what you are asking the Court to include in the final judgment of dissolution of marriage.)

Petitioner requests that the Court enter an order dissolving the marriage **and**:

[√ **all** that apply]

____ 1. distributing marital assets and liabilities as requested in Section I of this petition;

____ 2. awarding spousal support (alimony) as requested in Section II of this petition;

___ 3. restoring Wife's former name as requested in Section III of this petition;
___ 4. awarding other relief as requested in Section III of this petition; and any other terms the Court deems necessary.

I understand that I am swearing or affirming under oath to the truthfulness of the claims made in this petition and that the punishment for knowingly making a false statement includes fines and/or imprisonment.

Dated: ____________________________

____
Signature of Petitioner
Printed Name: ______________________________
Address: __________________________________
City, State, Zip: ____________________________
Telephone Number: __________________________
Fax Number: _______________________________

STATE OF FLORIDA
COUNTY OF _______________

Sworn to or affirmed and signed before me on ________ by____.

____
NOTARY PUBLIC or DEPUTY CLERK

____
[Print, type, or stamp commissioned name of notary or deputy clerk.]

___ Personally known
___ Produced identification
Type of identification produced ___________________________

IF A NONLAWYER HELPED YOU FILL OUT THIS FORM, HE/SHE MUST FILL IN THE BLANKS BELOW: [fill in **all** blanks]
I, *{full legal name and trade name of nonlawyer}* ____,
a nonlawyer, located at *{street}* __________________________________, *{city}* ____________________,
{state} ______________, *{phone}* ___________, helped *{name}* __________________________________,
who is the petitioner, fill out this form.

IN THE CIRCUIT COURT OF THE ________________________ JUDICIAL CIRCUIT,
IN AND FOR ________________________ COUNTY, FLORIDA

Case No.:______________________________
Division: ______________________________

__________________________________,
Petitioner,

and

__________________________________,
Respondent.

PETITION FOR DISSOLUTION OF MARRIAGE
WITH NO DEPENDENT OR MINOR CHILD(REN) OR PROPERTY

I, *{full legal name}* ____, the [√ **one** only] ( ) Husband ( ) Wife, being sworn, certify that the following statements are true:

1. JURISDICTION/RESIDENCE
( ) Husband ( ) Wife ( ) Both has (have) lived in Florida for at least 6 months before the filing of this Petition for Dissolution of Marriage.

2. The husband [√ **one** only] ( ) is ( ) is not a member of the military service.
The wife [√ **one** only] ( ) is ( ) is not a member of the military service.

3. MARRIAGE HISTORY
Date of marriage: *{month, day, year}* ____
Place of marriage: *{city, state, country}* ______________________________________
Date of separation: *{month, day, year}* ______________________________(√ **if** approximate)

4. THERE ARE NO MINOR (under 18) OR DEPENDENT CHILD(REN) COMMON TO BOTH PARTIES AND THE WIFE IS NOT PREGNANT.

5. A completed Notice of Social Security Number, Florida Supreme Court Approved Family Law Form 12.902(j), is filed with this petition.

6. THIS PETITION FOR DISSOLUTION OF MARRIAGE SHOULD BE GRANTED BECAUSE: [√ **one** only]
___ a. The marriage is irretrievably broken.
___ b. One of the parties has been adjudged mentally incapacitated for a period of 3 years before the filing of this petition. A copy of the Judgment of Incapacity is attached.

7. THERE ARE NO MARITAL ASSETS OR LIABILITIES.

8. **PETITIONER FOREVER GIVES UP HIS/HER RIGHTS TO SPOUSAL SUPPORT (ALIMONY) FROM RESPONDENT.**

9. [If Petitioner is also the Wife, √ **one** only] ( ) yes ( ) no Petitioner/Wife wants to be known by her former name, which was *{full legal name}* ________________________________

10. Other relief *{specify}*: ______________________________
____
____
____
____
____

PETITIONER'S REQUEST (This section summarizes what you are asking the Court to include in the final judgment of dissolution of marriage.)

Petitioner requests that the Court enter an order dissolving the marriage **and**:
[√ **all** that apply]
___ 1. restoring Wife's former name as specified in paragraph 9 of this petition;
___ 2. awarding other relief as specified in paragraph 10 of this petition; and any other terms the Court deems necessary.

I understand that I am swearing or affirming under oath to the truthfulness of the claims made in this petition and that the punishment for knowingly making a false statement includes fines and/or imprisonment.

Dated: ____________________ ______________________________

Signature of Petitioner
Printed Name: ______________________________
Address: ______________________________
City, State, Zip: ______________________________
Telephone Number: ______________________________
Fax Number: ______________________________

STATE OF FLORIDA
COUNTY OF ____________

Sworn to or affirmed and signed before me on ________ by ______________________________.

____
NOTARY PUBLIC or DEPUTY CLERK

____
[Print, type, or stamp commissioned name of notary or clerk.]

___ Personally known
___ Produced identification
Type of identification produced ________________

IF A NONLAWYER HELPED YOU FILL OUT THIS FORM, HE/SHE MUST FILL IN THE BLANKS BELOW: [fill in **all** blanks]
I, *{full legal name and trade name of nonlawyer}* ______________________________,
a nonlawyer, located at *{street}* ______________________________
{state} ____________, *{phone}* ____________, helped *{name}* ______________________________,
who is the petitioner, fill out this form.

IN THE CIRCUIT/COUNTY COURT OF THE ---------------- JUDICIAL CIRCUIT
IN AND FOR -------------- COUNTY, FLORIDA

CASE NO.________________________________

____
Plaintiff/Petitioner or In the Interest Of
vs.

____
Defendant//Respondent

APPLICATION FOR DETERMINATION OF CIVIL INDIGENT STATUS

Notice to Applicant: If you qualify for civil indigence you must enroll in the Clerk's Office payment plan and pay a one-time administrative fee of $25.00.

1. **I have ______dependents.** *(Do not include children not living at home and do not include a working spouse or yourself.)*

2. **I have a take home income of $____________** paid ( ) weekly ( ) bi-weekly ( ) semi-monthly ( ) monthly ( ) yearly
(Take home income equals salary, wages, bonuses, commissions, allowances, overtime, tips and similar payments, ***minus*** *deductions required by law and other court ordered support payments)*

3. **I have other income** paid ( ) weekly ( ) bi-weekly ( ) semi-monthly ( ) monthly ( ) yearly: *(Circle "Yes" and fill in the amount if you have this kind of income, otherwise circle "No")*

Social Security benefits........................... Yes $______________ No
Unemployment compensation.................. Yes $______________ No
Union Funds.. Yes $______________ No
Workers compensation........................... Yes $______________ No
Retirement/pensions............................... Yes $______________ No
Trusts or gifts.. Yes $______________ No

Veterans' benefits.............................. Yes $______________ No
Child support or other regular support
from family members/spouse.......... Yes $______________ No
Rental income.................................. Yes $______________ No
Dividends or interest.......................... Yes $______________ No
Other kinds of income not on the list...... Yes $______________ No

4. **I have other assets:** *(Circle "yes" and fill in the value of the property, otherwise circle "No")*

Cash... Yes $______________ No
Bank account(s).................................. Yes $______________ No
Certificates of deposit or
money market accounts................ Yes $______________ No
*Equity in Motor vehicles/Boats/
Other tangible property.................. Yes $______________ No

Savings.. Yes $______________ No
Stocks/bonds... Yes $______________ No
*Equity in Real estate (excluding homestead) Yes $______________ No
*include expectancy of an interest in such property

5. **I have a total amount of liabilities and debts in the amount of $______________.**

6. **I have a private lawyer in this case**.. Yes No

A person who knowingly provides false information to the clerk or the court in seeking a determination of indigent status under s. 57.082, F.S. commits a misdemeanor of the first degree, punishable as provided in s.775.082, F.S. or s. 775.083, F.S. **I attest that the information I have provided on this application is true and accurate to the best of my knowledge.**

Signed this ________ day of ______________, 20____.

____
Signature of Applicant for Indigent Status

____
Date of Birth

Print Full Legal Name________________________________

____
Drivers License or ID Number

____
Address, P O Address, Street, City, State, Zip Code
Phone Number: ________________________________

NOTICE: If the applicant is determined by the clerk to be Not Indigent, you may seek judicial review by filing a petition with the court.

CLERK'S DETERMINATION

Based on the information in this Application, I have determined the applicant to be ( ) Indigent ( ) Not Indigent, according to s. 57.082, F.S.

Dated this ________ day of ______________, 20 ____.

Clerk of the Circuit court

This form was completed with the assistance of
______________Clerk/Deputy Clerk/Other authorized person.

Final approval by The Florida Supreme Court on June 30, 2005.

IN THE CIRCUIT COURT OF THE _________________________ JUDICIAL CIRCUIT,
IN AND FOR _________________________ COUNTY, FLORIDA

Case No.: ______________________________
Division: ______________________________

____________________________________,
Petitioner,

and

____________________________________,
Respondent.

FAMILY LAW FINANCIAL AFFIDAVIT (SHORT FORM)
(Under $50,000 Individual Gross Annual Income)

I, *{full legal name}*_________________________, being sworn, certify that the following information is true:

My Occupation: ____________ Employed by: ____________________________________

Business Address: ____

Pay rate: $ ________ ( ) every week ( ) every other week ( ) twice a month ( ) monthly ( ) other: _______
Check here if unemployed and explain on a separate sheet your efforts to find employment.

SECTION I. PRESENT MONTHLY GROSS INCOME:

All amounts must be MONTHLY. See the instructions with this form to figure out money amounts for anything that is NOT paid monthly. Attach more paper, if needed. Items included under "other" should be listed separately with separate dollar amounts.

1. Monthly gross salary or wages — 1. $_________
2. Monthly bonuses, commissions, allowances, overtime, tips, and similar payments — 2. _________
3. Monthly business income from sources such as self-employment, partnerships, close corporations, and/or independent contracts (gross receipts minus ordinary and necessary expenses required to produce income) (□ Attach sheet itemizing such income and expenses.) — 3. _________
4. Monthly disability benefits/SSI — 4. _________
5. Monthly Workers' Compensation — 5. _________
6. Monthly Unemployment Compensation — 6. _________
7. Monthly pension, retirement, or annuity payments — 7. _________
8. Monthly Social Security benefits — 8. _________
9. Monthly alimony actually received
   - 9a. From this case: $ _______
   - 9b. From other case(s): _______ Add 9a and 9b — 9. _________
10. Monthly interest and dividends — 10. _________
11. Monthly rental income (gross receipts minus ordinary and necessary expenses required to produce income) (□ Attach sheet itemizing such income and expense items.) — 11. _________
12. Monthly income from royalties, trusts, or estates — 12. _________
13. Monthly reimbursed expenses and in-kind payments to the extent that they reduce personal living expenses — 13. _________
14. Monthly gains derived from dealing in property (not including nonrecurring gains) — 14. _________
15. Any other income of a recurring nature (list source) ___________________ — 15. _________
16. ____ — 16. _________

17. PRESENT MONTHLY GROSS INCOME (Add lines 1–16) **TOTAL:** **17. $** ______________

PRESENT MONTHLY DEDUCTIONS:

18. Monthly federal, state, and local income tax (corrected for filing status and allowable dependents and income tax liabilities)
    a. Filing Status ___________
    b. Number of dependents claimed _______ 18. $_________
19. Monthly FICA or self-employment taxes 19. _________
20. Monthly Medicare payments 20. _________
21. Monthly mandatory union dues 21. _________
22. Monthly mandatory retirement payments 22. _________
23. Monthly health insurance payments (including dental insurance), excluding portion paid for any minor children of this relationship 23. _________
24. Monthly court-ordered child support actually paid for children from another relationship 24. _________
25. Monthly court-ordered alimony actually paid
    25a. from this case: $ _______
    25b. from other case(s): _______ Add 25a and 25b 25. _________

26. TOTAL DEDUCTIONS ALLOWABLE UNDER SECTION 61.30, FLORIDA STATUTES (Add lines 18 through 25) **TOTAL: 26. $** _______________

PRESENT NET MONTHLY INCOME (Subtract line 26 from line 17) **27. $** _______________

SECTION II. AVERAGE MONTHLY EXPENSES

A. HOUSEHOLD:

Mortgage or rent	$ ____________
Property taxes	$ ____________
Utilities	$ ____________
Telephone	$ ____________
Food	$ ____________
Meals outside home	$ ____________
Maintenance/Repairs	$ ____________
Other: ____________	$ ____________

B. AUTOMOBILE

Gasoline	$ ____________
Repairs	$ ____________
Insurance	$ ____________

C. CHILD(REN)'S EXPENSES

Day care	$ ____________
Lunch money	$ ____________
Clothing	$ ____________
Grooming	$ ____________
Gifts for holidays	$ ____________
Medical/Dental (uninsured)	$ ____________
Other: ____________	$ ____________

D. INSURANCE

Medical/Dental	$ ____________
Child(ren)'s medical/dental	$ ____________
Life	$ ____________
Other: ____________	$ ____________

E. OTHER EXPENSES NOT LISTED ABOVE

Clothing	$ ____________
Medical/Dental (uninsured)	$ ____________
Grooming	$ ____________
Entertainment	$ ____________
Gifts	$ ____________
Religious organizations	$ ____________
Miscellaneous	$ ____________
Other: ____________	$ ____________
____________	$ ____________
____________	$ ____________
____________	$ ____________
____________	$ ____________
____________	$ ____________
____________	$ ____________

F. PAYMENTS TO CREDITORS

CREDITOR:	MONTHLY PAYMENT
____________	$ ____________
____________	$ ____________
____________	$ ____________
____________	$ ____________
____________	$ ____________
____________	$ ____________
____________	$ ____________
____________	$ ____________
____________	$ ____________
____________	$ ____________
____________	$ ____________

28. TOTAL MONTHLY EXPENSES (add **ALL** monthly amounts in A through F above) **28.** $ ____________

SUMMARY

29. TOTAL PRESENT MONTHLY NET INCOME
(from line 27 of SECTION I. INCOME) **29. $**____________

30. TOTAL MONTHLY EXPENSES (from line 28 above) **30. $**____________

31. SURPLUS (If line 29 is more than line 30, subtract line 30 from line 29. This is the amount of your surplus. Enter that amount here.) **31. $**____________

32. (DEFICIT) (If line 30 is more than line 29, subtract line 29 from line 30. This is the amount of your deficit. Enter that amount here.) **32. ($**____________**)**

SECTION III. ASSETS AND LIABILITIES

Use the nonmarital column only if this is a petition for dissolution of marriage and you believe an item is "nonmarital," meaning it belongs to only one of you and should not be divided. You should indicate to whom you believe the item(s) or debt belongs. (Typically, you will only use this column if property/debt was owned/owed by one spouse before the marriage. See the **"General Information for Self-Represented Litigants"** found at the beginning of these forms and section 61.075(1), Florida Statutes, for definitions of "marital" and "nonmarital" assets and liabilities.)

A. ASSETS:

DESCRIPTION OF ITEM(S). List a description of each separate item owned by you (and/or your spouse, if this is a petition for dissolution of marriage). DO NOT LIST ACCOUNT NUMBERS. √ the box next to any asset(s) which you are requesting the judge award to you.	**Current Fair Market Value**	**Nonmarital (√ correct column)**	
		husband	wife
□ Cash (on hand)	$		
□ Cash (in banks or credit unions)			
□ Stocks, Bonds, Notes			
□ Real estate: (Home)			
□ (Other)			
□ Automobiles			
□ Other personal property			
□ Retirement plans (Profit Sharing, Pension, IRA, 401(k)s, etc.)			
□ Other			
□			
□			
□			
□			
□			
□			
√ here if additional pages are attached.			
Total Assets (add next column)	$________		

B. LIABILITIES:

DESCRIPTION OF ITEM(S). List a description of each separate debt owed by you (and/or your spouse, if this is a petition for dissolution of marriage). DO NOT LIST ACCOUNT NUMBERS. √ the box next to any debt(s) for which you believe you should be responsible.	**Current Amount Owed**	**Nonmarital (√ correct column)**	
		husband	wife
□ Mortgages on real estate: First mortgage on home	$		
□ Second mortgage on home			
□ Other mortgages			
□			
□ Auto loans			
□			
□ Charge/credit card accounts			
□			
□			
□			
□ Other			
□			
□			
□			
□ √ here if additional pages are attached.			
Total Debts (add next column)	$ ________		

C. CONTINGENT ASSETS AND LIABILITIES:

INSTRUCTIONS: If you have any **POSSIBLE assets** (income potential, accrued vacation or sick leave, bonus, inheritance, etc.) or **POSSIBLE liabilities** (possible lawsuits, future unpaid taxes, contingent tax liabilities, debts assumed by another), you must list them here.

Contingent Assets **√ the box next to any contingent asset(s) which you are requesting the judge award to you.**	**Possible Value**	**Nonmarital (√ correct column)**	
		husband	wife
□	$		
□			
Total Contingent Assets	$ ________		

Contingent Liabilities **√ the box next to any contingent debt(s) for which you believe you should be responsible.**	**Possible Amount Owed**	**Nonmarital (√ correct column)**	
		husband	wife
□	$		
□			
Total Contingent Liabilities	$ ________		

SECTION IV. CHILD SUPPORT GUIDELINES WORKSHEET
(Florida Family Law Rules of Procedure Form 12.902(e), Child Support Guidelines Worksheet, MUST be filed with the court at or prior to a hearing to establish or modify child support. This requirement cannot be waived by the parties.)

[√ **one** only]
___ **A Child Support Guidelines Worksheet IS or WILL BE filed in this case.** This case involves the establishment or modification of child support.
___ **A Child Support Guidelines Worksheet IS NOT being filed in this case.** The establishment or modification of child support is not an issue in this case.

I certify that a copy of this document was [√ **one** only] ( ) mailed ( ) faxed and mailed ( ) hand delivered to the person(s) listed below on *{date}* ______________________________.

Other party or his/her attorney:
Name: ______________________________
Address: ______________________________
City, State, Zip: ______________________________
Fax Number: ______________________________

I understand that I am swearing or affirming under oath to the truthfulness of the claims made in this affidavit and that the punishment for knowingly making a false statement includes fines and/or imprisonment.

Dated: ____________________

____
Signature of Party
Printed Name: ______________________________
Address: ______________________________
City, State, Zip: ______________________________
Telephone Number: ______________________________
Fax Number: ______________________________

STATE OF FLORIDA
COUNTY OF ______________

Sworn to or affirmed and signed before me on ________________ by ______________________________.

____
NOTARY PUBLIC or DEPUTY CLERK

____
[Print, type, or stamp commissioned name of notary or deputy clerk.]

___ Personally known
___ Produced identification
Type of identification produced ____________________

IF A NONLAWYER HELPED YOU FILL OUT THIS FORM, HE/SHE MUST FILL IN THE BLANKS BELOW: [fill in **all** blanks]
I, *{full legal name and trade name of nonlawyer}*______________________________,
a nonlawyer, located at *{street}* ______________________________, *{city}* ____________________,
{state} ________, *{phone}* __________, helped *{name}* ______________________________,
who is the [√ **one** only] ___ petitioner **or** ___ respondent, fill out this form.

IN THE CIRCUIT COURT OF THE ________________________ JUDICIAL CIRCUIT,
IN AND FOR ________________________ COUNTY, FLORIDA

Case No.: ____________________________
Division: ____________________________

________________________________,
Petitioner,

and

________________________________,
Respondent.

FAMILY LAW FINANCIAL AFFIDAVIT
($50,000 or more Individual Gross Annual Income)

I, *{full legal name}* ____, being sworn, certify that the following information is true:

SECTION I. INCOME

1. Date of Birth: ________________

2. My occupation is: ____

3. I am currently

[√ **all** that apply]

___ a. Unemployed

Describe your efforts to find employment, how soon you expect to be employed, and the pay you expect to receive: ____

____

___ b. Employed by: ____

Address: ____

City, State, Zip code: ____

Telephone Number: ____

Pay rate: $ __________ ( ) every week ( ) every other week ( ) twice a month

( ) monthly ( ) other: ____

If you are expecting to become unemployed or change jobs soon, describe the change you expect and why and how it will affect your income: ____

____

□ Check here if you currently have more than one job. List the information above for the second job(s) on a separate sheet and attach it to this affidavit.

___ c. Retired. Date of retirement: ________________________

Employer from whom retired: ____

Address: ____

City, State, Zip code: ____________________ Telephone Number: ______________

LAST YEAR'S GROSS INCOME: Your Income Other Party's Income *(if known)*

YEAR _______ $ _______________ $ __________

PRESENT MONTHLY GROSS INCOME:

All amounts must be MONTHLY. See the instructions with this form to figure out money amounts for anything that is NOT paid monthly. Attach more paper, if needed. Items included under "other" should be listed separately with separate dollar amounts.

1. Monthly gross salary or wages — 1. $________
2. Monthly bonuses, commissions, allowances, overtime, tips, and similar payments — 2. ________
3. Monthly business income from sources such as self-employment, partnerships, close corporations, and/or independent contracts (Gross receipts minus ordinary and necessary expenses required to produce income.) (□ Attach sheet itemizing such income and expenses.) — 3. ________
4. Monthly disability benefits/SSI — 4. ________
5. Monthly Workers' Compensation — 5. ________
6. Monthly Unemployment Compensation — 6. ________
7. Monthly pension, retirement, or annuity payments — 7. ________
8. Monthly Social Security benefits — 8. ________
9. Monthly alimony actually received
   - 9a. From this case: $ _______
   - 9b. From other case(s): _______ Add 9a and 9b — 9. ________
10. Monthly interest and dividends — 10. ________
11. Monthly rental income (gross receipts minus ordinary and necessary expenses required to produce income) (□ Attach sheet itemizing such income and expense items.) — 11. ________
12. Monthly income from royalties, trusts, or estates — 12. ________
13. Monthly reimbursed expenses and in-kind payments to the extent that they reduce personal living expenses (□ Attach sheet itemizing each item and amount.) — 13. ________
14. Monthly gains derived from dealing in property (not including nonrecurring gains) — 14. ________

Any other income of a recurring nature (identify source)

15. ____ 15. ________
16. ____ 16. ________

17. PRESENT MONTHLY GROSS INCOME (Add lines 1–16) **TOTAL: 17. $** ____________

PRESENT MONTHLY DEDUCTIONS:

All amounts must be MONTHLY. See the instructions with this form to figure out money amounts for anything that is NOT paid monthly.

18. Monthly federal, state, and local income tax (corrected for filing status and allowable dependents and income tax liabilities)
    - a. Filing Status ____________
    - b. Number of dependents claimed __________ — 18. $________
19. Monthly FICA or self-employment taxes — 19. ________
20. Monthly Medicare payments — 20. ________

21. Monthly mandatory union dues — 21. ______
22. Monthly mandatory retirement payments — 22. ______
23. Monthly health insurance payments (including dental insurance), excluding portion paid for any minor children of this relationship — 23. ______
24. Monthly court-ordered child support actually paid for children from another relationship — 24. ______
25. Monthly court-ordered alimony actually paid
    25a. from this case: $______
    25b. from other case(s): ______ Add 25a and 25b — 25. ______

26. TOTAL DEDUCTIONS ALLOWABLE UNDER SECTION 61.30, FLORIDA STATUTES (Add lines 18 through 25) **TOTAL:** **26. $** ______

27. PRESENT NET MONTHLY INCOME (Subtract line 26 from line 17) **27. $** ______

SECTION II. AVERAGE MONTHLY EXPENSES

Proposed/Estimated Expenses. If this is a dissolution of marriage case **and** your expenses as listed below do not reflect what you actually pay currently, you should write "estimate" next to each amount that is estimated.

HOUSEHOLD:

1. Monthly mortgage or rent payments — 1. $______
2. Monthly property taxes (if not included in mortgage) — 2. ______
3. Monthly insurance on residence (if not included in mortgage) — 3. ______
4. Monthly condominium maintenance fees and homeowner's association fees — 4. ______
5. Monthly electricity — 5. ______
6. Monthly water, garbage, and sewer — 6. ______
7. Monthly telephone — 7. ______
8. Monthly fuel oil or natural gas — 8. ______
9. Monthly repairs and maintenance — 9. ______
10. Monthly lawn care — 10. ______
11. Monthly pool maintenance — 11. ______
12. Monthly pest control — 12. ______
13. Monthly misc. household — 13. ______
14. Monthly food and home supplies — 14. ______
15. Monthly meals outside home — 15. ______
16. Monthly cable t.v. — 16. ______
17. Monthly alarm service contract — 17. ______
18. Monthly service contracts on appliances — 18. ______
19. Monthly maid service — 19. ______

Other:

20. ______________________ — 20. ______
21. ______________________ — 21. ______
22. ______________________ — 22. ______
23. ______________________ — 23. ______
24. ______________________ — 24. ______

25. **SUBTOTAL** (add lines 1 through 24) **25. $** ____________

AUTOMOBILE:

26. Monthly gasoline and oil 26. $________
27. Monthly repairs 27. ________
28. Monthly auto tags and emission testing 28. ________
29. Monthly insurance 29. ________
30. Monthly payments (lease or financing) 30. ________
31. Monthly rental/replacements 31. ________
32. Monthly alternative transportation (bus, rail, car pool, etc.) 32. ________
33. Monthly tolls and parking 33. ________
34. Other: ______________________________ 34. ________

35. **SUBTOTAL** (add lines 26 through 34) **35. $**____________

MONTHLY EXPENSES FOR CHILDREN COMMON TO BOTH PARTIES:

36. Monthly nursery, babysitting, or day care 36. $ ________
37. Monthly school tuition 37. ________
38. Monthly school supplies, books, and fees 38. ________
39. Monthly after school activities 39. ________
40. Monthly lunch money 40. ________
41. Monthly private lessons or tutoring 41. ________
42. Monthly allowances 42. ________
43. Monthly clothing and uniforms 43. ________
44. Monthly entertainment (movies, parties, etc.) 44. ________
45. Monthly health insurance 45. ________
46. Monthly medical, dental, prescriptions (nonreimbursed only) 46. ________
47. Monthly psychiatric/psychological/counselor 47. ________
48. Monthly orthodontic 48. ________
49. Monthly vitamins 49. ________
50. Monthly beauty parlor/barber shop 50. ________
51. Monthly nonprescription medication 51. ________
52. Monthly cosmetics, toiletries, and sundries 52. ________
53. Monthly gifts from child(ren) to others (other children, relatives, teachers, etc.) 53. ________
54. Monthly camp or summer activities 54. ________
55. Monthly clubs (Boy/Girl Scouts, etc.) 55. ________
56. Monthly access expenses (for nonresidential parent) 56. ________
57. Monthly miscellaneous 57. ________

58. **SUBTOTAL** (add lines 36 through 57) **58. $**____________

MONTHLY EXPENSES FOR CHILD(REN) FROM ANOTHER RELATIONSHIP: (other than court-ordered child support)

59. ______________________________ 59. $________
60. ______________________________ 60. ________
61. ______________________________ 61. ________
62. ______________________________ 62. ________

63. **SUBTOTAL** (add lines 59 through 62) **63. $**______________

MONTHLY INSURANCE:

64. Health insurance, excluding portion paid for any minor child(ren) of this relationship 64. $__________
65. Life insurance 65. __________
66. Dental insurance 66. __________

Other:

67. ______________________________ 67. __________
68. ______________________________ 68. __________

69. **SUBTOTAL** (add lines 64 through 68) **69. $**______________

OTHER MONTHLY EXPENSES NOT LISTED ABOVE:

70. Monthly dry cleaning and laundry 70. $__________
71. Monthly clothing 71. __________
72. Monthly medical, dental, and prescription (unreimbursed only) 72. __________
73. Monthly psychiatric, psychological, or counselor (unreimbursed only) 73. __________
74. Monthly non-prescription medications, cosmetics, toiletries, and sundries 74. __________
75. Monthly grooming 75. __________
76. Monthly gifts 76. __________
77. Monthly pet expenses 77. __________
78. Monthly club dues and membership 78. __________
79. Monthly sports and hobbies 79. __________
80. Monthly entertainment 80. __________
81. Monthly periodicals/books/tapes/CD's 81. __________
82. Monthly vacations 82. __________
83. Monthly religious organizations 83. __________
84. Monthly bank charges/credit card fees 84. __________
85. Monthly education expenses 85. __________

Other: (include any usual and customary expenses not otherwise mentioned in the items listed above)

86. ______________________________ 86. __________
87. ______________________________ 87. __________
88. ______________________________ 88. __________
89. ______________________________ 89. __________

90. **SUBTOTAL** (add lines 70 through 89) **90. $**______________

MONTHLY PAYMENTS TO CREDITORS: (only when payments are currently made by you on outstanding balances)

NAME OF CREDITOR(s):

91. ______________________________ 91. $__________
92. ______________________________ 92. __________
93. ______________________________ 93. __________
94. ______________________________ 94. __________
95. ______________________________ 95. __________
96. ______________________________ 96. __________
97. ______________________________ 97. __________
98. ______________________________ 98. __________

99. ______________________________ 99. ________
100. ______________________________ 100. ________
101. ______________________________ 101. ________
102. ______________________________ 102. ________
103. ______________________________ 103. ________

104. **SUBTOTAL** (add lines 91 through 103) **104. $**__________

105. TOTAL MONTHLY EXPENSES:
(add lines 25, 35, 58, 63, 69, 90, and 104 of Section II, Expenses) **105. $** __________

SUMMARY

106. TOTAL PRESENT MONTHLY NET INCOME
(from line 27 of SECTION I. INCOME) **106. $**__________

107. TOTAL MONTHLY EXPENSES (from line 105 above) **107. $**__________

108. SURPLUS (If line 106 is more than line 107, subtract line 107 from line 106. This is the amount of your surplus. Enter that amount here.) **108. $**__________

109. (DEFICIT) (If line 107 is more than line 106, subtract line 106 from line 107. This is the amount of your deficit. Enter that amount here.) **109. ($**__________)

SECTION III. ASSETS AND LIABILITIES

A. ASSETS (This is where you list what you OWN.)

INSTRUCTIONS:

STEP 1: In column A, list a description of each separate item owned by you (and/or your spouse, if this is a petition for dissolution of marriage). Blank spaces are provided if you need to list more than one of an item.

STEP 2: If this is a petition for dissolution of marriage, check the box **in Column A** next to any item that you are requesting the judge award to you.

STEP 3: In column B, write what you believe to be the current fair market value of all items listed.

STEP 4: Use column C only if this is a petition for dissolution of marriage and you believe an item is "nonmarital," meaning it belongs to only one of you and should not be divided. You should indicate to whom you believe the item belongs. (Typically, you will only use Column C if property was owned by one spouse before the marriage. See the **"General Information for Self-Represented Litigants"** found at the beginning of these forms and section 61.075(1), Florida Statutes, for definitions of "marital" and "nonmarital" assets and liabilities.)

A ASSETS: DESCRIPTION OF ITEM(S) DO NOT LIST ACCOUNT NUMBERS. √ the box next to any asset(s) which you are requesting the judge award to you.	B Current Fair Market Value	C Nonmarital (√ correct column) husband	 wife
☐ Cash (on hand)	$		
☐ Cash (in banks or credit unions)			
☐			
☐ Stocks/Bonds			
☐			

A ASSETS: DESCRIPTION OF ITEM(S) DO NOT LIST ACCOUNT NUMBERS. √ the box next to any asset(s) which you are requesting the judge award to you.	B Current Fair Market Value	C Nonmarital (√ correct column) husband	 wife
☐			
☐ Notes (money owed to you in writing)			
☐			
☐			
☐ Money owed to you (not evidenced by a note)			
☐			
☐			
☐ Real estate: (Home)			
☐ (Other)			
☐			
☐			
☐			
☐			
☐			
☐ Business interests			
☐			
☐			
☐			
☐			
☐ Automobiles			
☐			
☐			
☐			
☐ Boats			
☐			
☐			
☐ Other vehicles			
☐			
☐			
☐ Retirement plans (Profit Sharing, Pension, IRA, 401(k)s, etc.)			
☐			
☐			
☐			
☐ Furniture & furnishings in home			
☐			
☐ Furniture & furnishings elsewhere			

A ASSETS: DESCRIPTION OF ITEM(S) DO NOT LIST ACCOUNT NUMBERS. √ the box next to any asset(s) which you are requesting the judge award to you.	B Current Fair Market Value	C Nonmarital (√ correct column) husband	 wife
☐			
☐ Collectibles			
☐			
☐ Jewelry			
☐			
☐ Life insurance (cash surrender value)			
☐			
☐			
☐ Sporting and entertainment (T.V., stereo, etc.) equipment			
☐			
☐			
☐			
☐			
☐ Other assets			
☐			
☐			
☐			
☐			
☐			
☐			
☐			
Total Assets (add column B)	**$** ________		

B. LIABILITIES/DEBTS (This is where you list what you OWE.)

INSTRUCTIONS:

STEP 1: In column A, list a description of each separate debt owed by you (and/or your spouse, if this is a petition for dissolution of marriage). Blank spaces are provided if you need to list more than one of an item.

STEP 2: If this is a petition for dissolution of marriage, check the box **in Column A** next to any debt(s) for which you believe you should be responsible.

STEP 3: In column B, write what you believe to be the current amount owed for all items listed.

STEP 4: Use column C only if this is a petition for dissolution of marriage and you believe an item is "nonmarital," meaning the debt belongs to only one of you and should not be divided. You should indicate to whom you believe the debt belongs. (Typically, you will only use Column C if the debt was owed by one spouse before the marriage. See the **"General Information for Self-Represented Litigants"** found at the beginning of these forms and section 61.075(1), Florida Statutes, for definitions of "marital" and "nonmarital" assets and liabilities.)

A LIABILITIES: DESCRIPTION OF ITEM(S) DO NOT LIST ACCOUNT NUMBERS. √ the box next to any debt(s) for which you believe you should be responsible.	B Current Amount Owed	C Nonmarital (√ correct column)	
		husband	wife
☐ Mortgages on real estate: First mortgage on home	$		
☐ Second mortgage on home			
☐ Other mortgages			
☐			
☐ Charge/credit card accounts			
☐			
☐			
☐			
☐			
☐			
☐ Auto loan			
☐ Auto loan			
☐ Bank/Credit Union loans			
☐			
☐			
☐			
☐ Money you owe (not evidenced by a note)			
☐			
☐ Judgments			
☐			
☐ Other			
☐			
☐			
☐			
☐			
☐			
☐			
Total Debts (add column B)	$ ________		

C. NET WORTH (excluding contingent assets and liabilities)

Total Assets (enter total of Column B in Asset Table; Section A) $ __________
Total Liabilities (enter total of Column B in Liabilities Table; Section B) $ __________

TOTAL NET WORTH (Total Assets minus Total Liabilities)
(excluding contingent assets and liabilities) **$__________**

D. CONTINGENT ASSETS AND LIABILITIES

INSTRUCTIONS:

If you have any **POSSIBLE assets** (income potential, accrued vacation or sick leave, bonus, inheritance, etc.) or **POSSIBLE liabilities** (possible lawsuits, future unpaid taxes, contingent tax liabilities, debts assumed by another), you must list them here.

A Contingent Assets √ the box next to any contingent asset(s) which you are requesting the judge award to you.	B Possible Value	C Nonmarital (√ correct column) husband	 wife
☐	$		
☐			
☐			
☐			
☐			
Total Contingent Assets	**$**_________		

A Contingent Liabilities √ the box next to any contingent debt(s) for which you believe you should be responsible.	B Possible Amount Owed	C Nonmarital (√ correct column) husband	 wife
☐	$		
☐			
☐			
☐			
☐			
Total Contingent Liabilities	**$** _________		

E. CHILD SUPPORT GUIDELINES WORKSHEET. Florida Family Law Rules of Procedure Form 12.902(e), Child Support Guidelines Worksheet, MUST be filed with the court at or prior to a hearing to establish or modify child support. This requirement cannot be waived by the parties.

[√ **one** only]

___ **A Child Support Guidelines Worksheet IS or WILL BE filed in this case.** This case involves the establishment or modification of child support.

___ **A Child Support Guidelines Worksheet IS NOT being filed in this case.** The establishment or modification of child support is not an issue in this case.

I certify that a copy of this financial affidavit was: (   ) mailed, (   ) faxed and mailed, or (   ) hand delivered to the person(s) listed below on *{date}* ______________________________.

Other party or his/her attorney:

Name: ______________________________

Address: ______________________________

City, State, Zip: ______________________________

Fax Number: ______________________________

I understand that I am swearing or affirming under oath to the truthfulness of the claims made in this affidavit and that the punishment for knowingly making a false statement includes fines and/or imprisonment.

Dated: ______________________

____
Signature of Party
Printed Name: ______________________________
Address: ______________________________
City, State, Zip: ______________________________
Telephone Number: ______________________________
Fax Number: ______________________________

STATE OF FLORIDA
COUNTY OF __________________

Sworn to or affirmed and signed before me on _____________ by __________________________.

____
NOTARY PUBLIC or DEPUTY CLERK

____
[Print, type, or stamp commissioned name of notary or deputy clerk .]

___ Personally known
___ Produced identification
Type of identification produced ____________________

IF A NONLAWYER HELPED YOU FILL OUT THIS FORM, HE/SHE MUST FILL IN THE BLANKS BELOW: [fill in **all** blanks]
I, *{full legal name and trade name of nonlawyer}* ______________________________________,
a nonlawyer, located at *{street}* ______________________________, *{city}* __________________,
{state} _____________, *{phone}* _________________, helped *{name}* _________________________,
who is the [√ **one** only] ___ petitioner **or** ___ respondent, fill out this form.

IN THE CIRCUIT COURT OF THE _______________ JUDICIAL CIRCUIT,
IN AND FOR _______________ COUNTY, FLORIDA

Case No.: _______________
Division: _______________

_______________,
Petitioner,

and

_______________,
Respondent.

UNIFORM CHILD CUSTODY JURISDICTION AND ENFORCEMENT ACT (UCCJEA) AFFIDAVIT

I, *{full legal name}* _______________, being sworn, certify that the following statements are true:

1. The number of minor child(ren) subject to this proceeding is ________. The name, place of birth, birth date, and sex of each child; the present address, periods of residence, and places where each child has lived **within the past five (5) years**; and the name, present address, and relationship to the child of each person with whom the child has lived during that time are:

THE FOLLOWING INFORMATION IS TRUE ABOUT CHILD # 1 :

Child's Full Legal Name: _______________
Place of Birth: ___________ Date of Birth: _______________ Sex: _______________

Child's Residence for the past 5 years:

Dates (From/To)	Address (including city and state) where child lived	Name and present address of person child lived with	Relationship to child
____ /present*			
____/____			
____/____			
____/____			
____/____			
____/____			

* **If you are the petitioner in an injunction for protection against domestic violence case and you have filed**

(Make as many copies of page 2 as necessary.)

Petitioner's Request for Confidential Filing of Address, ✎ ❑ Florida Supreme Court Approved Family Law Form 12.980(i), you should write "confidential" in any space on this form that would require you to enter the address where you are currently living.

THE FOLLOWING INFORMATION IS TRUE ABOUT CHILD # ____:

Child's Full Legal Name: ______________________________
Place of Birth: ____________ Date of Birth: ________________ Sex: ________________

Child's Residence for the past 5 years:

Dates (From/To)	Address (including city and state) where child lived	Name and present address of person child lived with	Relationship to child
____/present			
____/____			
____/____			
____/____			
____/____			
____/____			

THE FOLLOWING INFORMATION IS TRUE ABOUT CHILD # ____:

Child's Full Legal Name: ______________________________
Place of Birth: ____________ Date of Birth: ________________ Sex: ________________

Child's Residence for the past 5 years:

Dates (From/To)	Address (including city and state) where child lived	Name and present address of person child lived with	Relationship to child
____/present			
____/____			
____/____			
____/____			
____/____			

___/___			

2. **Participation in custody proceeding(s):**

[√ **one** only]

____ I HAVE NOT participated as a party, witness, or in any capacity in any other litigation or custody proceeding in this or any other state, concerning custody of a child subject to this proceeding.

____ I HAVE participated as a party, witness, or in any capacity in any other litigation or custody proceeding in this or another state, concerning custody of a child subject to this proceeding. Explain:

a. Name of each child: ______________________________

b. Type of proceeding: ______________________________

c. Court and state: ______________________________

d. Date of court order or judgment (if any): ______________________________

3. **Information about custody proceeding(s):**

[√ **one** only]

____ I HAVE NO INFORMATION of any custody proceeding pending in a court of this or any other state concerning a child subject to this proceeding.

____ I HAVE THE FOLLOWING INFORMATION concerning a custody proceeding pending in a court of this or another state concerning a child subject to this proceeding, other than set out in item 2. Explain:

a. Name of each child: ______________________________

b. Type of proceeding: ______________________________

c. Court and state: ______________________________

d. Date of court order or judgment (if any): ______________________________

4. **Persons not a party to this proceeding:**

[√ **one** only]

____ I DO NOT KNOW OF ANY PERSON not a party to this proceeding who has physical custody or claims to have custody or visitation rights with respect to any child subject to this proceeding.

____ I KNOW THAT THE FOLLOWING NAMED PERSON(S) not a party to this proceeding has (have) physical custody or claim(s) to have custody or visitation rights with respect to any child subject to this proceeding:

a. Name and address of person: ______________________________

____

(   ) has physical custody (   ) claims custody rights (   ) claims visitation rights.

Name of each child: ______________________________

b. Name and address of person: ______________________________

____

(   ) has physical custody (   ) claims custody rights (   ) claims visitation rights.

Name of each child: ______________________________

c. Name and address of person: ______________________________

____

(   ) has physical custody (   ) claims custody rights (   ) claims visitation rights.

Name of each child: ______________________________

5. **Knowledge of prior child support proceedings:**
[√ **one** only]

____ The child(ren) described in this affidavit are NOT subject to existing child support order(s) in this or any state or territory.

____ The child(ren) described in this affidavit are subject to the following existing child support order(s):

a. Name of each child: ____________________
b. Type of proceeding: ____________________
c. Court and address: ____________________
d. Date of court order/judgment (if any): ____________________
e. Amount of child support paid and by whom: ____________________

6. **I acknowledge that I have a continuing duty to advise this Court of any custody, visitation, child support, or guardianship proceeding (including dissolution of marriage, separate maintenance, child neglect, or dependency) concerning the child(ren) in this state or any other state about which information is obtained during this proceeding.**

I certify that a copy of this document was [√ **one** only] ( ) mailed ( ) faxed and mailed ( ) hand delivered to the person(s) listed below on *{date}* ____________________.

Other party or his/her attorney:
Name: ____________________
Address: ____________________
City, State, Zip: ____________________
Fax Number: ____________________

I understand that I am swearing or affirming under oath to the truthfulness of the claims made in this affidavit and that the punishment for knowingly making a false statement includes fines and/or imprisonment.

Dated: ____________________

____
Signature of Party
Printed Name: ____________________
Address: ____________________
City, State, Zip: ____________________
Telephone Number: ____________________
Fax Number: ____________________

STATE OF FLORIDA
COUNTY OF ____________________

Sworn to or affirmed and signed before me on ______________ by ____________________.

____
NOTARY PUBLIC or DEPUTY CLERK

____

[Print, type, or stamp commissioned name of notary or clerk.]

____ Personally known
____ Produced identification
Type of identification produced ____________________

IF A NONLAWYER HELPED YOU FILL OUT THIS FORM, HE/SHE MUST FILL IN THE BLANKS BELOW: [✍ fill in **all** blanks]
I, *{full legal name and trade name of nonlawyer}* ______________________________,
a nonlawyer, located at *{street}* ________________________, *{city}* ______________,
{state} ______________, *{phone}* ______________, helped *{name}* ______________,
who is the [√ **one** only] ___ petitioner **or** ___ respondent, fill out this form.

IN THE CIRCUIT COURT OF THE ______________________ JUDICIAL CIRCUIT,
IN AND FOR ________________________ COUNTY, FLORIDA

Case No.: ____________________________________
Division: _____________________________________

________________________________,
Petitioner,

and

________________________________,
Respondent.

NOTICE OF FILING CHILD SUPPORT GUIDELINES WORKSHEET

PLEASE TAKE NOTICE, that {name}____________________________, is filing his/her Child Support Guidelines Worksheet attached and labeled Exhibit 1.

CERTIFICATE OF SERVICE

I certify that a copy of this Notice of Filing with the Child Support Guidelines Worksheet was [√ **one** only] ( ) mailed ( ) faxed and mailed ( ) hand delivered to the person(s) listed below on *{date}* _______.

Other party or his/her attorney:
Name: ____
Address: ____
City, State, Zip: _______________________________________
Fax Number: ____
Date: _____________________

____
Signature of Party
Printed Name: ____________________________________
Address: ____
City, State, Zip: __________________________________
Telephone Number: ________________________________
Fax Number: ______________________________________

CHILD SUPPORT GUIDELINES WORKSHEET			
	A. FATHER	**B.** MOTHER	TOTAL
1. Present Net Monthly Income Enter the amount from line number 27, Section I of ✎❑ Florida Family Law Rules of Procedure Form 12.902(b) or (c), Financial Affidavit.			
2. Basic Monthly Obligation There is (are) *{number}* ________ minor child(ren) common to the parties. Using the total amount from line 1, enter the appropriate amount from the child support guidelines chart.			
3. Percent of Financial Responsibility Divide the amount on line 1A by the total amount on line 1 to get Father's percentage financial responsibility. Enter answer on line 3A. Divide the amount on line 1B by the total amount on line 1 to get Mother's percentage financial responsibility. Enter answer on line 3B.	.%	. %	
4. Share of Basic Monthly Obligation Multiply the number on line 2 by the percentage on line 3A to get Father's share of basic obligation. Enter answer on line 4A. Multiply the number on line 2 by the percentage on line 3B to get Mother's share of basic obligation. Enter answer on line 4B.			
Additional Support — Health Insurance, Child Care & Other			
5a. 75% of Monthly Child Care Costs [Child care costs should not exceed the level required to provide quality care from a licensed source for the child(ren). See section 61.30(7), Fla. Stat. for more information.]			
5b. Total Monthly Child(ren)'s Health Insurance Cost [This is only amounts actually paid for health insurance on the child(ren).]			
5c. Total Monthly Child(ren)'s Noncovered Medical, Dental and Prescription Medication Costs			
5d. Total Monthly Child Care & Health Costs [Add lines 5a+5b+5c]			
6. Additional Support Payments Multiply the number on line 5d by the percentage on line 3A to determine the Father's share. Enter answer on line 6A. Multiply the number on line 5d by the percentage on line 3B to determine the Mother's share. Enter answer on line 6B.			
Statutory Adjustments/Credits			
7a. Monthly child care payments actually made			
7b. Monthly health insurance payments actually made			
7c. Other payments/credits actually made for any noncovered medical, dental and prescription medication expenses of the child(ren) not ordered to be separately paid on a percentage basis. [See § 61.30 (8), Florida Statutes]			
8. Total Support Payments actually made [Add 7a through 7c]			
9. MINIMUM CHILD SUPPORT OBLIGATION FOR EACH PARENT [Line 4 plus line 6; minus line 8]			
Substantial Shared Parenting (GROSS UP METHOD) If the noncustodial parent exercises visitation at least 40 percent of the overnights in the year (146 overnights in the year), complete Nos. 10 through 21			
10. Basic Monthly Obligation x 150% [Multiply line 2by 1.5]			

CHILD SUPPORT GUIDELINES WORKSHEET			
	A. FATHER	B. MOTHER	TOTAL
11. Increased Basic Obligation for each parent Multiply the number on line 10 by the percentage on line 3A to determine the Father's share. Enter answer on line 11A. Multiply the number on line 10 by the percentage on line 3B to determine the Mother's share. Enter answer on line 11B.			
12. Percentage of overnight stays with each parent The child(ren) spend(s)_____ overnight stays with the father each year. Using the number on the above line, multiply it by 100 and divide by 365. Enter this number on line 12A. The child(ren) spend(s)_____ overnight stays with the mother each year. Using the number on the above line, multiply it by 100 and divide by 365. Enter this number on line 12B.	%	%	
13. Parent's support multiplied by other Parent's percentage of overnights [Multiply line 11A by line 12B. Enter this number in 13A. Multiply line 11B by line 12A. Enter this number in 13B.]			
Additional Support — Health Insurance, Child Care & Other			
14a. Total Monthly Child Care Costs [Child care costs should not exceed the level required to provide quality care from a licensed source for the child(ren). See section 61.30(7), Fla. Stat. for more information.]			
14b. Total Monthly Child(ren)'s Health Insurance Cost [This is only amounts actually paid for health insurance on the child(ren).]			
14c. Total Monthly Child(ren)'s Noncovered Medical, Dental and Prescription Medication Costs			
14d. Total Monthly Child Care & Health Costs [Add lines 14a+14b+14c]			
15. Additional Support Payments Multiply the number on line 14d by the percentage on line 3A to determine the Father's share. Enter answer on line 15A. Multiply the number on line 14d by the percentage on line 3B to determine the Mother's share. Enter answer on line 15B.			
Statutory Adjustments/Credits			
16a. Monthly child care payments actually made			
16b. Monthly health insurance payments actually made			
16c. Other payments/credits actually made for any noncovered medical, dental and prescription medication expenses of the child(ren) not ordered to be separately paid on a percentage basis. [See § 61.30 (8), Florida Statutes]			
17. Total Support Payments actually made [Add 16a through 16c]			
18. Total Additional Support Transfer Amount [Line 15 minus line 17; Enter any negative number as zero]			
19. Total Child Support Owed from Father to Mother [Add line 13A+18A]			
20. Total Child Support Owed from Mother to Father [Add line 13B+18B]			
21. Actual Child Support to Be Paid. [Comparing lines 19 and 20, Subtract the smaller amount owed from the larger amount owed and enter the result in the column for the parent that owes the larger amount of support]	$_________-or- $ _________		

ADJUSTMENTS TO GUIDELINES AMOUNT. If you or the other parent is requesting the Court to award a child support amount that is more or less than the child support guidelines, you must complete and file Motion to Deviate from Child Support Guidelines, ✎❒ Florida Supreme Court Approved Family Law Form 12.943.

[√ **one** only]

___ a. **Deviation from the guidelines amount is requested.** The Motion to Deviate from Child Support Guidelines, ✎❒ Florida Supreme Court Approved Family Law Form 12.943, is attached.

___ b. **Deviation from the guidelines amount is NOT requested.** The Motion to Deviate from Child Support Guidelines, ✎❒ Florida Supreme Court Approved Family Law Form 12.943, is not attached.

IF A NONLAWYER HELPED YOU FILL OUT THIS FORM, HE/SHE MUST FILL IN THE BLANKS BELOW:

[✍ fill in **all** blanks]

I, *{full legal name and trade name of nonlawyer}* ______________________________,
a nonlawyer, located at *{street}* ______________________, *{city}* ______________________,
{state} ____________, *{phone}* ____________, helped *{name}* ______________________________,
who is the [√ **one** only] ___ petitioner **or** ___ respondent, fill out this form.

IN THE CIRCUIT COURT OF THE ___________________________ JUDICIAL CIRCUIT,
IN AND FOR ____________________________ COUNTY, FLORIDA

Case No.: ______________________________
Division: ______________________________

____________________________________,
Petitioner,

and

____________________________________,
Respondent.

MOTION TO DEVIATE FROM CHILD SUPPORT GUIDELINES

( ) Petitioner ( ) Respondent requests that the Court enter an order granting the following:

SECTION I
[√ **one** only]

____ a. **MORE** child support than the amount required by the child support guidelines. The Court should order MORE child support than the amount required by the child support guidelines because of:

[√ **all** that apply to your situation]

____ 1. Extraordinary medical, psychological, educational, or dental expenses;
____ 2. Seasonal variations in one or both parent's income;
____ 3. Age(s) of the child(ren), taking into consideration the greater needs of older child(ren);
____ 4. Special needs that have been met traditionally within the family budget even though the fulfilling of those needs will cause support to exceed the guidelines;
____ 5. The amount of time each child will spend with each parent under the shared parental arrangement;
____ 6. The direct and indirect financial expenses for each child as set forth in s. 61.30(11)(b)3, Florida Statutes;
____ 7. Total available assets of mother, father, and child(ren);
____ 8. Impact of IRS dependency exemption and waiver of that exemption;
____ 9. Residency of subsequently born or adopted child(ren) with the obligor, including consideration of the subsequent spouse's income;
____ 10. The comparative income of each parent, considering all relevant factors, as provided in s. 61.30(2)(a), Florida Statutes;
____ 11. The station in life of each parent and each child;
____ 12. The standard of living experienced by the entire family during the marriage;
____ 13. The financial status and ability of each parent; and/or
____ 14. Any other adjustment that is needed to achieve an equitable result, which may include reasonable and necessary expenses jointly incurred during the marriage.

Explain any items marked above: ____
____
____.

____ b. **LESS** child support than the amount required by the child support guidelines. The Court should order LESS child support than the amount required by the child support guidelines because of:

[√ **all** that apply to your situation]

____ 1. Extraordinary medical, psychological, educational, or dental expenses;
____ 2. Independent income of child(ren), excluding the child(ren)'s SSI income;
____ 3. Payment of both child support and spousal support to a parent that regularly has been paid and for which there is a demonstrated need;

____ 4. Seasonal variations in one or both parent's income;
____ 5. Age of the child(ren), taking into consideration the greater needs of older child(ren);
____ 6. The amount of time each child will spend with each parent under the shared parental arrangement;
____ 7. The direct and indirect financial expenses for each child as set forth in s. 61.30(11)(b), Florida Statutes;
____ 8. The comparative income of each parent, considering all relevant factors, as provided in s. 61.30(2)(a), Florida Statutes;
____ 9. Total available assets of obligee, obligor, and child(ren);
____ 10. Impact of IRS dependency exemption and waiver of that exemption;
____ 11. Application of the child support guidelines requires the obligor to pay more than 55% of gross income for a single support order;
____ 12. The station in life of each parent and each child;
____ 13. The standard of living experienced by the entire family during the marriage;
____ 14. The financial status and ability of each parent; and/or
____ 15. Any other adjustment that is needed to achieve an equitable result, which may include reasonable and necessary expenses jointly incurred during the marriage.

Explain any items marked above:____
____
____.

SECTION II. INCOME AND ASSETS OF CHILD(REN) COMMON TO BOTH PARTIES

List the total of any independent income or assets of the child(ren) common to both parties (income from Social Security, gifts, stocks/bonds, employment, trust fund(s), investment(s), etc.). Attach an explanation.

TOTAL VALUE OF ASSETS OF CHILD(REN)	**$ __________**
TOTAL MONTHLY INCOME OF CHILD(REN)	**$ __________**

SECTION III. EXPENSES FOR CHILD(REN) COMMON TO BOTH PARTIES

All amounts must be MONTHLY. See the instructions with this form to figure out money amounts for anything that is NOT paid monthly. Attach more paper, if needed. Items included under "other" should be listed separately with separate dollar amounts.

1.	Monthly nursery, babysitting, or other child care	1. $ __________
2.	Monthly after-school care	2. $ __________
3.	Monthly school tuition	3. $ __________
4.	Monthly school supplies, books, and fees	4. $ __________
5.	Monthly after-school activities	5. $ __________
6.	Monthly lunch money	6. $ __________
7.	Monthly private lessons/tutoring	7. $ __________
8.	Monthly allowance	8. $ __________
9.	Monthly clothing	9. $ __________
10.	Monthly uniforms	10. $ __________
11.	Monthly entertainment (movies, birthday parties, etc.)	11. $ __________
12.	Monthly health and dental insurance premiums	12. $ __________
13.	Monthly medical, dental, prescription charges (unreimbursed)	13. $ __________
14.	Monthly psychiatric/psychological/counselor (unreimbursed)	14. $ __________
15.	Monthly orthodontic (unreimbursed)	15. $ __________
16.	Monthly grooming	16. $ __________
17.	Monthly non-prescription medications/cosmetics/toiletries/sundries	17. $ __________
18.	Monthly gifts from children to others (other children, relatives, teachers, etc.)	18. $ __________
19.	Monthly camp or other summer activities	19. $ __________

20. Monthly clubs (Boy/Girl Scouts, etc.) or recreational fees 20. $ ________
21. Monthly visitation expenses (for nonresidential parent)
Explain: ______________________________ 21. $ ________
22. Monthly insurance (life, etc.) *{explain}*: ______________ 22. $ ________

Other *{explain}*: 23. $ ________
23. ______________________________ 24. $ ________
24. ______________________________ 25. $ ________
25. ______________________________

26. TOTAL EXPENSES FOR CHILD(REN) COMMON TO BOTH PARTIES
(add lines 1 through 25) **26. $** ________

I have filed, will file, or am filing with this form the following additional documents:

1. Florida Family Law Family Law Financial Affidavit ✎ ❑ Florida Family Law Rules of Procedure Form 12.902(b) or (c).

2. Child Support Guidelines Worksheet ✎ ❑ Florida Family Law Rules of Procedure Form 12.902(e).

I certify that a copy of this document was [√ **one** only] ( ) mailed ( ) faxed and mailed ( ) hand delivered to the person(s) listed below on *{date}* ______________________.

Other party or his/her attorney:
Name: ______________________
Address: ______________________
City, State, Zip: ______________________
Fax Number: ______________________

I understand that I am swearing or affirming under oath to the truthfulness of the claims made in this motion and that the punishment for knowingly making a false statement includes fines and/or imprisonment.

Dated: ______________

____
Signature
Printed Name: ______________________
Address: ______________________
City, State, Zip: ______________________
Telephone Number: ______________________
Fax Number: ______________________

STATE OF FLORIDA
COUNTY OF ______________

Sworn to or affirmed and signed before me on ______________ by ______________________.

____
NOTARY PUBLIC or DEPUTY CLERK

____
[Print, type, or stamp commissioned name of notary or clerk.]

____ Personally known
____ Produced identification
Type of identification produced ______________________

IF A NONLAWYER HELPED YOU FILL OUT THIS FORM, HE/SHE MUST FILL IN THE BLANKS BELOW: [✍ fill in **all** blanks]

I, *{full legal name and trade name of nonlawyer}*____,
a nonlawyer, located at *{street}*__________________________________, *{city}* ____________________,
{state} ____________________, *{phone}* __________________, helped *{name}* ____________________,
who is the [√ **one** only] ___ petitioner **or** ___ respondent, fill out this form.

IN THE CIRCUIT COURT OF THE ________________________ JUDICIAL CIRCUIT,
IN AND FOR __________________________ COUNTY, FLORIDA

Case No.: ______________________________
Division: ______________________________

____________________________________,
Petitioner,

and

____________________________________,
Respondent.

MARITAL SETTLEMENT AGREEMENT FOR SIMPLIFIED DISSOLUTION OF MARRIAGE

We, *{Husband's full legal name}* ____,
and *{Wife's full legal name}* ____,
being sworn, certify that the following statements are true:

1. We were married to each other on *{date}* ______________________.
2. Because of irreconcilable differences in our marriage (no chance of staying together), we have made this agreement to settle once and for all what we owe to each other and what we can expect to receive from each other. Each of us states that nothing has been held back, that we have honestly included everything we could think of in listing our assets (everything we own and that is owed to us) and our debts (everything we owe), and that we believe the other has been open and honest in writing this agreement.
3. We have both filed a Financial Affidavit, ✎ ☐ Florida Family Law Rules of Procedure Form 12.902(b) or (c). Because we have voluntarily made full and fair disclosure to each other of all our assets and debts, we waive any further disclosure under rule 12.285, Florida Family Law Rules of Procedure.
4. Each of us agrees to execute and exchange any papers that might be needed to complete this agreement, including deeds, title certificates, etc.

SECTION I. MARITAL ASSETS AND LIABILITIES

A. Division of Assets. We divide our assets (everything we own and that is owed to us) as follows: Any personal item(s) not listed below is the property of the party currently in possession of the item(s).

1. Wife shall receive as her own and Husband shall have no further rights or responsibilities regarding these assets:

ASSETS: DESCRIPTION OF ITEM(S) WIFE SHALL RECEIVE (To avoid confusion at a later date, describe each item as clearly as possible. You do not need to list account numbers. Where applicable, include whether the name on any title/deed/account described below is wife's, husband's, or both.)	Current Fair Market Value
☐ Cash (on hand)	$
☐ Cash (in banks/credit unions)	
☐	
☐ Stocks/Bonds	
☐	
☐ Notes (money owed to you in writing)	

ASSETS: DESCRIPTION OF ITEM(S) WIFE SHALL RECEIVE (To avoid confusion at a later date, describe each item as clearly as possible. You do not need to list account numbers. Where applicable, include whether the name on any title/deed/account described below is wife's, husband's, or both.)	Current Fair Market Value
☐	
☐	
☐ Money owed to you (not evidenced by a note)	
☐	
☐	
☐ Real estate: (Home)	
☐ (Other)	
☐	
☐ Business interests	
☐	
☐ Automobiles	
☐	
☐	
☐ Boats	
☐ Other vehicles	
☐	
☐ Retirement plans (Profit Sharing, Pension, IRA, 401(k)s, etc.)	
☐	
☐	
☐ Furniture & furnishings in home	
☐	
☐ Furniture & furnishings elsewhere	
☐	
☐ Collectibles	
☐	
☐ Jewelry	
☐	
☐ Life insurance (cash surrender value)	
☐	
☐ Sporting and entertainment (T.V., stereo, etc.) equipment	
☐	
☐	
☐	
☐ Other assets	
☐	
☐	
☐	
☐	
☐	

ASSETS: DESCRIPTION OF ITEM(S) WIFE SHALL RECEIVE (To avoid confusion at a later date, describe each item as clearly as possible. You do not need to list account numbers. Where applicable, include whether the name on any title/deed/account described below is wife's, husband's, or both.)	**Current Fair Market Value**
▯	
Total Assets to Wife	**$ ________**

2. Husband shall receive as his own and Wife shall have no further rights or responsibilities regarding these assets:

ASSETS: DESCRIPTION OF ITEM(S) HUSBAND SHALL RECEIVE (To avoid confusion at a later date, describe each item as clearly as possible. You do not need to list account numbers. Where applicable, include whether the name on any title/deed/account described	**Current Fair Market Value**
▯ Cash (on hand)	$
▯ Cash (in banks/credit unions)	
▯	
▯ Stocks/Bonds	
▯	
▯ Notes (money owed to you in writing)	
▯	
▯	
▯ Money owed to you (not evidenced by a note)	
▯	
▯	
▯ Real estate: (Home)	
▯ (Other)	
▯	
▯ Business interests	
▯	
▯ Automobiles	
▯	
▯	
▯ Boats	
▯ Other vehicles	
▯	
▯ Retirement plans (Profit Sharing, Pension, IRA, 401(k)s, etc.)	
▯	
▯	
▯ Furniture & furnishings in home	
▯	
▯ Furniture & furnishings elsewhere	
▯	
▯ Collectibles	
▯	
▯ Jewelry	

ASSETS: DESCRIPTION OF ITEM(S) HUSBAND SHALL RECEIVE (To avoid confusion at a later date, describe each item as clearly as possible. You do not need to list account numbers. Where applicable, include whether the name on any title/deed/account described	Current Fair Market Value
☐	
☐ Life insurance (cash surrender value)	
☐	
☐ Sporting and entertainment (T.V., stereo, etc.) equipment	
☐	
☐	
☐	
☐ Other assets	
☐	
☐	
☐	
☐	
Total Assets to Husband	$ ___________

B. Division of Liabilities/Debts. We divide our liabilities (everything we owe) as follows:

1. Wife shall pay as her own the following and will not at any time ask Husband to pay these debts/bills:

LIABILITIES: DESCRIPTION OF DEBT(S) TO BE PAID BY WIFE (To avoid confusion at a later date, describe each item as clearly as possible. You do not need to list account numbers. Where applicable, include whether the name on any mortgage, note, or account described below is wife's, husband's, or both.)	Monthly Payment	Current Amount Owed
☐ Mortgages on real estate: (Home)	$	$
☐ (Other)		
☐		
☐ Charge/credit card accounts		
☐		
☐		
☐		
☐		
☐		
☐ Auto loan		
☐ Auto loan		
☐ Bank/credit union loans		
☐		
☐		
☐		
☐ Money you owe (not evidenced by a note)		
☐		
☐ Judgments		

LIABILITIES: DESCRIPTION OF DEBT(S) TO BE PAID BY WIFE (To avoid confusion at a later date, describe each item as clearly as possible. You do not need to list account numbers. Where applicable, include whether the name on any mortgage, note, or account described below is wife's, husband's, or both.)	Monthly Payment	Current Amount Owed
☐		
☐ Other		
☐		
☐		
☐		
☐		
Total Debts to Be Paid by Wife	**$ ________**	**$ ________**

2. Husband shall pay as his own the following and will not at any time ask Wife to pay these debts/bills:

LIABILITIES: DESCRIPTION OF DEBT(S) TO BE PAID BY HUSBAND (To avoid confusion at a later date, describe each item as clearly as possible. You do not need to list account numbers. Where applicable, include whether the name on any mortgage, note or account described below is wife's, husband's, or both.)	Monthly Payment	Current Amount Owed
☐ Mortgages on real estate: (Home)	$	$
☐ (Other)		
☐		
☐ Charge/credit card accounts		
☐		
☐		
☐		
☐		
☐		
☐ Auto loan		
☐ Auto loan		
☐ Bank/credit union loans		
☐		
☐		
☐		
☐ Money you owe (not evidenced by a note)		
☐		
☐ Judgments		
☐		
☐ Other		
☐		
☐		
☐		
☐		
☐		
☐		

LIABILITIES: DESCRIPTION OF DEBT(S) TO BE PAID BY HUSBAND (To avoid confusion at a later date, describe each item as clearly as possible. You do not need to list account numbers. Where applicable, include whether the name on any mortgage, note or account described below is wife's, husband's, or both.)	Monthly Payment	Current Amount Owed
Total Debts to Be Paid by Husband	$ ______	$ ______

C. Contingent Assets and Liabilities (listed in Section III of our Financial Affidavits) will be divided as follows: ______________________________

____

____

____

____

SECTION II. SPOUSAL SUPPORT (ALIMONY). Each of us forever gives up any right to spousal support (alimony) that we may have.

SECTION III. OTHER

____

____

____

____

____

I certify that I have been open and honest in entering into this settlement agreement. I am satisfied with this agreement and intend to be bound by it.

Dated: ______________________ ______________________________

Signature of Husband
Printed Name: ______________________
Address: ______________________
City, State, Zip: ______________________
Telephone Number: ______________________
Fax Number: ______________________

STATE OF FLORIDA
COUNTY OF ______________________

Sworn to or affirmed and signed before me on ______________ by ______________________.

____
NOTARY PUBLIC or DEPUTY CLERK

____
[Print, type, or stamp commissioned name of notary or deputy clerk.]

____ Personally known
____ Produced identification
Type of identification produced ______________________

IF A NONLAWYER HELPED YOU FILL OUT THIS FORM, HE/SHE MUST FILL IN THE

BLANKS BELOW: [✍ fill in **all** blanks]
I, *{full legal name and trade name of nonlawyer}* ________________________________,
a nonlawyer, located at *{street}* ______________________, *{city}* ______________,
{state} ______________, *{phone}* ____________, helped *{**Husband's** name}* ________,
who is the [√ **one** only] ___ petitioner **or** ___ respondent, fill out this form.

I certify that I have been open and honest in entering into this settlement agreement. I am satisfied with this agreement and intend to be bound by it.

Dated: ____________________ ______________________________

Signature of Wife
Printed Name: ______________________________
Address: ______________________________
City, State, Zip: ______________________________
Telephone Number: ______________________________
Fax Number: ______________________________

STATE OF FLORIDA
COUNTY OF ________________

Sworn to or affirmed and signed before me on ____________ by ______________________.

____
NOTARY PUBLIC or DEPUTY CLERK

____
[Print, type, or stamp commissioned name of notary or clerk.]

___ Personally known
___ Produced identification
Type of identification produced ____________________

IF A NONLAWYER HELPED YOU FILL OUT THIS FORM, HE/SHE MUST FILL IN THE BLANKS BELOW: [✍ fill in **all** blanks]
I, *{full legal name and trade name of nonlawyer}*________________________________,
a nonlawyer, located at *{street}* ______________________, *{city}* ______________,
{state} ______________, *{phone}* ____________, helped *{**Wife's** name}* __________,
who is the [√ **one** only] ___ petitioner **or** ___ respondent, fill out this form.

IN THE CIRCUIT COURT OF THE ______________________ JUDICIAL CIRCUIT,
IN AND FOR ______________________ COUNTY, FLORIDA

Case No.: ______________
Division: ______________

______________________________,
Petitioner,

and

______________________________,
Respondent.

MARITAL SETTLEMENT AGREEMENT FOR DISSOLUTION OF MARRIAGE WITH DEPENDENT OR MINOR CHILD(REN)

We, *{Husband's full legal name}* ______________________________,
and *{Wife's full legal name}* ______________________________,
being sworn, certify that the following statements are true:

1. We were married to each other on *{date}* ______________________.
2. Because of irreconcilable differences in our marriage (no chance of staying together), we have made this agreement to settle once and for all what we owe to each other and what we can expect to receive from each other. Each of us states that nothing has been held back, that we have honestly included everything we could think of in listing our assets (everything we own and that is owed to us) and our debts (everything we owe), and that we believe the other has been open and honest in writing this agreement.
3. We have both filed a Family Law Financial Affidavit, ✎ ❑Florida Family Law Rules of Procedure Form 12.902(b) or (c). Because we have voluntarily made full and fair disclosure to each other of all our assets and debts, we waive any further disclosure under rule 12.285, Florida Family Law Rules of Procedure.
4. Each of us agrees to execute and exchange any papers that might be needed to complete this agreement, including deeds, title certificates, etc.

SECTION I. MARITAL ASSETS AND LIABILITIES

A. Division of Assets. We divide our assets (everything we own and that is owed to us) as follows: Any personal item(s) not listed below is the property of the party currently in possession of the item(s).

1. Wife shall receive as her own and Husband shall have no further rights or responsibilities regarding these assets:

ASSETS: DESCRIPTION OF ITEM(S) WIFE SHALL RECEIVE (To avoid confusion at a later date, describe each item as clearly as possible. You do not need to list account numbers. Where applicable, include whether the name on any title/deed/account described below is wife's, husband's, or both.)	**Current Fair Market Value**
☐ Cash (on hand)	$
☐ Cash (in banks/credit unions)	
☐	
☐ Stocks/Bonds	
☐	

ASSETS: DESCRIPTION OF ITEM(S) WIFE SHALL RECEIVE (To avoid confusion at a later date, describe each item as clearly as possible. You do not need to list account numbers. Where applicable, include whether the name on any title/deed/account described below is wife's, husband's, or both.)	Current Fair Market Value
▯ Notes (money owed to you in writing)	
▯	
▯	
▯ Money owed to you (not evidenced by a note)	
▯	
▯	
▯ Real estate: (Home)	
▯ (Other)	
▯	
▯ Business interests	
▯	
▯ Automobiles	
▯	
▯	
▯ Boats	
▯ Other vehicles	
▯	
▯ Retirement plans (Profit Sharing, Pension, IRA, 401(k)s, etc.)	
▯	
▯	
▯ Furniture & furnishings in home	
▯	
▯ Furniture & furnishings elsewhere	
▯	
▯ Collectibles	
▯	
▯ Jewelry	
▯	
▯ Life insurance (cash surrender value)	
▯	
▯ Sporting and entertainment (T.V., stereo, etc.) equipment	
▯	
▯	
▯	
▯ Other assets	
▯	
▯	
▯	
▯	
▯	

ASSETS: DESCRIPTION OF ITEM(S) WIFE SHALL RECEIVE (To avoid confusion at a later date, describe each item as clearly as possible. You do not need to list account numbers. Where applicable, include whether the name on any title/deed/account described below is wife's, husband's, or both.)	Current Fair Market Value
☐	
Total Assets to Wife	**$ ________**

2. Husband shall receive as his own and Wife shall have no further rights or responsibilities regarding these assets:

ASSETS: DESCRIPTION OF ITEM(S) HUSBAND SHALL RECEIVE (To avoid confusion at a later date, describe each item as clearly as possible. You do not need to list account numbers. Where applicable, include whether the name on any title/deed/account described below is wife's, husband's or both.)	Current Fair Market Value
☐ Cash (on hand)	$
☐ Cash (in banks/credit unions)	
☐	
☐ Stocks/Bonds	
☐	
☐ Notes (money owed to you in writing)	
☐	
☐	
☐ Money owed to you (not evidenced by a note)	
☐	
☐	
☐ Real estate: (Home)	
☐ (Other)	
☐	
☐ Business interests	
☐	
☐ Automobiles	
☐	
☐	
☐ Boats	
☐ Other vehicles	
☐	
☐ Retirement plans (Profit Sharing, Pension, IRA, 401(k)s, etc.)	
☐	
☐	
☐ Furniture & furnishings in home	
☐	
☐ Furniture & furnishings elsewhere	
☐	
☐ Collectibles	
☐	
☐ Jewelry	

ASSETS: DESCRIPTION OF ITEM(S) HUSBAND SHALL RECEIVE (To avoid confusion at a later date, describe each item as clearly as possible. You do not need to list account numbers. Where applicable, include whether the name on any title/deed/account described below is wife's, husband's or both.)	Current Fair Market Value
☐	
☐ Life insurance (cash surrender value)	
☐	
☐ Sporting and entertainment (T.V., stereo, etc.) equipment	
☐	
☐	
☐	
☐ Other assets	
☐	
☐	
☐	
☐	
☐	
Total Assets to Husband	$ ________

B. Division of Liabilities/Debts. We divide our liabilities (everything we owe) as follows:

1. Wife shall pay as her own the following and will not at any time ask Husband to pay these debts/bills:

LIABILITIES: DESCRIPTION OF DEBT(S) TO BE PAID BY WIFE (To avoid confusion at a later date, describe each item as clearly as possible. You do not need to list account numbers. Where applicable, include whether the name on any mortgage, note, or account described below is wife's, husband's, or both.)	Monthly Payment	Current Amount Owed
☐ Mortgages on real estate: (Home)	$	$
☐ (Other)		
☐		
☐ Charge/credit card accounts		
☐		
☐		
☐		
☐		
☐		
☐ Auto loan		
☐ Auto loan		
☐ Bank/credit union loans		
☐		
☐		
☐		
☐ Money you owe (not evidenced by a note)		
☐		

LIABILITIES: DESCRIPTION OF DEBT(S) TO BE PAID BY WIFE (To avoid confusion at a later date, describe each item as clearly as possible. You do not need to list account numbers. Where applicable, include whether the name on any mortgage, note, or account described below is wife's, husband's, or both.)	Monthly Payment	Current Amount Owed
☐ Judgments		
☐		
☐ Other		
☐		
☐		
☐		
Total Debts to Be Paid by Wife	$	$

2. Husband shall pay as his own the following and will not at any time ask Wife to pay these debts/bills:

LIABILITIES: DESCRIPTION OF DEBT(S) TO BE PAID BY HUSBAND (To avoid confusion at a later date, describe each item as clearly as possible. You do not need to list account numbers. Where applicable, include whether the name on any mortgage, note or account described below is wife's, husband's, or both.)	Monthly Payment	Current Amount Owed
☐ Mortgages on real estate: (Home)	$	$
☐ (Other)		
☐		
☐ Charge/credit card accounts		
☐		
☐		
☐		
☐		
☐		
☐ Auto loan		
☐ Auto loan		
☐ Bank/credit union loans		
☐		
☐		
☐		
☐ Money you owe (not evidenced by a note)		
☐		
☐ Judgments		
☐		
☐ Other		
☐		
☐		
☐		
☐		

LIABILITIES: DESCRIPTION OF DEBT(S) TO BE PAID BY HUSBAND (To avoid confusion at a later date, describe each item as clearly as possible. You do not need to list account numbers. Where applicable, include whether the name on any mortgage, note or account described below is wife's, husband's, or both.)	Monthly Payment	Current Amount Owed
Total Debts to Be Paid by Husband	$	$

C. Contingent Assets and Liabilities (listed in Section III of our Family Law Financial Affidavits) will be divided as follows: ______________________________

____

____

____

____

____

SECTION II. SPOUSAL SUPPORT (ALIMONY) (If you have not agreed on this matter, write "n/a" on the lines provided.)

[√ **one** only]

____ 1. **Each of us forever gives up any right to spousal support (alimony) that we may have.**

____ 2. ( ) HUSBAND ( ) WIFE agrees to pay spousal support (alimony) in the amount of $ _____ every ( ) week ( ) other week ( ) month, beginning *{date}* ______________ and continuing until *{date or event}* ______________________________.
Explain type of alimony (temporary, permanent, rehabilitative, and/or lump sum) and any other specifics: ______________________________

____

____

____

____

____

[√ **if** applies] ( ) Life insurance in the amount of $ __________ to secure the above support, will be provided by the obligor.

SECTION III. CHILD CUSTODY, PARENTAL RESPONSIBILITY, AND VISITATION
(If you have **not** reached an agreement on any of these issues, write "n/a" on the lines provided. The Court reserves the right to modify any agreement(s) concerning the minor child(ren).)

1. **The parties' minor child(ren) are:**

Name	**Birth date**

2. **Parental responsibility** for the minor child(ren) will be:
____ a. shared *{explain any exceptions}* ______________________________

____

____

____ b. sole to ( ) Father ( ) Mother *{explain reasons}* ____________________

____

____

3. **The primary residential parent** will be ( ) Father ( ) Mother and the other parent will be the secondary residential parent **OR** the primary residential parent will be ( ) undesignated ( ) rotating.

4. **Secondary Residential Responsibility, Visitation, or Time Sharing** will be as follows: *{explain schedule (days and times, holidays, etc.)}* ____________________

____

____

____

____

____

{explain how parents will communicate regarding arrangements or any other issues relating to the child(ren)} ____________________

____

____

____

____

____

{explain how parents will handle situations when one parent is unable to meet the schedule, for example, notice requirements to the other parent} ____________________

____

____

____

____

____

{explain how the child(ren) will be exchanged, for example, location(s), by third parties, etc.}

____

____

____

____

____

____

{explain any other agreed-upon arrangements} ____________________

____

____

____

____

____

____

____

5. Neither parent shall take the child(ren) from the custody of the other parent or any child care

provider or other person entrusted by the other parent with the care of the child(ren) without the agreement of the other party during the other party's time of parental responsibility or visitation.

SECTION IV. CHILD SUPPORT

1. ( ) Mother ( ) Father will pay child support, under Florida's child support guidelines, section 61.30, Florida Statutes, to the primary residential or sole parent named above. Child Support Guidelines Worksheet ✎ ❑ Florida Family Law Rules of Procedure Form 12.902(e), is completed and attached. This parent shall be obligated to pay child support in the amount of $____________, every ( ) week ( ) other week ( ) month, beginning *{date}* _______________ and continuing until modified by court order, the youngest child turns 18, becomes emancipated, marries, dies, otherwise becomes self-supporting or, if after the age of 18, until *{date}* _______________. If the child support amount above deviates from the guidelines by 5% or more, explain the reason(s) here: _________
____
____
____

2. **Child Support Arrearage.** There currently is a child support arrearage of $ _______________ for retroactive child support and/or $___________ for previously ordered unpaid child support. The total of $ ________ in child support arrearage shall be repaid at the rate of $ ________ every ( ) week ( ) other week ( ) month, beginning *{date}* _________, until paid in full including statutory interest.

3. **Health Insurance.** ( ) Mother ( ) Father will maintain health insurance coverage for the parties' minor child(ren). The party providing coverage will provide insurance cards to the other party showing coverage. **OR** ( ) Health insurance is not reasonably available at this time. Any uninsured/ unreimbursed medical costs for the minor child(ren) shall be assessed as follows:
   ____ a. Shared equally by both parents.
   ____ b. Prorated according to the child support guideline percentages.
   ____ c. Other *{explain}*: ____
   ____

   As to these uninsured/unreimbursed medical expenses, the party who incurs the expense shall submit a request for reimbursement to the other party within 30 days, and the other party, within 30 days of receipt, shall submit the applicable reimbursement for that expense, according to the schedule of reimbursement set out in this paragraph.

4. **Dental Insurance.** ( ) Mother ( ) Father will maintain ( ) dental insurance coverage for the parties' minor child(ren). The party providing coverage will provide insurance cards to the other party showing coverage. **OR** ( ) dental insurance is not reasonably available at this time. Any uninsured/ unreimbursed dental costs for the minor child(ren) shall be assessed as follows:
   ____ a. Shared equally by both parents.
   ____ b. Prorated according to the child support guideline percentages.
   ____ c. Other *{explain}*: ____
   ____

   As to these uninsured/unreimbursed dental expenses, the party who incurs the expense shall submit a request for reimbursement to the other party within 30 days, and the other party, within 30 days of receipt, shall submit the applicable reimbursement for that expense, according to the schedule of reimbursement set out in this paragraph.

5. **Life Insurance.** ( ) Mother ( ) Father shall be required to maintain life insurance coverage for the benefit of the parties' minor child(ren) in the amount of $ __________ until the youngest child turns 18, becomes emancipated, marries, dies, or otherwise becomes self-supporting.

6. **IRS Income Tax Deduction(s).** The parent granted primary residential responsibility or sole parental responsibility of the parties' minor child(ren) shall have the benefit of any tax deductions for the child(ren) or as follows: *{explain}* ____
____
The other parent will convey any applicable IRS form regarding the income tax deduction.

7. Other provisions relating to child support (e.g., uninsured medical/dental expenses, insurance coverage, life insurance to secure child support, orthodontic payments, college fund, etc.): _______
____
____
____
____
____
____
____
____
____

SECTION V. OTHER

____
____
____
____
____
____

SECTION VI. We have not agreed on the following issues:

____
____
____
____
____
____
____
____
____

I certify that I have been open and honest in entering into this settlement agreement. I am satisfied with this agreement and intend to be bound by it.

Dated: ______________________

____
Signature of Husband
Printed Name: ______________________
Address: ______________________
City, State, Zip: ______________________
Telephone Number: ______________________
Fax Number: ______________________

STATE OF FLORIDA
COUNTY OF ________________

Sworn to or affirmed and signed before me on ____________ by ______________________.

____
NOTARY PUBLIC or DEPUTY CLERK

____
[Print, type, or stamp commissioned name of notary or clerk.]

____ Personally known
____ Produced identification
Type of identification produced ______________________

IF A NONLAWYER HELPED YOU FILL OUT THIS FORM, HE/SHE MUST FILL IN THE BLANKS BELOW: [✍ fill in **all** blanks]
I, *{full legal name and trade name of nonlawyer}* ______________________,
a nonlawyer, located at *{street}* ______________________, *{city}* ______________,
{state} ______________, *{phone}* ______________, helped ***{Husband's** name}* ________,
who is the [√ **one** only] ___ petitioner **or** ___ respondent, fill out this form.

I certify that I have been open and honest in entering into this settlement agreement. I am satisfied with this agreement and intend to be bound by it.

Dated: ______________________

____
Signature of Wife
Printed Name: ______________________
Address: ______________________
City, State, Zip: ______________________
Telephone Number: ______________________
Fax Number: ______________________

STATE OF FLORIDA
COUNTY OF ________________

Sworn to or affirmed and signed before me on ________________ by ____________________________.

____
NOTARY PUBLIC or DEPUTY CLERK

____
[Print, type, or stamp commissioned name of notary or clerk.]

____ Personally known
____ Produced identification
Type of identification produced ________________________

IF A NONLAWYER HELPED YOU FILL OUT THIS FORM, HE/SHE MUST FILL IN THE BLANKS BELOW: [✍ fill in **all** blanks]
I, *{full legal name and trade name of nonlawyer}* ____,
a nonlawyer, located at *{street}* ________________________________, *{city}* ____________________,
{state} ___________________, *{phone}* _________________, helped *{**Wife's** name}* ____________,
who is the [√ **one** only] ___ petitioner **or** ___ respondent, fill out this form.

IN THE CIRCUIT COURT OF THE ____________________ JUDICIAL CIRCUIT,
IN AND FOR ____________________ COUNTY, FLORIDA

Case No.: ____________________
Division: ____________________

____________________,
Petitioner,

and

____________________,
Respondent.

MARITAL SETTLEMENT AGREEMENT FOR DISSOLUTION OF MARRIAGE WITH PROPERTY BUT NO DEPENDENT OR MINOR CHILD(REN)

We, *{Husband's full legal name}* ____________________,
and *{Wife's full legal name}* ____________________,
being sworn, certify that the following statements are true:

1. We were married to each other on *{date}* ____________________.
2. Because of irreconcilable differences in our marriage (no chance of staying together), we have made this agreement to settle once and for all what we owe to each other and what we can expect to receive from each other. Each of us states that nothing has been held back, that we have honestly included everything we could think of in listing our assets (everything we own and that is owed to us) and our debts (everything we owe), and that we believe the other has been open and honest in writing this agreement.
3. We have both filed a Family Law Financial Affidavit, ✎ ❑Florida Family Law Rules of Procedure Form 12.902(b) or (c). Because we have voluntarily made full and fair disclosure to each other of all our assets and debts, we waive any further disclosure under rule 12.285, Florida Family Law Rules of Procedure.
4. Each of us agrees to execute and exchange any papers that might be needed to complete this agreement, including deeds, title certificates, etc.

SECTION I. MARITAL ASSETS AND LIABILITIES

A. Division of Assets. We divide our assets (everything we own and that is owed to us) as follows: Any personal item(s) not listed below is the property of the party currently in possession of the item(s).

1. Wife shall receive as her own and Husband shall have no further rights or responsibilities regarding these assets:

ASSETS: DESCRIPTION OF ITEM(S) WIFE SHALL RECEIVE (To avoid confusion at a later date, describe each item as clearly as possible. You do not need to list account numbers. Where applicable, include whether the name on any title/deed/account described below is wife's, husband's or both.)	**Current Fair Market Value**
☐ Cash (on hand)	$
☐ Cash (in banks/credit unions)	
☐	

ASSETS: DESCRIPTION OF ITEM(S) WIFE SHALL RECEIVE (To avoid confusion at a later date, describe each item as clearly as possible. You do not need to list account numbers. Where applicable, include whether the name on any title/deed/account described below is wife's, husband's or both.)	**Current Fair Market Value**
☐ Stocks/Bonds	
☐	
☐ Notes (money owed to you in writing)	
☐	
☐	
☐ Money owed to you (not evidenced by a note)	
☐	
☐	
☐ Real estate: (Home)	
☐ (Other)	
☐	
☐ Business interests	
☐	
☐ Automobiles	
☐	
☐	
☐ Boats	
☐ Other vehicles	
☐	
☐ Retirement plans (Profit Sharing, Pension, IRA, 401(k)s, etc.)	
☐	
☐	
☐ Furniture & furnishings in home	
☐	
☐ Furniture & furnishings elsewhere	
☐	
☐ Collectibles	
☐	
☐ Jewelry	
☐	
☐ Life insurance (cash surrender value)	
☐	
☐ Sporting and entertainment (T.V., stereo, etc.) equipment	
☐	
☐	
☐	
☐ Other assets	
☐	
☐	

ASSETS: DESCRIPTION OF ITEM(S) WIFE SHALL RECEIVE (To avoid confusion at a later date, describe each item as clearly as possible. You do not need to list account numbers. Where applicable, include whether the name on any title/deed/account described below is wife's, husband's or both.)	Current Fair Market Value
☐	
☐	
☐	
☐	
Total Assets to Wife	**$**

2. Husband shall receive as his own and Wife shall have no further rights or responsibilities regarding these assets:

ASSETS: DESCRIPTION OF ITEM(S) HUSBAND SHALL RECEIVE (To avoid confusion at a later date, describe each item as clearly as possible. You do not need to list account numbers. Where applicable, include whether the name on any title/deed/account described below is wife's, husband's or both.)	Current Fair Market Value
☐ Cash (on hand)	$
☐ Cash (in banks/credit unions)	
☐	
☐ Stocks/Bonds	
☐	
☐ Notes (money owed to you in writing)	
☐	
☐	
☐ Money owed to you (not evidenced by a note)	
☐	
☐	
☐ Real estate: (Home)	
☐ (Other)	
☐	
☐ Business interests	
☐	
☐ Automobiles	
☐	
☐	
☐ Boats	
☐ Other vehicles	
☐	
☐ Retirement plans (Profit Sharing, Pension, IRA, 401(k)s, etc.)	
☐	
☐	
☐ Furniture & furnishings in home	
☐	
☐ Furniture & furnishings elsewhere	
☐	

ASSETS: DESCRIPTION OF ITEM(S) HUSBAND SHALL RECEIVE (To avoid confusion at a later date, describe each item as clearly as possible. You do not need to list account numbers. Where applicable, include whether the name on any title/deed/account described below is wife's, husband's or both.)	Current Fair Market Value
☐ Collectibles	
☐	
☐ Jewelry	
☐	
☐ Life insurance (cash surrender value)	
☐	
☐ Sporting and entertainment (T.V., stereo, etc.) equipment	
☐	
☐	
☐	
☐ Other assets	
☐	
☐	
☐	
☐	
Total Assets to Husband	$ __________

B. Division of Liabilities/Debts. We divide our liabilities (everything we owe) as follows:

1. Wife shall pay as her own the following and will not at any time ask Husband to pay these debts/bills:

LIABILITIES: DESCRIPTION OF DEBT(S) TO BE PAID BY WIFE (To avoid confusion at a later date, describe each item as clearly as possible. You do not need to list account numbers. Where applicable, include whether the name on any mortgage, note, or account described below is wife's, husband's, or both.)	Monthly Payment	Current Amount Owed
☐ Mortgages on real estate: (Home)	$	$
☐ (Other)		
☐		
☐ Charge/credit card accounts		
☐		
☐		
☐		
☐		
☐		
☐ Auto loan		
☐ Auto loan		
☐ Bank/credit union loans		
☐		
☐		
☐		

LIABILITIES: DESCRIPTION OF DEBT(S) TO BE PAID BY WIFE (To avoid confusion at a later date, describe each item as clearly as possible. You do not need to list account numbers. Where applicable, include whether the name on any mortgage, note, or account described below is wife's, husband's, or both.)	Monthly Payment	Current Amount Owed
☐ Money you owe (not evidenced by a note)		
☐		
☐ Judgments		
☐		
☐ Other		
☐		
☐		
☐		
☐		
Total Debts to Be Paid by Wife	**$**	**$**

2. Husband shall pay as his own the following and will not at any time ask Wife to pay these debts/bills:

LIABILITIES: DESCRIPTION OF DEBT(S) TO BE PAID BY HUSBAND (To avoid confusion at a later date, describe each item as clearly as possible. You do not need to list account numbers. Where applicable, include whether the name on any mortgage, note or account described below is wife's, husband's, or both.)	Monthly Payment	Current Amount Owed
☐ Mortgages on real estate: (Home)	$	$
☐ (Other)		
☐		
☐ Charge/credit card accounts		
☐		
☐		
☐		
☐		
☐		
☐ Auto loan		
☐ Auto loan		
☐ Bank/credit union loans		
☐		
☐		
☐		
☐ Money you owe (not evidenced by a note)		
☐		
☐ Judgments		
☐		
☐ Other		
☐		
☐		
☐		

LIABILITIES: DESCRIPTION OF DEBT(S) TO BE PAID BY HUSBAND (To avoid confusion at a later date, describe each item as clearly as possible. You do not need to list account numbers. Where applicable, include whether the name on any mortgage, note or account described below is wife's, husband's, or both.)	Monthly Payment	Current Amount Owed
☐		
Total Debts to Be Paid by Husband	$	$

C. Contingent Assets and Liabilities (listed in Section III of our Family Law Financial Affidavits) will be divided as follows: ____

____

____

____

____

____

SECTION II. SPOUSAL SUPPORT (ALIMONY) (If you have not agreed on this matter, write "n/a" on the lines provided.)
[√ **one** only]

____ 1. **Each of us forever gives up any right to spousal support (alimony) that we may have.**

____ 2. ( ) HUSBAND ( ) WIFE agrees to pay spousal support (alimony) in the amount of $ _____ every ( ) week ( ) other week ( ) month, beginning *{date}* ______________ and continuing until *{date or event}* ______________________________
Explain type of alimony (temporary, permanent, rehabilitative, and/or lump sum) and any other specifics: ____

____

____

____

[√ **if** applies] ( ) Life insurance in the amount of $ __________ to secure the above support, will be provided by the obligor.

SECTION III. OTHER

____

____

____

____

SECTION IV. We have not agreed on the following issues:

____

____

____

I certify that I have been open and honest in entering into this settlement agreement. I am satisfied with this agreement and intend to be bound by it.

Dated: ____________________________ ______________________________

Signature of Husband
Printed Name: ______________________________
Address: ______________________________

City, State, Zip: ___________________________
Telephone Number: ___________________________
Fax Number: ___________________________

STATE OF FLORIDA
COUNTY OF ____________________

Sworn to or affirmed and signed before me on ______________ by ________________________.

____
NOTARY PUBLIC or DEPUTY CLERK

____
[Print, type, or stamp commissioned name of notary or clerk.]

____ Personally known
____ Produced identification
Type of identification produced ______________________

IF A NONLAWYER HELPED YOU FILL OUT THIS FORM, HE/SHE MUST FILL IN THE BLANKS BELOW: [✍ fill in **all** blanks]
I, *{full legal name and trade name of nonlawyer}* ______________________________________,
a nonlawyer, located at *{street}* ____________________________, *{city}* __________________,
{state} __________________, *{phone}* ________________, helped *{**Husband's** name}* ________,
who is the [√ **one** only] ___ petitioner **or** ___ respondent, fill out this form.

I certify that I have been open and honest in entering into this settlement agreement. I am satisfied with this agreement and intend to be bound by it.

Dated: ____________________

____
Signature of Wife
Printed Name: ___________________________
Address: ___________________________
City, State, Zip: ___________________________
Telephone Number: ___________________________
Fax Number: ___________________________

STATE OF FLORIDA
COUNTY OF ____________________

Sworn to or affirmed and signed before me on ______________ by ________________________.

____
NOTARY PUBLIC or DEPUTY CLERK

____
[Print, type, or stamp commissioned name of notary or clerk.]

____ Personally known
____ Produced identification
Type of identification produced ________________________

IF A NONLAWYER HELPED YOU FILL OUT THIS FORM, HE/SHE MUST FILL IN THE BLANKS BELOW: [✍ fill in **all** blanks]
I, *{full legal name and trade name of nonlawyer}* ____,
a nonlawyer, located at *{street}* ________________________________, *{city}* ___________________,
{state} ___________________, *{phone}* _________________, helped *{**Wife's** name}* ____________,
who is the [√ **one** only] ___ petitioner **or** ___ respondent, fill out this form.

IN THE CIRCUIT COURT OF THE ___________________________ JUDICIAL CIRCUIT,
IN AND FOR ___________________________ COUNTY, FLORIDA

Case No.: ______________________________
Division: ______________________________

________________________________,
Petitioner,

and

________________________________,
Respondent.

AFFIDAVIT OF CORROBORATING WITNESS

I, *{full legal name}* ________________________________, being sworn, certify that the following statements are true: I have known *{name}* ____________________________ since *{approximate date}*_________________; to the best of my understanding the petition in this action was filed on *{date}*______________; and I know of my own personal knowledge that this person has resided in the State of Florida for at least 6 months immediately before *{date}* ____________.

I understand that I am swearing or affirming under oath to the truthfulness of the claims made in this affidavit and that the punishment for knowingly making a false statement includes fines and/or imprisonment.

Dated: __________________________

____
Signature of Corroborating Witness
Printed Name:______________________
Address: __________________________
City, State, Zip: ___________________
Telephone Number: _________________

STATE OF FLORIDA
COUNTY OF ___________________

Sworn to or affirmed and signed before me on ____________________ by ______________________.

____
NOTARY PUBLIC or DEPUTY CLERK

____
[Print, type, or stamp commissioned name of notary or clerk.]

____ Personally known
____ Produced identification
Type of identification produced ___________________

IF A NONLAWYER HELPED YOU FILL OUT THIS FORM, HE/SHE MUST FILL IN THE BLANKS BELOW:[fill in **all** blanks]
I, *{full legal name and trade name of nonlawyer}* ________________________________,
a nonlawyer, located at *{street}* ________________________, *{city}* ________________________,
{state} ______________, *{phone}* _________________, helped *{name}* ________________________,
who is the affiant, fill out this form.

IN THE CIRCUIT COURT OF THE ____________________________ JUDICIAL CIRCUIT,
IN AND FOR ____________________________ COUNTY, FLORIDA

Case No.: ______________________________
Division: ______________________________

______________________________________,
Petitioner,

and

______________________________________,
Respondent.

NOTICE OF SOCIAL SECURITY NUMBER

I, *{full legal name}* ____, certify that my social security number is ______________________, as required in section 61.052(7), sections 61.13(9) or (10), section 742.031(3), sections 742.032(1)–(3), and/or sections 742.10(1)–(2), Florida Statutes. My date of birth is ______________________________.

[√ **one** only]

___ 1. This notice is being filed in a dissolution of marriage case in which the parties have **no** minor children in common.

___ 2. This notice is being filed in a paternity or child support case, or in a dissolution of marriage in which the parties have minor children in common. The minor child(ren)'s name(s), date(s) of birth, and social security number(s) is/are:

Name	**Birth date**	**Social Security Number**
________________________	__________	________________
________________________	__________	________________
________________________	__________	________________
________________________	__________	________________
________________________	__________	________________
________________________	__________	________________
________________________	__________	________________
________________________	__________	________________

{Attach additional pages if necessary.}

Disclosure of social security numbers shall be limited to the purpose of administration of the Title IV-D program for child support enforcement.

I understand that I am swearing or affirming under oath to the truthfulness of the claims made in this notice and that the punishment for knowingly making a false statement includes fines and/or imprisonment.

Dated: ____________________________ ____

Signature
Printed Name: ____
Address: ____
City, State, Zip: ______________________________________
Telephone Number:_____________________________________
Fax Number: ____

STATE OF FLORIDA
COUNTY OF ________

Sworn to or affirmed and signed before me on ______________ by ____________________________.

____
NOTARY PUBLIC or DEPUTY CLERK

____
[Print, type, or stamp commissioned name of notary or clerk]

____ Personally known
____ Produced identification
Type of identification produced __________________________

IF A NONLAWYER HELPED YOU FILL OUT THIS FORM, HE/SHE MUST FILL IN THE BLANKS BELOW: [✍ fill in **all** blanks]

I, *{full legal name and trade name of nonlawyer}*____,
a nonlawyer, located at *{street}*_________________________________, *{city}* ____________________,
{state} __________, *{phone}* ______________, helped *{name}* ____________________________________,
who is the [√ **one** only] ___ petitioner **or** ___ respondent, fill out this form.

IN THE CIRCUIT COURT OF THE _________________________ JUDICIAL CIRCUIT,
IN AND FOR _________________________ COUNTY, FLORIDA

Case No.: ____________________________
Division: ____________________________

____,
Petitioner,

and

____,
Respondent.

ANSWER, WAIVER, AND REQUEST FOR COPY OF FINAL JUDGMENT OF DISSOLUTION OF MARRIAGE

I, *{full legal name}* ______________________________, Respondent, being sworn, certify that the following information is true:

1. Respondent answers the Petition for Dissolution of Marriage filed in this action and admits all the allegations. By admitting all of the allegations in the petition, respondent agrees to all relief requested in the petition including any requests regarding child custody and visitation, child support, alimony, distribution of marital assets and liabilities, and temporary relief.

2. Respondent waives notice of hearing as well as all future notices in connection with the Petition for Dissolution of Marriage, as filed. Respondent also waives appearance at the final hearing.

3. Respondent requests that a copy of the Final Judgment of Dissolution of Marriage entered in this case be forwarded to Respondent at the address below.

4. If this case involves minor child(ren), a completed Uniform Child Custody Jurisdiction and Enforcement Act (UCCJEA) Affidavit, ✎ ❑Florida Supreme Court Approved Family Law Form 12.902(d), is filed with this answer.

5. A completed Notice of Social Security Number, ✎ ❑Florida Supreme Court Approved Family Law Form 12.902(j), is filed with this answer.

6. A completed Family Law Financial Affidavit, ✎ ❑Florida Family Law Rules of Procedure Form 12.902(b) or (c), is filed with this answer.

I certify that a copy of this document was [√**one** only] ( ) mailed ( ) faxed and mailed ( ) hand delivered to the person(s) listed below on *{date}* ____.

Other party or his/her attorney:
Name: ________________________________
Address: ______________________________
City, State, Zip: _________________________

Fax Number: ______________________

I understand that I am swearing or affirming under oath to the truthfulness of the claims made in this answer and waiver and that the punishment for knowingly making a false statement includes fines and/or imprisonment.

Dated: ______________________

____
Signature of Respondent
Printed Name: ______________________
Address: ______________________
City, State, Zip: ______________________
Telephone Number: ______________________
Fax Number: ______________________

STATE OF FLORIDA
COUNTY OF ______________

Sworn to or affirmed and signed before me on ____________ by ______________________.

____
NOTARY PUBLIC or DEPUTY CLERK

____
[Print, type, or stamp commissioned name of notary or clerk.]

____ Personally known
____ Produced identification
Type of identification produced ______________________

IF A NONLAWYER HELPED YOU FILL OUT THIS FORM, HE/SHE MUST FILL IN THE BLANKS BELOW: [✍ fill in **all** blanks]
I, *{full legal name and trade name of nonlawyer}* ______________________,
a nonlawyer, located at *{street}* ______________________, *{city}* ______________,
{state} ______________, *{phone}* ______________, helped *{name}* ______________,
who is the respondent, fill out this form.

IN THE CIRCUIT COURT OF THE ______________________ JUDICIAL CIRCUIT,
IN AND FOR ______________________ COUNTY, FLORIDA

Case No.: ______________________
Division: ______________________

______________________,
Petitioner,

and

______________________,
Respondent.

SUMMONS: PERSONAL SERVICE ON AN INDIVIDUAL
ORDEN DE COMPARECENCIA: SERVICIO PERSONAL EN UN INDIVIDUO
CITATION: L'ASSIGNATION PERSONAL SUR UN INDIVIDUEL

TO/PARA/A: *{enter other party's full legal name}* ______________________,
{address(including city and state)/location for service} ______________________.

IMPORTANT

A lawsuit has been filed against you. You have **20 calendar days** after this summons is served on you to file a written response to the attached complaint/petition with the clerk of this circuit court, located at: *{street address}* ______________________.
A phone call will not protect you. Your written response, including the case number given above and the names of the parties, must be **filed** if you want the Court to hear your side of the case.

If you do not file your written response on time, you may lose the case, and your wages, money, and property may be taken thereafter without further warning from the Court. There are other legal requirements. You may want to call an attorney right away. If you do not know an attorney, you may call an attorney referral service or a legal aid office (listed in the phone book).

If you choose to file a written response yourself, at the same time you file your written response to the Court, you must also mail or take a copy of your written response to the party serving this summons at:
{Name and address of party serving summons} ______________________

______________________.

Copies of all court documents in this case, including orders, are available at the Clerk of the Circuit Court's office. You may review these documents, upon request.

You must keep the Clerk of the Circuit Court's office notified of your current address. (You may file Notice of Current Address, ✎❐ Florida Supreme Court Approved Family Law Form 12.915.) Future papers in this lawsuit will be mailed to the address on record at the clerk's office.

WARNING: **Rule 12.285, Florida Family Law Rules of Procedure, requires certain automatic disclosure of documents and information. Failure to comply can result in sanctions,**

including dismissal or striking of pleadings.

IMPORTANTE

Usted ha sido demandado legalmente. Tiene veinte (20) dias, contados a partir del recibo de esta notificacion, para contestar la demanda adjunta, por escrito, y presentarla ante este tribunal. Localizado en: ____. Una llamada telefonica no lo protegera. Si usted desea que el tribunal considere su defensa, debe presentar su respuesta por escrito, incluyendo el numero del caso y los nombres de las partes interesadas. Si usted no contesta la demanda a tiempo, pudiese perder el caso y podria ser despojado de sus ingresos y propiedades, o privado de sus derechos, sin previo aviso del tribunal. Existen otros requisitos legales. Si lo desea, usted puede consultar a un abogado inmediatamente. Si no conoce a un abogado, puede llamar a una de las oficinas de asistencia legal que aparecen en la guia telefonica.

Si desea responder a la demanda por su cuenta, al mismo tiempo en que presente su respuesta ante el tribunal, usted debe enviar por correo o entregar una copia de su respuesta a la persona denominada abajo.

Si usted elige presentar personalmente una respuesta por escrito, en el mismo momento que usted presente su respuesta por escrito al Tribunal, usted debe enviar por correo o llevar una copia de su respuesta por escrito a la parte entregando esta orden de comparencencia a:

Nombre y direccion de la parte que entrega la orden de comparencencia: ____________________________

____.

Copias de todos los documentos judiciales de este caso, incluyendo las ordenes, estan disponibles en la oficina del Secretario de Juzgado del Circuito [Clerk of the Circuit Court's office]. Estos documentos pueden ser revisados a su solicitud.

Usted debe de manener informada a la oficina del Secretario de Juzgado del Circuito de su direccion actual. (Usted puede presentar ______ el Formulario: Ley de Familia de la Florida 12.915, [✎❒ Florida Supreme Court Approved Family Law Form 12.915], Notificacion de la Direccion Actual [Notice of Current Address].) Los papelos que se presenten en el futuro en esta demanda judicial seran env ados por correo a la direccion que este registrada en la oficina del Secretario.

ADVERTENCIA: Regla 12.285 (Rule 12.285), de las Reglas de Procedimiento de Ley de Familia de la Florida [Florida Family Law Rules of Procedure], requiere cierta revelacion automatica de documentos e informacion. El incumplimient, puede resultar en sanciones, incluyendo la desestimacion o anulacion de los alegatos.

IMPORTANT

Des poursuites judiciaries ont ete entreprises contre vous. Vous avez 20 jours consecutifs a partir de la date de l'assignation de cette citation pour deposer une reponse ecrite a la plainte ci-jointe aupres de ce tribunal. Qui se trouve a: *{L'Adresse}* ________________________________. Un simple coup de telephone est insuffisant pour vous proteger; vous etes obliges de deposer votre reponse ecrite, avec mention du numero de dossier ci-dessus et du nom des parties nommees ici, si vous souhaitez que le tribunal entende votre cause. Si vous ne deposez pas votre reponse ecrite dans le delai requis, vous risquez de perdre la cause ainsi que votre salaire, votre argent, et vos biens peuvent etre saisis par la suite, sans aucun preavis ulterieur du tribunal. Il y a d'autres obligations juridiques et vous pouvez requerir les services immediats d'un avocat. Si vous ne connaissez pas d'avocat, vous pourriez telephoner a un service de reference d'avocats ou a un bureau d'assistance juridique (figurant a l'annuaire de telephones).

Si vous choisissez de deposer vous-meme une reponse ecrite, il vous faudra egalement, en meme temps que cette formalite, faire parvenir ou expedier une copie au carbone ou une photocopie de votre reponse ecrite a la partie qui vous depose cette citation.

Nom et adresse de la partie qui depose cette citation: ______________________________
____

Les photocopies de tous les documents tribunals de cette cause, y compris des arrets, sont disponible au bureau du greffier. Vous pouvez revue ces documents, sur demande.

Il faut aviser le greffier de votre adresse actuelle. (Vous pouvez deposer ✎❒ Florida Supreme_Court Approved Family Law Form 12.915, Notice of Current Address.) Les documents de l'avenir de ce proces seront envoyer a l' adresse que vous donnez au bureau du greffier.

ATTENTION: La regle 12.285 des regles de procedure du droit de la famille de la Floride exige que l'on remette certains renseignements et certains documents a la partie adverse. Tout refus de les fournir pourra donner lieu a des sanctions, y compris le rejet ou la suppression d'un ou de plusieurs actes de procedure.

THE STATE OF FLORIDA
TO EACH SHERIFF OF THE STATE: You are commanded to serve this summons and a copy of the complaint in this lawsuit on the above-named person.

DATED: ______________________

CLERK OF THE CIRCUIT COURT

(SEAL)

By: ______________________________
Deputy Clerk

IN THE CIRCUIT COURT OF THE ____________________ JUDICIAL CIRCUIT,
IN AND FOR ____________________ COUNTY, FLORIDA

Case No.: ____________________
Division: ____________________

______________________________,
Petitioner,

and

______________________________,
Respondent.

PROCESS SERVICE MEMORANDUM

TO: ( ) Sheriff of ______________ County, Florida; ______________ Division
( ) Private process server: ______________________________
Please serve the *{name of document(s)}* ______________________________
____
in the above-styled cause upon:
Party: *{full legal name}* ______________________________
Address or location for service: ______________________________
____
Work Address: ______________________________
____

If the party to be served owns, has, and/or is known to have guns or other weapons, describe what type of weapon(s): ______________________________

SPECIAL INSTRUCTIONS: ______________________________
____
____
____

Dated: ____________________ ______________________________
Signature of Party
*Printed Name: ______________________________
*Address: ______________________________
*City, State, Zip: ______________________________
*Telephone Number: ______________________________
*Fax Number: ______________________________

*** If this is a domestic violence case, do not enter this information if your address or telephone number need to be kept confidential for safety reasons; instead write "confidential" in the spaces provided and file**
✎ ❑ Florida Supreme Court Approved Family Law Form 12.980(i), Petitioner's Request for Confidential Filing of Address.

IF A NONLAWYER HELPED YOU FILL OUT THIS FORM, HE/SHE MUST FILL IN THE BLANKS BELOW: [✍ fill in **all** blanks]
I, *{full legal name and trade name of nonlawyer}*____,
a nonlawyer, located at *{street}* __________________________, *{city}* __________________________,
{state} ____________________, *{phone}* __________________, helped *{name}* ____________________,
who is the petitioner, fill out this form.

IN THE CIRCUIT COURT OF THE __________________________ JUDICIAL CIRCUIT,
IN AND FOR __________________________ COUNTY, FLORIDA

Case No.: __________________________
Division: __________________________

________________________________,
Petitioner,

and

________________________________,
Respondent.

MEMORANDUM FOR CERTIFICATE OF MILITARY SERVICE

TO:
( ) U.S. Coast Guard Commander (CGPC-ADM-3), Coast Guard Personnel Command, 2100 2nd St., S.W., Room 1616, Washington, D. C. 20593
( ) AFPC MSIMDL, 550 C Street, W., Suite 50, Randolph AFB, TX 78150-4752
( ) BUPERS, PERS 02116, 2 Navy Annex, Washington, D. C. 20370-0216
( ) USMC-CMC, HQMC-MMSB-10, 2008 Elliot Road, Room 201, Quantico, VA 22134-5030
( ) Surgeon General, U.S. Public Health Service, Div. of Comm., Off. Personnel, 5600 Fishers Lane, Room 4-21, Rockville, MD 20857
( ) Army World Wide Locator, U.S. Army Enlisted Records and Evaluation Center, 8899 East 56th Street, Indianapolis, IN 46249-5301

RE: __________________________ __________________________
{Name of Respondent} *{Respondent's Social Security Number}*

This case involves a family matter. It is imperative that a determination be made whether the above- named individual, who has an interest in these proceedings, is presently in the military service of the United States, and the dates of induction and discharge, if any. This information is requested under section 581 of the Soldiers' and Sailors' Civil Relief Act of 1940, as amended. Please supply a verification as soon as possible. My check for $__________ for your search fee and a self-addressed, stamped envelope are enclosed.

Dated: __________________________ ________________________________

Signature of Petitioner
Printed Name: __________________________
Address: __________________________
City, State, Zip: __________________________
Telephone Number: __________________________
Fax Number: __________________________

Florida Supreme Court Approved Family Law Form 12.912(a), Memorandum for Certificate of Military Service (9/00)

IF A NONLAWYER HELPED YOU FILL OUT THIS FORM, HE/SHE MUST FILL IN THE BLANKS BELOW: [✍ fill in **all** blanks]
I, *{full legal name and trade name of nonlawyer}* ____,
a nonlawyer, located at *{street}* ______________________________, *{city}* ___________________,
{state} ____________________, *{phone}* _________________, helped *{name}* __________________,
who is the petitioner, fill out this form.

IN THE CIRCUIT COURT OF THE ________________________ JUDICIAL CIRCUIT,
IN AND FOR ________________________ COUNTY, FLORIDA

Case No.: ________________________
Division: ________________________

__________________________________,
Petitioner,

and

__________________________________,
Respondent.

NONMILITARY AFFIDAVIT

I, *{full legal name}* ____________________________________, being sworn, certify that the following information is true:
[√ **all** that apply]

____ 1. I know of my own personal knowledge that Respondent is not on active duty in the armed services of the United States.

____ 2. I have inquired of the armed services of the United States and the U.S. Public Health Service to determine whether the Respondent is a member of the armed services and am attaching certificates stating that Respondent is not now in the armed services.

I understand that I am swearing or affirming under oath to the truthfulness of the claims made in this affidavit and that the punishment for knowingly making a false statement includes fines and/or imprisonment.

DATED: ____________________

____
Signature of Petitioner
Printed Name: ____________________________
Address: ________________________________
City, State, Zip: __________________________
Telephone Number: _________________________
Fax Number: ______________________________

STATE OF FLORIDA
COUNTY OF ____________________
Sworn to or affirmed and signed before me on ______________ by ________________________.

____
NOTARY PUBLIC or DEPUTY CLERK

____
[Print, type, or stamp commissioned name of notary or clerk.]

____ Personally known
____ Produced identification
Type of identification produced _________________________

IF A NONLAWYER HELPED YOU FILL OUT THIS FORM, HE/SHE MUST FILL IN THE BLANKS BELOW: [✍ fill in **all** blanks]
I, *{full legal name and trade name of nonlawyer}* ____,
a nonlawyer, located at *{street}* ________________________________, *{city}* ____________________,
{state} __________________, *{phone}* __________________, helped *{name}* __________________,
who is the petitioner, fill out this form.

IN THE CIRCUIT COURT OF THE _______________ JUDICIAL CIRCUIT,
IN AND FOR _______________ COUNTY, FLORIDA

Case No.: _______________
Division: _______________

_______________,
Petitioner

and

_______________,
Respondent.

NOTICE OF ACTION FOR DISSOLUTION OF MARRIAGE

TO: *{name of Respondent}* _______________
{Respondent's last known address} _______________

YOU ARE NOTIFIED that an action has been filed against you and that you are required to serve a copy of your written defenses, if any, to it on *{name of Petitioner}* _______________, whose address is _______________
on or before *{date}* _______________, and file the original with the clerk of this Court at *{clerk's address}* _______________,
before service on Petitioner or immediately thereafter. **If you fail to do so, a default may be entered against you for the relief demanded in the petition.**

Copies of all court documents in this case, including orders, are available at the Clerk of the Circuit Court's office. You may review these documents upon request.

You must keep the Clerk of the Circuit Court's office notified of your current address. (You may file Notice of Current Address, Florida Supreme Court Approved Family Law Form 12.915.) Future papers in this lawsuit will be mailed to the address on record at the clerk's office.

WARNING: Rule 12.285, Florida Family Law Rules of Procedure, requires certain automatic disclosure of documents and information. Failure to comply can result in sanctions, including dismissal or striking of pleadings.

Dated:_______________________________.   CLERK OF THE CIRCUIT COURT

By: ____
Deputy Clerk

IF A NONLAWYER HELPED YOU FILL OUT THIS FORM, HE/SHE MUST FILL IN THE BLANKS BELOW: [fill in **all** blanks]
I, *{full legal name and trade name of nonlawyer}* ____,
a nonlawyer, located at *{street}* ____
{state} ______________, *{phone}*____________, helped *{name}*____________________________________,
who is the petitioner, fill out this form.

IN THE CIRCUIT COURT OF THE __________________________ JUDICIAL CIRCUIT,
IN AND FOR __________________________ COUNTY, FLORIDA

Case No.: ______________________________
Division: ______________________________

____________________________________,
Petitioner,

and

____________________________________,
Respondent.

AFFIDAVIT OF DILIGENT SEARCH AND INQUIRY

I, *{full legal name}* ____, being sworn, certify that the following information is true:

1. I have made diligent search and inquiry to discover the name and current residence of Respondent: *{Specify details of search}* **Refer to checklist below and identify all actions taken (any additional information included such as the date the action was taken and the person with whom you spoke is helpful) (attach additional sheet if necessary):**

[√ **all** that apply]

____ United States Post Office inquiry through Freedom of Information Act for current address or any relocations.

____ Last known employment of Respondent, including name and address of employer. You should also ask for any addresses to which W-2 Forms were mailed, and, if a pension or profit-sharing plan exists, then for any addresses to which any pension or plan payment is and/or has been mailed.

____ Unions from which Respondent may have worked or that governed particular trade or craft.

____ Regulatory agencies, including professional or occupational licensing.

____ Names and addresses of relatives and contacts with those relatives, and inquiry as to Respondent's last known address. You are to follow up any leads of any addresses where Respondent may have moved. Relatives include, but are not limited to: parents, brothers, sisters, aunts, uncles, cousins, nieces, nephews, grandparents, great-grandparents, former in-laws, stepparents, stepchildren.

____ Information about the Respondent's possible death and, if dead, the date and location of the death.

____ Telephone listings in the last known locations of Respondent's residence.

___ Internet at http://www.switchboard.com or other Internet people finder or the library checked for me.

____ Law enforcement arrest and/or criminal records in the last known residential area of Respondent.

____ Highway Patrol records in the state of Respondent's last known address.

____ Department of Motor Vehicle records in the state of Respondent's last known address.

____ Department of Corrections records in the state of Respondent's last known address.

____ Title IV-D (child support enforcement) agency records in the state of Respondent's last known address.

____ Hospitals in the last known area of Respondent's residence.

____ Utility companies, which include water, sewer, cable TV, and electric, in the last known area of Respondent's residence.

____ Letters to the Armed Forces of the U.S. and their response as to whether or not there is any information about Respondent. (See Memorandum for Certificate of Military Service, ✎ ❑Florida

Supreme Court Approved Family Law Form 12.912(a).)

____ Tax Assessor's and Tax Collector's Office in the area where Respondent last resided.

____ Other: *{explain}* ____

____

____

____

____

2. The age of Respondent is [√ **one** only] ( ) known *{enter age}* ____________ **or** ( ) unknown.

3. **Respondent's current residence**

[√ **one** only]

____ a. Respondent's current residence is unknown to me.

____ b. Respondent's current residence is in some state or country other than Florida, and Respondent's last known address is: ____.

____

____ c. The Respondent, having residence in Florida, has been absent from Florida for more than 60 days prior to the date of this affidavit, or conceals him(her)self so that process cannot be served personally upon him or her, and I believe there is no person in the state upon whom service of process would bind this absent or concealed Respondent.

I understand that I am swearing or affirming under oath to the truthfulness of the claims made in this affidavit and that the punishment for knowingly making a false statement includes fines and/or imprisonment.

Dated: ________________________

____
Signature of Petitioner
Printed Name: ______________________________
Address: ______________________________
City, State, Zip: ______________________________
Telephone Number: ______________________________
Fax Number: ______________________________

STATE OF FLORIDA
COUNTY OF ____________________

Sworn to or affirmed and signed before me on ______________ by ______________________.

____
NOTARY PUBLIC or DEPUTY CLERK

____
[Print, type, or stamp commissioned name of notary or clerk.]

____

____ Personally known

____ Produced identification

Type of identification produced ______________________

IF A NONLAWYER HELPED YOU FILL OUT THIS FORM, HE/SHE MUST FILL IN THE

BLANKS BELOW: [✍ fill in **all** blanks]
I, *{full legal name and trade name of nonlawyer}* ____,
a nonlawyer, located at *{street}* ____________________________, *{city}* ___________________,
{state} ___________________, *{phone}* _________________, helped *{name}* ___________________,
who is the petitioner, fill out this form.

IN THE CIRCUIT COURT OF THE ________________________ JUDICIAL CIRCUIT,
IN AND FOR _________________________ COUNTY, FLORIDA

Case No.: ___________________________
Division: ____________________________

__________________________________,
Petitioner,

and

__________________________________,
Respondent.

CERTIFICATE OF SERVICE

I certify that a copy of *{name of document(s)}* ___________________________________
____
was [√ **one** only] ( ) mailed ( ) faxed and mailed ( ) hand delivered to the person listed below on *{date}* _______________________.

Other party or his/her attorney:
Name: ____
Address: ___________________________________
City, State, Zip: ____________________________
Fax Number: _______________________________

____
Signature of Party
Printed Name: ______________________________
Address: __________________________________
City, State, Zip: ____________________________
Telephone Number: __________________________
Fax Number: ________________________________

IF A NONLAWYER HELPED YOU FILL OUT THIS FORM, HE/SHE MUST FILL IN THE BLANKS BELOW: [✍ fill in **all** blanks]
I, *{full legal name and trade name of nonlawyer}* ________________________________,
a nonlawyer, located at *{street}* ____________________________, *{city}* _________________,
{state} _________________, *{phone}* _________________, helped *{name}* _________________,
wh√is the [**one** only] ____ petitioner **or** ____ respondent, fill out this form.

IN THE CIRCUIT COURT OF THE ________________________ JUDICIAL CIRCUIT,
IN AND FOR _________________________ COUNTY, FLORIDA

Case No.: ___________________________
Division: ____________________________

____________________________________,
Petitioner,

and

____________________________________,
Respondent.

NOTICE OF CURRENT ADDRESS

I, *{full legal name}* ____________________________________, being sworn, certify that my current address is: *{street}* ____ *{City}*____________________, *{State}* _____ *{Zip}* _______ *{Telephone No.}* ________________ *{Fax No.}* ________________.

I understand that I must keep the clerk's office notified of my current address and that all future papers in this lawsuit will be mailed to the address on record at the clerk's office.

I certify that a copy of this document was [√ **one** only] (   ) mailed (   ) faxed and mailed (   ) hand-delivered to the person(s) listed below on *{date}* ______________________________________.

Other party or his/her attorney:
Name: ____
Address: _____________________________________
City, State, Zip: ______________________________
Fax Number: __________________________________

Dated: ________________________________ ______________________________________
Signature of Party

STATE OF FLORIDA
COUNTY OF ______________________
Sworn to or affirmed and signed before me on ________________ by __________________________.

____
NOTARY PUBLIC or DEPUTY CLERK

[Print, type, or stamp commissioned name of notary or clerk.]

___ Personally known
___ Produced identification
Type of identification produced ______________________________

IF A NONLAWYER HELPED YOU FILL OUT THIS FORM, HE/SHE MUST FILL IN THE BLANKS BELOW: [fill in **all** blanks]
I, *{full legal name and trade name of nonlawyer}* ____,
a nonlawyer, located at *{street}* ______________________________, *{city}* __________________,
{state} __________________, *{phone}* ________________, helped *{name}* ________________,
who is the [√ **one** only] ___ petitioner **or** ___ respondent, fill out this form.

IN THE CIRCUIT COURT OF THE ____________________________ JUDICIAL CIRCUIT,
IN AND FOR ____________________________ COUNTY, FLORIDA

Case No.: ______________________________
Division: ______________________________

______________________________________,
Petitioner,

and

______________________________________,
Respondent.

CERTIFICATE OF COMPLIANCE WITH MANDATORY DISCLOSURE

I, *{full legal name}* ____, certify that I have complied with the mandatory disclosure required by Florida Family Law Rule 12.285 as follows:

1. FOR TEMPORARY FINANCIAL RELIEF, ONLY:
The date the following documents were served: ____.
[√ **all** that apply]

___ a. Financial Affidavit (Filing of a Financial Affidavit cannot be waived.)
( ) Florida Family Law Rules of Procedure Form 12.902(b) (short form)
( ) Florida Family Law Rules of Procedure Form 12.902(c) (long form)

___ b. ( ) All personal (1040) federal tax, gift tax, and intangible personal property tax returns for the preceding year; or
( ) Transcript of tax return as provided by IRS form 4506-T; or
( ) IRS forms W-2, 1099, and K-1 for the past year because the income tax return for the past year has not been prepared.

___ c. Pay stubs or other evidence of earned income for the 3 months before the service of the financial affidavit.

2. FOR INITIAL, SUPPLEMENTAL, AND PERMANENT FINANCIAL RELIEF:
The date the following documents were served: ____.
[√ **all** that apply]

___ a. Financial Affidavit (Filing of a Financial Affidavit cannot be waived.)
( ) Florida Family Law Rules of Procedure Form 12.902(b) (short form)
( ) Florida Family Law Rules of Procedure Form 12.902(c) (long form)

___ b. ( ) All personal (1040) federal and state tax income returns, gift tax returns, and intangible personal property tax returns for the preceding 3 years;
( ) IRS forms W-2, 1099, and K-1 for the past year because the income tax return for the past year has not been prepared.

___ c. Pay stubs or other evidence of earned income for the 3 months before the service of the financial affidavit.

___ d. A statement identifying the source and amount of all income for the 3 months before the service of the financial affidavit, if not reflected on the pay stubs produced.

___ e. All loan applications and financial statements prepared for any purpose or used for any purpose within the 12 months preceding the service of the financial affidavit.

___ f. All deeds to real estate in which I presently own or owned an interest within the past 3 years.

All promissory notes in which I presently own or owned an interest within the last 12 months. All present leases in which I own an interest.

___ g. All periodic statements for the last 3 months for all checking accounts and for the last year for all savings accounts, money market funds, certificates of deposit, etc.

___ h. All brokerage account statements for the last 12 months.

___ i. Most recent statement for any pension, profit sharing, deferred compensation, or retirement plan (for example, IRA, 401(k), 403(b), SEP, KEOGH, etc.) and summary plan description for any such plan in which I am a participant or alternate payee.

___ j. The declaration page, the last periodic statement, and the certificate for any group insurance for all life insurance policies insuring my life or the life of me or my spouse.

___ k. All health and dental insurance cards covering either me or my spouse and/or our dependent child(ren).

___ l. Corporate, partnership, and trust tax returns for the last 3 tax years, in which I have an ownership or interest greater than or equal to 30%.

___ m. All credit card and charge account statements and other records showing my (our) indebtedness as of the date of the filing of this action and for the prior 3 months. All promissory notes on which I presently owe or owned within the past year. All lease agreements I presently owe.

n. All premarital and marital agreements between the parties to this case.

___ o. If a modification proceeding, all written agreements entered into between the parties at any time since the order to be modified was entered.

___ p. All documents and tangible evidence relating to claims for special equity or nonmarital status of an asset or debt.

___ q. Any court order directing that I pay or receive spousal support (alimony) or child support.

I certify that a copy of this document was [√ **one** only] ( ) mailed ( ) faxed and mailed ( ) hand delivered to the person(s) listed below on *{date}* ______________________________.

I understand that I am swearing or affirming under oath to the accuracy of my compliance with the mandatory disclosure requirements of Fla. Fam. L. R. P. 12.285 and that, unless otherwise indicated with specificity, this disclosure is complete. I further understand that the punishment for knowingly making a false statement or incomplete disclosure includes fines and/or imprisonment.

Other party or his/her attorney:
Name: ______________________________
Address: ______________________________
City, State, Zip: ______________________________
Fax Number: ______________________________
Dated: ______________________

____
Signature of Party
Printed Name: ______________________
Address: ______________________
City, State, Zip: ______________________
Telephone Number: ______________________
Fax Number: ______________________

STATE OF FLORIDA
COUNTY OF ___________

Sworn to or affirmed and signed before me on ______________ by ________________.

____
NOTARY PUBLIC or DEPUTY CLERK

____
[Print, type, or stamp commissioned name of notary or clerk.]

____ Personally known
____ Produced identification
Type of identification produced:____________________

IF A NONLAWYER HELPED YOU FILL OUT THIS FORM, HE/SHE MUST FILL IN THE BLANKS BELOW: [fill in **all** blanks]
I, *{full legal name and trade name of nonlawyer}* ______________________________________,
a nonlawyer, located at *{street}* __________________________, *{city}* ____________________,
{state} ______________, *{phone}* ____________, helped *{name}* ___________________________,
who is the [√ **one** only] ___ petitioner **or** ___ respondent, fill out this form.

IN THE CIRCUIT COURT OF THE ______________________ JUDICIAL CIRCUIT,
IN AND FOR ______________________ COUNTY, FLORIDA

Case No.: ______________________
Division: ______________________

______________________________,
Petitioner,

and

______________________________,
Respondent.

MOTION FOR DEFAULT

TO THE CLERK OF THE CIRCUIT COURT:

PLEASE ENTER A DEFAULT AGAINST RESPONDENT WHO HAS FAILED TO RESPOND TO THE PETITION.

I certify that a copy of this document was [√ **one** only] ( ) mailed ( ) faxed and mailed ( ) hand delivered to the person(s) listed below on *{date}* ______________________.

Other party or his/her attorney:
Name: ______________________
Address: ______________________
City, State, Zip: ______________________
Fax Number: ______________________

Dated: ______________

____
Signature of Petitioner
Printed Name: ______________________
Address: ______________________
City, State, Zip: ______________________
Telephone Number: ______________________
Fax Number: ______________________

IF A NONLAWYER HELPED YOU FILL OUT THIS FORM, HE/SHE MUST FILL IN THE BLANKS BELOW: [✍ fill in **all** blanks]
I, *{full legal name and trade name of nonlawyer}* ______________________,
a nonlawyer, located at *{street}* ______________________, *{city}* ______________,
{state} ______________, *{phone}* ______________, helped *{name}* ______________,
who is the petitioner, fill out this form.

IN THE CIRCUIT COURT OF THE _________________________ JUDICIAL CIRCUIT,
IN AND FOR _________________________ COUNTY, FLORIDA

Case No.: ___________________________
Division: ___________________________

____,
Petitioner,

and

____,
Respondent.

DEFAULT

A default is entered in this action against Respondent for failure to serve or file a response or any paper as is required by law.

Dated: ____________

CLERK OF THE CIRCUIT COURT

(SEAL)

By: ______________________________________
Deputy Clerk

I certify that a copy of this document was [√ **one** only] ( ) mailed ( ) faxed and mailed ( ) hand delivered to the person(s) listed below on *{date}* ______________________________.

Other party or his/her attorney:

Name: ______________________________
Address: ______________________________
City, State, Zip: ______________________________
Fax Number: ______________________________

Dated: __________________

____
Signature of Petitioner
Printed Name: ______________________________
Address: ______________________________
City, State, Zip: ______________________________
Telephone Number: ______________________________
Fax Number: ______________________________

IF A NONLAWYER HELPED YOU FILL OUT THIS FORM, HE/SHE MUST FILL IN THE BLANKS BELOW: [✍ fill in **all** blanks]
I, *{full legal name and trade name of nonlawyer}* ______________________________,
a nonlawyer, located at *{street}* ______________________________, *{city}* ____________,
{state} ____________, *{phone}* ____________, helped *{name}* ____________,
who is the petitioner, fill out this form.

IN THE CIRCUIT COURT OF THE ______________________ JUDICIAL CIRCUIT,
IN AND FOR ______________________ COUNTY, FLORIDA

Case No.: ______________________
Division: ______________________

______________________,
Petitioner,

and

______________________,
Respondent.

NOTICE OF SERVICE OF STANDARD FAMILY LAW INTERROGATORIES

I, *{full legal name}* ______________________, have on *{date}* __________, served upon *{name of person served}* ______________________, to be answered under oath within 30 days after service, the Standard Family Law Interrogatories for [√ **one** only]

( ) **Original or Enforcement Proceedings** ( ) **Modification Proceedings**

I am requesting that the following standard questions be answered: [√ **all** that apply]

___ 1	___ 2	___ 3	___ 4	___ 5	___ 6	___ 7
Background Information	Education	Employment	Assets	Liabilities	Miscellaneous	Long Form Affidavit

In addition, I am requesting that the attached *{#}* __________ questions be answered.

I certify that a copy of this document was [√ **one** only] ( ) mailed ( ) faxed and mailed ( ) hand delivered to the person(s) listed below on *{date}* ______________________.

Other party or his/her attorney:
Name: ______________________
Address: ______________________
City, State, Zip: ______________________
Fax Number: ______________________

Dated: ______________________

____
Signature of Party
Printed Name: ______________________
Address: ______________________
City, State, Zip: ______________________
Telephone Number: ______________________
Fax Number: ______________________

IF A NONLAWYER HELPED YOU FILL OUT THIS FORM, HE/SHE MUST FILL IN THE BLANKS BELOW: [✍ fill in **all** blanks]
I, *{full legal name and trade name of nonlawyer}* ______________________, a nonlawyer, located at *{street}* ______________________, *{city}* ______________________, *{state}* __________, *{phone}* __________, helped *{name}* ______________________, who is the [√ **one** only] ___ petitioner **or** ___ respondent, fill out this form.

IN THE CIRCUIT COURT OF THE ________________________ JUDICIAL CIRCUIT,
IN AND FOR __________________________ COUNTY, FLORIDA

Case No.: ______________________________
Division: ______________________________

____________________________________,
Petitioner,

and

____________________________________,
Respondent.

STANDARD FAMILY LAW INTERROGATORIES FOR ORIGINAL OR ENFORCEMENT PROCEEDINGS

TO BE COMPLETED BY THE PARTY SERVING THESE INTERROGATORIES

I am requesting that the following standard questions be answered: [√ **all** that apply]

____ 1	____ 2	____ 3	____ 4	____ 5	____ 6	____ 7
Background Information	Education	Employment	Assets	Liabilities	Miscellaneous	Long Form Affidavit

In addition, I am requesting that the attached *{#}* _____ questions be answered.

The answers to the following questions are intended to supplement the information provided in the Financial Affidavits, ✎❐ Florida Family Law Rules of Procedure Form 12.902(b) or (c). You should answer the group of questions indicated in the above shaded box. The questions should be answered in the blank space provided below each separately numbered question. If sufficient space is not provided, you may attach additional papers with the answers and refer to them in the space provided in the interrogatories. You should be sure to make a copy for yourself. Each question must be answered separately and as completely as the available information permits. All answers are to be made under oath or affirmation as to their truthfulness.

I, *{name of person answering interrogatories}* ______________________________________, being sworn, certify that the following information is true:

1. **BACKGROUND INFORMATION:**
   a. State your full legal name and any other name by which you have been known.
   b. State your present residence and telephone numbers.
   c. State your place and date of birth.

2. **EDUCATION:**

a. List all business, commercial, and professional licenses that you have obtained.

b. List all of your education including, but not limited to, vocational or specialized training, including the following:

(1) name and address of each educational institution.

(2) dates of attendance.

(3) degrees or certificates obtained or anticipated dates of same.

3. **EMPLOYMENT:**

a. For each place of your employment or self-employment during the last 3 years, state the following:

(1) name, address, and telephone number of your employer.

(2) dates of employment.

(3) job title and brief description of job duties.

(4) starting and ending salaries.

(5) name of your direct supervisor.

(6) all benefits received, including, for example, health, life, and disability insurance; expense account; use of automobile or automobile expense reimbursement; reimbursement for travel, food, or lodging expenses; payment of dues in any clubs or associations; and pension or profit sharing plans.

b. Other than as an employee, if you have been engaged in or associated with any business, commercial, or professional activity within the last 3 years that was not detailed above, state for each such activity the following:

(1) name, address, and telephone number of each activity.

(2) dates you were connected with such activity.

(3) position title and brief description of activities.

(4) starting and ending compensation.

(5) name of all persons involved in the business, commercial, or professional activity with you.

(6) all benefits and compensation received, including, for example, health, life, and disability insurance; expense account; use of automobile or automobile expense reimbursement; reimbursement for travel, food, or lodging expenses; payment of dues in any clubs or associations; and pension or profit sharing plans.

c. If you have been unemployed at any time during the last 3 years, state the dates of unemployment. If you have not been employed at any time in the last 3 years, give the information requested above in question 3.a for your last period of employment.

4. **ASSETS:**

a. **Real Estate.** State the street address, if any, and if not, the legal description of all real property that you own or owned during the last 3 years. For each property, state the following:

(1) the names and addresses of any other persons or entities holding any interest and their percentage of interest.

(2) the purchase price, the cost of any improvements made since it was purchased, and the amount of any depreciation taken.

(3) the fair market value on the date of your separation from your spouse.

(4) the fair market value on the date of the filing of the petition for dissolution of marriage.

b. **Tangible Personal Property.** List all items of tangible personal property that are owned by you or in which you have had any interest during the last 3 years including, but not limited to, motor vehicles, tools, furniture, boats, jewelry, art objects or other collections, and collectibles whose fair market value exceeds $100. For each item, state the following:

(1) the percentage and type interest you hold.

d. **Retirement Accounts:** List all information regarding each retirement account/plan, including but not limited to defined benefit plans, 401k, 403B, IRA accounts, pension plans, Florida Retirement System plans (FRS), Federal Government plans, money purchase plans, HR10 (Keogh) plans, profit sharing plans, annuities, employee savings plans, etc. that you have established and/or that have been established for you by you, your employer, or any previous employer. For each account, state the following:

(1) the name and account number of each account/plan and where it is located.

(2) the type of account/plan.

(3) the name and address of the fiduciary plan administrator/service representative.

(4) the fair market value of your interest in each account/plan.

(a) present value

(b) value on the date of separation

(c) value on the date of filing of the petition for dissolution of marriage

(5) whether you are vested or not vested; and if vested, in what amount, as of a certain date and the schedule of future vesting.

(6) the date at which you became/become eligible to receive some funds in this account/plan.

(7) monthly benefits of the account/plan if no fair market value is ascertained.

(8) beneficiary(ies) and/or alternate payee(s).

e. **Financial Accounts.** For all financial accounts (checking, savings, money market, credit union accounts, or other such cash management accounts) listed in your Financial Affidavit, in which you have had any legal or equitable interest, regardless of whether the interest is or was held in your own name individually, in your name with another person, or in any other name, give the following:

(1) name and address of each institution.

(2) name in which the account is or was maintained.

(3) account numbers.

(4) name of each person authorized to make withdrawals from the accounts.

(5) highest balance within each of the preceding 3 years.

(6) lowest balance within each of the preceding 3 years.

You may comply with this interrogatory (4.e) by providing copies of all periodic (monthly, quarterly, semi-annual, or annual) account statements for each such account for the preceding 3 years. You do not have to resubmit account statements previously furnished pursuant to rule 12.285 (Mandatory Disclosure).

f. **Closed Financial Accounts.** For all financial accounts (checking, savings, money market, credit union accounts, or other such cash management accounts) closed within the last 3 years, in which you have had any legal or equitable interest, regardless of whether the interest is or was held in your own name individually, in your name with another person, or in any other name, give the following:

(1) name and address of each institution.

(2) name in which the account is or was maintained.

(3) account numbers.

(4) name of each person authorized to make withdrawals from the accounts.

(5) date account was closed.

g. **Trust.** For any interest in an estate, trust, insurance policy, or annuity, state the following:

(1) If you are the beneficiary of any estate, trust, insurance policy, or annuity, give for each one the following:

(a) identification of the estate, trust, insurance policy, or annuity.

(b) the nature, amount, and frequency of any distributions of benefits.

(c) the total value of the beneficiaries' interest in the benefit.

(d) whether the benefit is vested or contingent.

(2) If you have established any trust or are the trustee of a trust, state the following:

(a) the date the trust was established.

(b) the names and addresses of the trustees.

(c) the names and addresses of the beneficiaries.

(d) the names and addresses of the persons or entities who possess the trust documents.

(e) each asset that is held in each trust, with its fair market value.

h. **Canceled Life Insurance Policies.** For all policies of life insurance within the preceding 3 years that you no longer hold, own, or have any interest in, state the following:

(1) name of company that issued the policy and policy number.
(2) name, address, and telephone number of agent who issued the policy.
(3) amount of coverage.
(4) name of insured.
(5) name of owner of policy.
(6) name of beneficiaries.
(7) premium amount.
(8) date the policy was surrendered.
(9) amount, if any, of monies distributed to the owner.

i. **Name of Accountant, Bookkeeper, or Records Keeper.** State the names, addresses, and telephone numbers of your accountant, bookkeeper, and any other persons who possess your financial records, and state which records each possesses.

j. **Safe Deposit Boxes, Lock Boxes, Vaults, Etc.** For all safe deposit boxes, lock boxes, vaults, or similar types of depositories, state the following:

(1) The names and addresses of all banks, depositories, or other places where, at any time during the period beginning 3 years before the initiation of the action, until the date of your answering this interrogatory, you did any of the following:

(a) had a safe deposit box, lock box, or vault.

(b) were a signatory or co-signatory on a safe deposit box, lock box, or vault.

(c) had access to a safe deposit box, lock box, or vault.

(d) maintained property.

(2) The box or identification numbers and the name and address of each person who has had access to any such depository during the same time period.

(3) All persons who have possession of the keys or combination to the safe deposit box, lock box, or vault.

(4) Any items removed from any safe deposit boxes, lock boxes, vaults, or similar types of depositories by you or your agent during that time, together with the present location and fair market value of each item.

(5) All items in any safe deposit boxes, lock boxes, vaults, or similar types of depositories and fair market value of each item.

5. **LIABILITIES:**

a. **Loans, Liabilities, Debts, and Other Obligations.** For all loans, liabilities, debts, and other obligations (other than credit cards and charge accounts) listed in your Financial Affidavit, indicate for each the following:

(1) name and address of the creditor.

(2) name in which the obligation is or was incurred.

(3) loan or account number, if any.

(4) nature of the security, if any.

(5) payment schedule.

(6) present balance and current status of your payments.

(7) total amount of arrearage, if any.

(8) balance on the date of your separation from your spouse.

(9) balance on the date of the filing of the petition for dissolution of marriage.

You may comply with this interrogatory (5.a) by providing copies of all periodic (monthly, quarterly, semi-annual, or annual) account statements for each such account for the preceding 3 years. You do not have to resubmit account statements previously furnished under rule 12.285 (Mandatory Disclosure).

b. **Credit Cards and Charge Accounts.** For all financial accounts (credit cards, charge accounts, or other such accounts) listed in your Financial Affidavit, in which you have had any legal or equitable interest, regardless of whether the interest is or was held in your own name individually, in your name with another person, or in any other name, give the following:

(1) name and address of the creditor.

(2) name in which the account is or was maintained.

(3) names of each person authorized to sign on the accounts.

(4) account numbers.

(5) present balance and current status of your payments.

(6) total amount of arrearage, if any.

(7) balance on the date of your separation from your spouse.

(8) balance on the date of the filing of the petition for dissolution of marriage.

(9) highest and lowest balance within each of the preceding 3 years.

You may comply with this interrogatory (5.b) by providing copies of all periodic (monthly quarterly, semi-annual, or annual) account statements for each such account for the preceding 3 years. You do not have to resubmit account statements previously furnished under rule 12.285 (Mandatory Disclosure).

(2) the names and addresses of any other persons or entities holding any interest.

(3) the date you acquired your interest.

(4) the purchase price.

(5) the present fair market value.

(6) the fair market value on the date of your separation from your spouse.

(7) the fair market value on the date of the filing of the petition for dissolution of marriage.

c. **Intangible Personal Property.** Other than the financial accounts (checking, savings, money market, credit union accounts, retirement accounts, or other such cash management accounts) listed in the answers to interrogatories 4.d and 4.e below, list all items of intangible personal property that are owned by you or in which you have had any ownership interest (including closed accounts) within the last 3 years, including but not limited to, partnership and business interests (including good will), deferred compensation accounts unconnected with retirement, including but not limited to stock options, sick leave, and vacation pay, stocks, stock funds, mutual funds, bonds, bond funds, real estate investment trust, receivables, certificates of deposit, notes, mortgages, and debts owed to you by another entity or person. For each item, state the following:

(1) the percentage and type interest you hold.

(2) the names and addresses of any other persons or entities holding any interest and the names and addresses of the persons and entities who are indebted to you.

(3) the date you acquired your interest.

(4) the purchase price, acquisition cost, or loaned amount.

(5) the fair market value or the amounts you claim are owned by or owed to you:

(a) presently, at the time of answering these interrogatories.

(b) on the date of your separation from your spouse.

(c) on the date of the filing of the petition for dissolution of marriage.

You may comply with this interrogatory (4.c) by providing copies of all periodic (monthly, quarterly, semi-annual, or annual) account statements for each such account for the preceding 3 years. However, if the date of acquisition, the purchase price and the market valuations are not clearly reflected in the periodic statements which are furnished then these questions must be answered separately. You do not have to resubmit any periodic statements previously furnished under rule 12.285 (Mandatory Disclosure).

c. **Closed Credit Cards and Charge Accounts.** For all financial accounts (credit cards, charge accounts, or other such accounts) closed with no remaining balance, within the last 3 years, in which you have had any legal or equitable interest, regardless of whether the interest is or was held in your own name individually, in your name with another person, or in any other name, give the following:

(1) name and address of each creditor.

(2) name in which the account is or was maintained.

(3) account numbers.

(4) names of each person authorized to sign on the accounts.

(5) date the balance was paid off.

(6) amount of final balance paid off.

You may comply with this interrogatory (5.c) by providing copies of all periodic (monthly, quarterly, semi-annual, or annual) account statements for each such account for the preceding 3 years. You do not have to resubmit account statements previously furnished under rule 12.285 (Mandatory Disclosure).

6. **MISCELLANEOUS:**

a. If you are claiming a special equity in any assets, list the asset, the amount claimed as special equity, and all facts upon which you rely in your claim.

b. If you are claiming an asset or liability is nonmarital, list the asset or liability and all facts upon which you rely in your claim.

c. If the mental or physical condition of a spouse or child is an issue, identify the person and state the name and address of all health care providers involved in the treatment of that person for said mental or physical condition.

d. If custody of minor children is an issue, state why, and the facts that support your contention that you should be the primary residential parent or have sole parental responsibility of the child(ren).

7. **LONG FORM AFFIDAVIT:** If you filed the short form affidavit, Florida Family Law Rules of Procedure Form 12.902(b), and you were specifically requested in the Notice of Service of Standard Family Law Interrogatories to file the Long Form Affidavit, Form12.902(c), you must do so within the time to serve the answers to these interrogatories.

I certify that a copy of this document was [√ **one** only] ( ) mailed ( ) faxed and mailed ( ) hand delivered to the person(s) listed below on *{date}* ____.

Other party or his/her attorney:
Name: ______________________________
Address: ____________________________
City, State, Zip: ______________________
Fax Number: _________________________

I understand that I am swearing or affirming under oath to the truthfulness of the answers to these interrogatories and that the punishment for knowingly making a false statement includes fines and/or imprisonment.

Dated: ______________________

____
Signature of Party
Printed Name: ____________________________
Address: ________________________________
City, State, Zip: __________________________
Telephone Number: ________________________
Fax Number: _____________________________

STATE OF FLORIDA
COUNTY OF __________________

Sworn to or affirmed and signed before me on _____________ by ___________________________.

____
NOTARY PUBLIC or DEPUTY CLERK

____
[Print, type, or stamp commissioned name of notary or clerk.]

___ Personally known

___ Produced identification
Type of identification produced ______________________

IF A NONLAWYER HELPED YOU FILL OUT THIS FORM, HE/SHE MUST FILL IN THE BLANKS BELOW: [✍ fill in **all** blanks]
I, *{full legal name and trade name of nonlawyer}* ______________________________,
a nonlawyer, located at *{street}* __________________________, *{city}* __________________________,
{state} __________, *{phone}* ______________, helped *{name}* ______________________________,
who is the [√ **one** only] ___ petitioner **or** ___ respondent, fill out this form.

IN THE CIRCUIT COURT OF THE ________________________ JUDICIAL CIRCUIT,
IN AND FOR ________________________ COUNTY, FLORIDA

Case No.: ________________________
Division: ________________________

________________________________,
Petitioner,

and

________________________________,
Respondent.

NOTICE OF PRODUCTION FROM NONPARTY

TO: ____
{all parties}

YOU ARE NOTIFIED that, after **10 days** from the date of service of this notice, the undersigned will apply to the clerk of this Court for issuance of the attached subpoena directed to *{name of person, organization, or agency}* ____________________________ , who is not a party, to produce the items listed at the time and place specified in the subpoena. Objections to the issuance of this subpoena must be filed with the clerk of the circuit court within **10 days**.

I certify that a copy of this document was [√ **one** only] ( ) mailed ( ) faxed and mailed ( ) hand delivered to the person(s) listed below on *{date}* ______________________.

Other party or his/her attorney (if represented)	Other
______________________ Printed Name	______________________ Printed Name
______________________ Address	______________________ Address
______________________ City State Zip	______________________ City State Zip
______________________ Telephone (area code and number)	______________________ Telephone (area code and number)
______________________ Fax (area code and number)	______________________ Fax (area code and number)

Dated: ______________________________

____
Signature of Party

Printed Name: ___________________________________
Address: ___________________________________
City, State, Zip: ___________________________________
Telephone Number: ___________________________________
Fax Number: ___________________________________

IF A NONLAWYER HELPED YOU FILL OUT THIS FORM, HE/SHE MUST FILL IN THE BLANKS BELOW: [✍ fill in **all** blanks]
I, *{full legal name and trade name of nonlawyer}* ______________________________,
a nonlawyer, located at *{street}* ______________________, *{city}* ______________,
{state} ______________, *{phone}* ______________, helped *{name}* ______________,
who is the [√ **one** only] ___ petitioner **or** ___ respondent, fill out this form.

IN THE CIRCUIT COURT OF THE ________________________ JUDICIAL CIRCUIT,
IN AND FOR ________________________ COUNTY, FLORIDA

Case No.:___________________________
Division: ___________________________

__________________________________,
Petitioner,

and

__________________________________,
Respondent.

SUBPOENA FOR PRODUCTION OF DOCUMENTS FROM NONPARTY

THE STATE OF FLORIDA
TO: ____

YOU **MUST** go to *{place}*____, on *{date}* _____________, at *{time}* _______________, a.m./p.m. and bring with you at that time and place the following:____

____

____

____

____

These items will be inspected and may be copied at that time. You will not have to leave the original items.

You may obey this subpoena by providing readable copies of the items to be produced to the party **or** his/her attorney whose name appears on this subpoena on or before the scheduled date of production. You may condition the preparation of the copies upon payment in advance of the reasonable cost of preparation. If you mail or deliver the copies to the attorney whose name appears on this subpoena before the date indicated above, you do not have to appear in person.

You may be in contempt of court if you fail to: (1) appear as specified; (2) furnish the records instead of appearing as provided above; or (3) object to this subpoena.

You can only be excused by the person whose name appears on this subpoena and, unless excused by that person or the Court, you shall respond as directed.

Dated: ______________

CLERK OF THE CIRCUIT COURT

(SEAL)

By:__________________________________
Deputy Clerk

This part to be filled out by the court or filled in with information you have obtained from the court:
If you are a person with a disability who needs any accommodation in order to participate in this proceeding, you are entitled, at no cost to you, to the provision of certain assistance. Please contact *{name}*____,
*{address}*____*{telephone}*
____________________,within 2 working days of your receipt of this subpoena. If you are hearing or voice impaired, call TDD 1-800-955-8771.

I CERTIFY that I gave notice to every other party to this action of my intent to serve a subpoena upon a person who is not a party to this action directing that person to produce documents or things without deposition. I also certify that no objection under Florida Rule of Civil Procedure 1.351 has been received by the undersigned within 10 days of service of this notice, if service was by hand delivery or appropriate facsimile transmission, and within 15 days if service was by mail.

Dated: _______________

____
Signature of Party
Printed Name: ____________________________
Address: ____________________________
City, State, Zip: ____________________________
Telephone Number: ____________________________
Fax Number: ____________________________

IF A NONLAWYER HELPED YOU FILL OUT THIS FORM, HE/SHE MUST FILL IN THE BLANKS BELOW: [✍ fill in **all** blanks]
I, *{full legal name and trade name of nonlawyer}*_____________________________,
a nonlawyer, located at *{street}*_____________________________, *{city}*__________,
*{state}*__________________, *{phone}*____________________, helped *{name}*__________,
who is the [√ **one** only] __ petitioner **or** __ respondent, fill out this form.

IN THE CIRCUIT COURT OF THE ___________________________ JUDICIAL CIRCUIT,
IN AND FOR ___________________________ COUNTY, FLORIDA

Case No.: ______________________________
Division: ______________________________

______________________________________,
Petitioner,

and

______________________________________,
Respondent.

NOTICE OF HEARING (GENERAL)

[✍ fill in **all** blanks]

TO: *{name of other party}* ____

There will be a hearing before Judge *{name}* ______________________________,
on *{date}* _________________, at *{time}* __________ m., in Room ________ of the______________
Courthouse, on the following issues: ____
____
____.
____________ hour(s)/ ______ minutes have been reserved for this hearing.

This part to be filled out by the court or to be filled in with information you obtained from the court: If you are a person with a disability who needs any accommodation in order to participate in this proceeding, you are entitled, at no cost to you, to the provision of certain assistance. Please contact *{name}* ____,
{address} ______________________________________, *{telephone}* ______________,
within 2 working days of your receipt of this Notice of Hearing. If you are hearing or voice impaired, call TDD 1-800-955-8771.

If you are represented by an attorney or plan to retain an attorney for this matter, you should notify the attorney of this hearing.

If this matter is resolved, the moving party shall contact the judge's office to cancel this hearing.

I certify that a copy of this document was [√ **one** only] ( ) mailed ( ) faxed and mailed ( ) hand delivered to the person(s) listed below on *{date}* ______________________________________.

Other party or his/her attorney:
Name: ______________________________________
Address: ____________________________________
City, State, Zip: ______________________________
Fax Number: _________________________________

Dated: ____________________

____
Signature of Party
Printed Name: ____________________________________
Address: ____
City, State, Zip: __________________________________
Telephone Number: ________________________________
Fax Number: ______________________________________

IF A NONLAWYER HELPED YOU FILL OUT THIS FORM, HE/SHE MUST FILL IN THE BLANKS BELOW: [✍ fill in **all** blanks]

I, *{full legal name and trade name of nonlawyer}* ______________________________________,
a nonlawyer, located at *{street}* ________________________________, *{city}* ____________________,
{state} ____________________, *{phone}* __________________, helped *{name}* ____________________,
who is the [√ **one** only] ___ petitioner **or** ___ respondent, fill out this form.

IN THE CIRCUIT COURT OF THE ____________________ JUDICIAL CIRCUIT,
IN AND FOR ____________________ COUNTY, FLORIDA

Case No.: ____________________
Division: ____________________

______________________________,
Petitioner,

and

______________________________,
Respondent.

NOTICE OF HEARING (CHILD SUPPORT ENFORCEMENT HEARING OFFICER)

TO: *{name of other party}* ____

There will be a hearing before Child Support Enforcement Hearing Officer *{name}* __________ ____________________, on *{date}* ______________, at *{time}* __________ m., in Room __________ of the ____ County Courthouse, on the following issues: ____ ____ ____.

__________ hour(s)/ _____ minutes have been reserved for this hearing.

If the matter before the Child Support Enforcement Hearing Officer is a Motion for Civil Contempt/Enforcement, **FAILURE TO APPEAR AT THE HEARING MAY RESULT IN THE COURT ISSUING A WRIT OF BODILY ATTACHMENT FOR YOUR ARREST. IF YOU ARE ARRESTED, YOU MAY BE HELD IN JAIL UP TO 48 HOURS BEFORE A HEARING IS HELD.**

This part to be filled out by the court or filled in with information you have obtained from the court:
If you are a person with a disability who needs any accommodation in order to participate in this proceeding, you are entitled, at no cost to you, to the provision of certain assistance. Please contact *{name}*____
*{address}*______________________________ *{telephone}* __________
within 2 working days of your receipt of this Notice of Hearing. If you are hearing or voice impaired, call TDD 1-800-955-8771.

If you are represented by an attorney or plan to retain an attorney for this matter, you should notify the attorney of this hearing.

If this matter is resolved, the moving party shall contact the hearing officer's office to cancel this hearing.

I certify that a copy of this document was [√ **one** only] ( ) mailed ( ) faxed and mailed ( ) hand delivered to the person(s) listed below on *{date}* ______________________.

Other party or his/her attorney:
Name: ______________________
Address: ______________________
City, State, Zip: ______________________
Fax Number: ______________________

Dated: ______________

____
Signature of Party
Printed Name: ______________________
Address: ______________________
City, State, Zip: ______________________
Telephone Number: ______________________
Fax Number: ______________________

IF A NONLAWYER HELPED YOU FILL OUT THIS FORM, HE/SHE MUST FILL IN THE BLANKS BELOW: [✍ fill in **all** blanks]

I, *{full legal name and trade name of nonlawyer}*______________________, a nonlawyer, located at *{street}*______________________, *{city}* ______________, *{state}* ______________, *{phone}* ______________, helped *{name}* ______________, who is the [√ **one** only] ___ petitioner **or** ___ respondent, fill out this form.

IN THE CIRCUIT COURT OF THE ________________________ JUDICIAL CIRCUIT,
IN AND FOR ________________________ COUNTY, FLORIDA

Case No.: ______________________________
Division: ______________________________

__________________________________,
Petitioner,

and

__________________________________,
Respondent.

MOTION FOR REFERRAL TO GENERAL MAGISTRATE

I, *{full legal name}* ________________________________, request that the Court enter an order referring this case to a general magistrate. The case should be referred to a general magistrate on the following issues: *{explain}* ____
____
____
____
____

I certify that a copy of this document was [√ **one** only] ( ) mailed ( ) faxed and mailed ( ) hand delivered to the person(s) listed below on *{date}* ________________________________.

Other party or his/her attorney:
Name: ______________________________
Address: ______________________________
City, State, Zip: ______________________________
Fax Number: ______________________________

Dated: ______________________

____
Signature of Party
Printed Name: ______________________________
Address: ______________________________
City, State, Zip: ______________________________
Telephone Number: ______________________________
Fax Number: ______________________________

IF A NONLAWYER HELPED YOU FILL OUT THIS FORM, HE/SHE MUST FILL IN THE BLANKS BELOW: [✍ fill in **all** blanks]
I, *{full legal name and trade name of nonlawyer}* ____,
a nonlawyer, located at *{street}* ___________________________, *{city}* ___________________________,
{state} ______________, *{phone}* __________________, helped *{name}* ___________________________,
who is the [√ **one** only] ___ petitioner **or** ___ respondent, fill out this form.

IN THE CIRCUIT COURT OF THE ________________________ JUDICIAL CIRCUIT,
IN AND FOR ________________________ COUNTY, FLORIDA

Case No.: ____________________________
Division: ____________________________

______________________________,
Petitioner,

and

______________________________,
Respondent.

ORDER OF REFERRAL TO GENERAL MAGISTRATE

THIS CASE IS REFERRED TO THE GENERAL MAGISTRATE on the following issues:

1. ____
2. ____
3. ____
4. ____

AND ANY OTHER MATTER RELATED THERETO.

IT IS FURTHER ORDERED that the above issues are referred to General Magistrate *{name}*____, for further proceedings, under rule 12.490 of the Florida Family Law Rules (✎ ❑cedure and current administrative orders of the Court. Financial Affidavits, ✎❑ Florida Family Law Rules of Procedure Form 12.902(b) or (c), shall be filed in accordance with Florida Family Law Rule of Procedure 12.285. The General Magistrate is authorized to administer oaths and conduct hearings, which may include taking of evidence, and shall file a report and recommendations that contain findings of fact, conclusions of law, and the name of the court reporter, if any.

The General Magistrate shall assign a time for the proceedings as soon as reasonably possible after this referral is made and shall give notice to each of the parties either directly or by directing counsel or a party to file and serve a notice of hearing.

Counties within the State of Florida may have different rules. Please consult the ( ) Clerk of the Court ( ) Family Law Intake Staff ( ) other __________________________ relating to this procedure.

A REFERRAL TO A GENERAL MAGISTRATE REQUIRES THE CONSENT OF ALL PARTIES. YOU ARE ENTITLED TO HAVE THIS MATTER HEARD BY A JUDGE. IF YOU DO NOT WANT TO HAVE THIS MATTER HEARD BY THE GENERAL MAGISTRATE, YOU MUST FILE A WRITTEN OBJECTION TO THE REFERRAL WITHIN 10 DAYS OF THE TIME OF SERVICE OF THIS ORDER. IF THE TIME SET FOR THE HEARING IS LESS THAN 10 DAYS AFTER SERVICE OF THIS ORDER, THE OBJECTION MUST BE MADE BEFORE THE HEARING. IF THIS ORDER IS SERVED WITHIN THE FIRST 20 DAYS AFTER SERVICE OF PROCESS, THE TIME TO FILE AN OBJECTION IS EXTENDED TO

THE TIME WITHIN WHICH A RESPONSIVE PLEADING IS DUE. FAILURE TO FILE A WRITTEN OBJECTION WITHIN THE APPLICABLE TIME PERIOD IS DEEMED TO BE A CONSENT TO THE REFERRAL.

If either party files a timely objection, this matter shall be returned to the undersigned judge with a notice stating the amount of time needed for hearing.

REVIEW OF THE REPORT AND RECOMMENDATIONS MADE BY THE GENERAL MAGISTRATE SHALL BE BY EXCEPTIONS AS PROVIDED IN RULE 12.490(f), FLORIDA FAMILY LAW RULES OF PROCEDURE. A RECORD, WHICH INCLUDES A TRANSCRIPT, MAY BE REQUIRED TO SUPPORT EXCEPTIONS.

YOU ARE ADVISED THAT IN THIS CIRCUIT:

____ a. electronic recording is provided by the court. A party may provide a court reporter at that party's expense.

____ b. a court reporter is provided by the court.

SHOULD YOU WISH TO SEEK REVIEW OF THE REPORT AND RECOMMENDATION MADE BY THE GENERAL MAGISTRATE, YOU MUST FILE EXCEPTIONS IN ACCORDANCE WITH RULE 12.490(f), FLORIDA FAMILY LAW RULES OF PROCEDURE. YOU WILL BE REQUIRED TO PROVIDE THE COURT WITH A RECORD SUFFICIENT TO SUPPORT YOUR EXCEPTIONS, OR YOUR EXCEPTIONS WILL BE DENIED. A RECORD ORDINARILY INCLUDES A WRITTEN TRANSCRIPT OF ALL RELEVANT PROCEEDINGS. THE PERSON SEEKING REVIEW MUST HAVE THE TRANSCRIPT PREPARED IF NECESSARY FOR THE COURT'S REVIEW.

ORDERED on ______________________.

____
CIRCUIT JUDGE

COPIES TO:
Petitioner (or his or her attorney)
Respondent (or his or her attorney)
General Magistrate

IN THE CIRCUIT COURT OF THE ________________________ JUDICIAL CIRCUIT,
IN AND FOR ________________________ COUNTY, FLORIDA

Case No.: ______________________
Division: ______________________

______________________________,
Petitioner,

and

______________________________,
Respondent.

NOTICE OF HEARING BEFORE GENERAL MAGISTRATE

[✍ fill in **all** blanks]
TO: ________________________________
____

There will be a hearing before General Magistrate *{name of general magistrate}* ____________, on *{date}* ________________, at *{time}* __________ m., in Room ________ of the ____________ Courthouse, on the following issues: ____
____
____.

____________ hour(s)/ _____ minutes have been reserved for this hearing.
PLEASE GOVERN YOURSELF ACCORDINGLY.

If the matter before the General Magistrate is a Motion for Civil Contempt/Enforcement, FAILURE TO APPEAR AT THE HEARING MAY RESULT IN THE COURT ISSUING A WRIT OF BODILY ATTACHMENT FOR YOUR ARREST. IF YOU ARE ARRESTED, YOU MAY BE HELD IN JAIL UP TO 48 HOURS BEFORE A HEARING IS HELD.

PLEASE GOVERN YOURSELF ACCORDINGLY.

This part to be filled out by the court or filled in with information you have obtained from the court:
If you are a person with a disability who needs any accommodation in order to participate in this proceeding, you are entitled, at no cost to you, to the provision of certain assistance. Please contact *{name}* ____,
{address} ______________________________________, *{telephone}* ______________,
within 2 working days of your receipt of this Notice of Hearing. If you are hearing or voice impaired, call TDD 1-800-955-8771.

SHOULD YOU WISH TO SEEK REVIEW OF THE REPORT AND RECOMMENDATION MADE BY THE GENERAL MAGISTRATE, YOU MUST FILE EXCEPTIONS IN ACCORDANCE WITH RULE 12.490(f), FLORIDA FAMILY LAW RULES OF PROCEDURE. YOU WILL BE REQUIRED TO PROVIDE THE COURT WITH A RECORD SUFFICIENT TO

SUPPORT YOUR EXCEPTIONS, OR YOUR EXCEPTIONS WILL BE DENIED. A RECORD ORDINARILY INCLUDES A WRITTEN TRANSCRIPT OF ALL RELEVANT PROCEEDINGS. THE PERSON SEEKING REVIEW MUST HAVE THE TRANSCRIPT PREPARED IF NECESSARY FOR THE COURT'S REVIEW.

YOU ARE HEREBY ADVISED THAT IN THIS CIRCUIT:

____ a. electronic recording is provided by the court. A party may provide a court reporter at that party's expense.

____ b. a court reporter is provided by the court.

If you are represented by an attorney or plan to retain an attorney for this matter you should notify the attorney of this hearing.

If this matter is resolved, the moving party shall contact the General Magistrate's Office to cancel this hearing.

I certify that a copy of this document was [√ **one** only] ( ) mailed ( ) faxed and mailed ( ) hand delivered to the person(s) listed below on *{date}* ____.

Other party or his/her attorney:
Name: ______________________________________
Address: ______________________________________
City, State, Zip: ________________________________
Fax Number: ___________________________________

Dated: ____________________

____
Signature of Party
Printed Name: ________________________________
Address: ____________________________________
City, State, Zip: _______________________________
Telephone Number: ______________________________
Fax Number: __________________________________

IF A NONLAWYER HELPED YOU FILL OUT THIS FORM, HE/SHE MUST FILL IN THE BLANKS BELOW: [✍ fill in **all** blanks]
I, *{full legal name and trade name of nonlawyer}* ____,
a nonlawyer, located at *{street}* _____________________________, *{city}* _____________________________,
{state} ______________, *{phone}* ____________________, helped *{name}* ,who is the [√ **one** only] ___ petitioner **or** ___ respondent, fill out this form.

IN THE CIRCUIT COURT OF THE ______________________ JUDICIAL CIRCUIT,
IN AND FOR ______________________ COUNTY, FLORIDA

Case No.: ______________________
Division: ______________________

______________________,
Petitioner,

and

______________________,
Respondent.

NOTICE FOR TRIAL

Pursuant to rule 12.440, Florida Family Law Rules of Procedure, the party signing below states that the case is ready to be set for trial. The estimated time needed for the parties to present their cases is: *{hours}* ______________.

I certify that a copy of this document was [√ one only] ( ) mailed ( ) faxed and mailed ( ) hand delivered to the person(s) listed below on *{date}* ______________________.

Other party or his/her attorney:
Name: ______________________
Address: ______________________
City, State, Zip: ______________________
Fax Number: ______________________

Dated: ______________________

____
Signature of Party
Printed Name: ______________________
Address: ______________________
City, State, Zip: ______________________
Telephone Number: ______________________
Fax Number: ______________________

IF A NONLAWYER HELPED YOU FILL OUT THIS FORM, HE/SHE MUST FILL IN THE BLANKS BELOW: [✍ fill in **all** blanks]
I, *{full legal name and trade name of nonlawyer}* ______________________,
a nonlawyer, located at *{street}* ______________________, *{city}* ______________,
{state} ______________, *{phone}* ______________, helped *{name}* ______________,
who is the [√ **one** only] ___ petitioner **or** ___ respondent, fill out this form.

IN THE CIRCUIT COURT OF THE ____________________ JUDICIAL CIRCUIT,
IN AND FOR ____________________ COUNTY, FLORIDA

Case No.: ____________________
Division: ____________________

______________________________,
Petitioner,

and

______________________________,
Respondent.

MOTION TO SET FINAL HEARING / TRIAL

The ❑ Petitioner ❑ Respondent moves the court for an order setting this matter for:

❑ Uncontested final hearing ❑ Non-jury trial ❑ Status Conference

pursuant to Rule 1.440, Florida Rules of Civil Procedure, and states:

1. This matter is at issue and ready to set for final hearing/trial.

2. The estimated time necessary to conduct the final hearing/trial is ________________ ____________________.

DATED: ____________________

____
Signature
Printed name: ____________________
Address: ____________________
City, State, Zip: ____________________
Telephone Number: ____________________
Fax Number: ____________________

IF A NONLAWYER HELPED YOU FILL OUT THIS FORM, HE/SHE MUST FILL IN THE BLANKS BELOW: [✍ fill in all blanks]

I, *{full legal name and trade name of nonlawyer}* ____________________, a nonlawyer, located at *{street}* ____________________, *{city}* ____________________, *{state}* ____________, *{phone}* ____________, helped *{name}* ____________________, who is the petitioner/respondent, fill out this form.

IN THE CIRCUIT COURT OF THE ____________________ JUDICIAL CIRCUIT,
IN AND FOR ____________________ COUNTY, FLORIDA

Case No.: ____________________
Division: ____________________

____________________,
Petitioner,
and

____________________,
Respondent.

ORDER SETTING MATTER FOR FINAL HEARING OR FOR STATUS CONFERENCE

The court having reviewed the file finds that:
____ The time to file an answer has expired, and therefore,

IT IS ORDERED that:
This case is set for uncontested final hearing before Judge *{name of judge}* ____________________ ____________________, on *{date}* ____________________, ________, at *{time}* __________, in Room ________ of the ____________________ Courthouse.

[✔ **one** only]
____ If no answer has been filed, please bring your default order. You will also need to bring proof of residency, i.e., a residency witness, affidavit of residency, valid Florida driver's license, or valid Florida voter registration card.
____ If an answer has been filed, this hearing will serve as a status conference.

The ( ) Petitioner ( ) Respondent, or attorney for the ( ) Petitioner ( ) Respondent, is required to notify all other parties immediately of this hearing.

FAILURE TO APPEAR MAY RESULT IN A DISMISSAL OF THIS CASE

DATED: ____________________

____
CIRCUIT JUDGE

This part to be filled in by court: In accordance with the Americans with Disabilities Act of 1990, persons needing a special accommodation to participate in this proceeding should contact ____________________ for proceedings in court or ____________________ at ______________ for out of court proceedings no later than 7 days before the proceeding. Telephone ______________ or ______________ for assistance. If hearing impaired, telephone (TDD) ____________________ for proceedings in court or Florida Relay Service 1-800-955-8771 for out of court proceedings.

cc:

Petitioner or their attorney (if represented)	Respondent of their attorney (if represented)
Name ____________________	Name ____________________
Address: ____________________	Address: ____________________
____________________	____________________
City State Zip	City State Zip
Telephone No. ____________________	Telephone No. ____________________
Fax No. ____________________	Fax No. ____________________

IF A NONLAWYER HELPED YOU FILL OUT THIS FORM TO GIVE TO THE JUDGE TO SIGN, THE NONLAWYER WHO HELPED YOU MUST FILL IN THE BLANKS BELOW: [✍ fill in all blanks]
I, *{full legal name and trade name of nonlawyer}* ____________________,
a nonlawyer, located at *{street}* ____________________.*{city}* ____________________,
{state} __________, *{phone}* ____________________, helped *{name}* ____________________,
who is the petitioner/respondent, fill out this form.

IN THE CIRCUIT COURT OF THE ____________________ JUDICIAL CIRCUIT,
IN AND FOR ____________________ COUNTY, FLORIDA

Case No.: ____________________
Division: ____________________

____________________,
Petitioner,

and

____________________,
Respondent.

MOTION FOR TESTIMONY AND ATTENDANCE OF MINOR CHILD(REN)

( ) Petitioner ( ) Respondent requests that the Court enter an order authorizing one or more of the actions listed below related to the following minor child(ren):

Name	**Birth date**	**Age**

[√ **all** that apply]

____ 1. Minor child(ren), *{name(s)}* ____________________, be subpoenaed to appear at hearing now scheduled for *{date}* ____________________.

____ 2. Minor child(ren), *{name(s)}* ____________________, attend deposition of *{name(s)}* ____________________ now scheduled for *{date}* ____________________ at *{location}* ____________________.

____ 3. Minor child(ren)'s, *{name(s)}* ____________________, deposition be taken on *{date}* ____________________ at *{location}* ____________________.

____ 4. Minor child(ren), *{name(s)}* ____________________, be brought to court to attend hearing now scheduled for *{date}* ____________________ at *{location}* ____________________.

____ 5. Minor child(ren), *{name(s)}* ____________________, be brought to court to testify in a hearing now scheduled for *{date}* ____________________ at *{location}* ____________________.

The Court should do this because: ____________________
____
____
____
____
____
____________________.

I certify that a copy of this document was [√ **one** only] ( ) mailed ( ) faxed and mailed ( ) hand delivered to the person(s) listed below on *{date}* ____________________.

Other party or his/her attorney:
Name: ___________________________________
Address: _________________________________
City, State, Zip: ___________________________
Fax Number: ______________________________

Dated: ________________________

____
Signature of Party
Printed Name: ______________________________
Address: ___________________________________
City, State, Zip: ____________________________
Telephone Number: __________________________
Fax Number: _______________________________

IF A NONLAWYER HELPED YOU FILL OUT THIS FORM, HE/SHE MUST FILL IN THE BLANKS BELOW: [✍ fill in **all** blanks]
I, *{full legal name and trade name of nonlawyer}* ________________________________,
a nonlawyer, located at *{street}* _____________________________, *{city}* _________________,
{state} __________________, *{phone}* _______________, helped *{name}* ________________,
who is the [√ **one** only] ___ petitioner **or** ___ respondent, fill out this form.

IN THE CIRCUIT COURT OF THE ______________________ JUDICIAL CIRCUIT,
IN AND FOR ______________________ COUNTY, FLORIDA

Case No.: ______________________
Division: ______________________

______________________,
Petitioner,

and

______________________,
Respondent.

ORDER FOR TESTIMONY AND ATTENDANCE OF MINOR CHILD(REN)

Upon motion of ( ) Petitioner ( ) Respondent for testimony or attendance of minor child(ren) in these proceedings, and the Court finding that a showing of good cause has been made in support of the motion, it is

ORDERED that

[√ **all** that apply]

____ 1. Minor child(ren), *{name(s)}* ______________________,
be subpoenaed to appear at hearing now scheduled for *{date}* ______________________.

____ 2. Minor child(ren), *{name(s)}* ______________________,
attend deposition of *{name(s)}* ______________ now scheduled for *{date}* __________
at *{location}* ______________________.

____ 3. Minor child(ren)'s, *{name(s)}* ______________________,
deposition be taken on *{date}* ______________ at *{location}* ______________________
______________________.

____ 4. Minor child(ren), *{name(s)}* ______________________,
be brought to court to attend hearing now scheduled for *{date}* ______________________ at *{location}* ______________________.

____ 5. Minor child(ren), *{name(s)}* ______________________,
be brought to court to testify in a hearing now scheduled for *{date}* ______________________ at *{location}* ______________________.

If the minor child or the person bringing the child is a person with a disability who needs any accommodation in order to participate in this proceeding, the child is entitled, at no cost, to the provision of certain assistance. Please contact *{name}* ______________________, *{address}* ______________________, *{telephone}* ______________, within 2 working days of your receipt of this order. If you are hearing or voice impaired, call TDD 1-800-955-8771.

Conditions or limitations concerning the minor child(ren), if any, include: ______________________
____
____
____
____
____
____
____
______________________.

ORDERED on ______________________.

____
CIRCUIT JUDGE

COPIES TO:
Petitioner (or his or her attorney)
Respondent (or his or her attorney)

IN THE CIRCUIT COURT OF THE __________________________ JUDICIAL CIRCUIT,
IN AND FOR ____________________________ COUNTY, FLORIDA

Case No.: ______________________________
Division: _______________________________

____________________________________,
Petitioner,

and

____________________________________,
Respondent.

FINAL JUDGMENT OF SIMPLIFIED DISSOLUTION OF MARRIAGE

This cause came before this Court for a hearing on the parties' Petition for Simplified Dissolution of Marriage. The Court, having reviewed the file and heard the testimony, makes these findings of fact and reaches these conclusions of law:

1. The Court has jurisdiction over the subject matter and the parties.
2. At least one party has been a resident of the State of Florida for more than 6 months immediately before filing the Petition for Simplified Dissolution of Marriage.
3. The parties have no minor or dependent children in common, and the wife is not pregnant.
4. The marriage between the parties is irretrievably broken. Therefore, the marriage between the parties is dissolved, and the parties are restored to the status of being single.
5. Marital Settlement Agreement.
   [√ **one** only]
   ____ a. The parties have voluntarily entered into a Marital Settlement Agreement, and each has filed the required Financial Affidavit. Therefore, the Marital Settlement Agreement is filed as "Exhibit A" in this case and is ratified and made a part of this final judgment. The parties are ordered to obey all of its provisions.
   ____ b. There is no marital property or marital debts to divide, as the parties previously have divided all of their personal property. Therefore, each is awarded the personal property he or she presently has in his or her possession. Each party shall be responsible for any debts in his or her own name.
6. ( ) yes ( ) no The wife's former name of *{full legal name}* ___________________________ is restored.
7. The Court reserves jurisdiction to enforce the marital settlement agreement.

ORDERED on _______________________.

____
CIRCUIT JUDGE

COPIES TO:
Petitioner (or his or her attorney)

Respondent (or his or her attorney)
Other: ____________________________

IN THE CIRCUIT COURT OF THE ____________________________ JUDICIAL CIRCUIT,
IN AND FOR ____________________________ COUNTY, FLORIDA

Case No.: ________________________________
Division: ________________________________

______________________________________,
Petitioner,

and

______________________________________,
Respondent.

FINAL JUDGMENT OF DISSOLUTION OF MARRIAGE WITH MINOR CHILD(REN) (UNCONTESTED)

This cause came before this Court for a hearing on a Petition for Dissolution of Marriage. The Court, having reviewed the file and heard the testimony, makes these findings of fact and reaches these conclusions of law:

1. The Court has jurisdiction over the subject matter and the parties.
2. At least one party has been a resident of the State of Florida for more than 6 months immediately before filing the Petition for Dissolution of Marriage.
3. The marriage between the parties is irretrievably broken. Therefore, the marriage between the parties is dissolved, and the parties are restored to the status of being single.
4. Marital Settlement Agreement. The parties have voluntarily entered into a Marital Settlement Agreement, and each has filed the required Family Law Financial Affidavit. Therefore, the Marital Settlement Agreement is filed as "Exhibit A" in this case and is ratified and made a part of this final judgment. The parties are ordered to obey all of its provisions.
5. The Court finds that the parties have the present ability to pay support as agreed to in the marital settlement agreement as ratified and made part of this final judgment.
6. ( ) yes ( ) no The wife's former name of *{full legal name}* ____________________________ is restored.
7. The Court reserves jurisdiction to modify and enforce this final judgment.

ORDERED on ______________________.

____
CIRCUIT JUDGE

COPIES TO:

Florida Supreme Court Approved Family Law Form 12.990(b)(1), Final Judgment of Dissolution of Marriage with Minor child(ren) (Uncontested) (9/00)

Petitioner (or his or her attorney)
Respondent (or his or her attorney)
Other: ______________________________

IN THE CIRCUIT COURT OF THE ______________________ JUDICIAL CIRCUIT,
IN AND FOR ______________________ COUNTY, FLORIDA

Case No.: ______________________
Division: ______________________

______________________,
Petitioner,

and

______________________,
Respondent.

FINAL JUDGMENT OF DISSOLUTION OF MARRIAGE WITH DEPENDENT OR MINOR CHILD(REN)

This cause came before this Court for a trial on a Petition for Dissolution of Marriage. The Court, having reviewed the file and heard the testimony, makes these findings of fact and reaches these conclusions of law:

1. The Court has jurisdiction over the subject matter and the parties.
2. At least one party has been a resident of the State of Florida for more than 6 months immediately before filing the Petition for Dissolution of Marriage.
3. The marriage between the parties is irretrievably broken. Therefore, the marriage between the parties is dissolved, and the parties are restored to the status of being single.

SECTION I. MARITAL ASSETS AND LIABILITIES

A. Date of Valuation of Property. The assets and liabilities listed below are divided as indicated. The date of valuation of these assets and liabilities is, unless otherwise indicated:

___ a. date of filing petition for dissolution of marriage ______________.
___ b. date of separation ______________.
___ c. date of divorce trial ______________.

B. Division of Assets.

1. **The assets listed below are nonmarital assets.** Each party shall keep, as his or her own, the assets found to be nonmarital, and the other party shall have no further rights or responsibilities regarding these assets.

ASSETS: DESCRIPTION OF ITEM(S) (Describe each item as clearly as possible. You do not need to list account numbers.)	Current Fair Market Value	Wife's Nonmarital Property	Husband's Nonmarital Property
	$	$	$

ASSETS: DESCRIPTION OF ITEM(S) (Describe each item as clearly as possible. You do not need to list account numbers.)	Current Fair Market Value	Wife's Nonmarital Property	Husband's Nonmarital Property
Total Nonmarital Assets	$	$	$

2. **The assets listed below are marital assets.** Each party shall keep, as his or her own, the assets awarded in this section, and the other party shall have no further rights or responsibilities regarding these assets. **Any personal item(s) not listed below are awarded to the party currently in possession or control of the item(s).**

ASSETS: DESCRIPTION OF ITEM(S) (Describe each item as clearly as possible. You do not need to list account numbers.)	Current Fair Market Value	Wife Shall Receive	Husband Shall Receive
Cash (on hand or in banks/credit unions)	$	$	$
Stocks/bonds			
Notes			
Business interests			
Real estate: (Home)			
Automobiles			
Boats			
Furniture & furnishings			
Jewelry			
Life insurance (cash surrender value)			
Retirement Plans (Profit sharing, Pension, IRA, 401(k)s, etc.)			
Other assets			

ASSETS: DESCRIPTION OF ITEM(S) (Describe each item as clearly as possible. You do not need to list account numbers.)	Current Fair Market Value	Wife Shall Receive	Husband Shall Receive
Total Marital Assets	$	$	$

C. Division of Liabilities/Debts.

1. **The liabilities listed below are nonmarital liabilities** and, therefore, are owed as indicated. Each party shall owe, as his or her own, the liabilities found to be nonmarital, and the other party shall have no responsibilities regarding these debts.

LIABILITIES: DESCRIPTION OF DEBT(S) (Describe each item as clearly as possible. You do not need to list account numbers.)	Current Amount Owed	Wife's Nonmarital Liability	Husband's Nonmarital Liability
	$	$	$
Total Nonmarital Liabilities	$	$	$

2. **The liabilities listed below are marital liabilities** and are divided as indicated. Each party shall hold the other party harmless and pay, as his or her own, the marital liabilities awarded below.

LIABILITIES: DESCRIPTION OF DEBT(S) (Describe each item as clearly as possible. You do not need to list account numbers.)	Current Amount Owed	Wife Shall Pay	Husband Shall Pay
Mortgages on real estate: (Home)	$	$	$
(Other)			
Charge/credit card accounts			

LIABILITIES: DESCRIPTION OF DEBT(S) (Describe each item as clearly as possible. You do not need to list account numbers.)	Current Amount Owed	Wife Shall Pay	Husband Shall Pay
Auto loan			
Auto loan			
Bank/Credit Union loans			
Other			
Total Marital Liabilities	$	$	$

D. Contingent assets and liabilities will be divided as follows: ______________________________
____
____

E. The distribution of assets and liabilities in this final judgment is equitable; if each party does not receive approximately one-half, the distribution is based on the following facts and reasoning: __________
____
____
____
____

SECTION II. EXCLUSIVE USE AND POSSESSION OF HOME

[√ **all** that apply]

____ 1. ( ) Petitioner ( ) Respondent, as a condition of support, shall have exclusive use and possession of the dwelling located at: ______________________________________ until *{date or event}* ______________________________________
____
____.

____ 2. ( ) Petitioner ( ) Respondent may make visits to the premises described in the paragraph above for the purpose of obtaining any items awarded in this Final Judgment. These visits shall occur after notice to the person granted exclusive use and possession of the dwelling and at the earliest convenience of both parties or as ordered in paragraph 4 below.

____ 3. Upon the termination of the right of exclusive use and possession, the dwelling shall be sold and the net proceeds divided _____% to Petitioner and ____% to Respondent, with the following credits and/or setoffs being allowed: ______________________________________
____
____

____ 4. Other: ____
____
____

SECTION III. CUSTODY OF AND VISITATION WITH DEPENDENT OR MINOR CHILD(REN)

1. **Jurisdiction.** The Court has jurisdiction to determine custody of and visitation with the parties' minor child(ren) listed in paragraph 2 below.

2. **The parties' dependent or minor child(ren) is (are):**

Name	**Birth date**

3. **Parental Responsibility for the Minor Child(ren).**

[√ **one** only]

____ a. The parties shall have **shared parental responsibility** for the parties' minor child(ren).
( ) Mother ( ) Father shall have **primary residential responsibility** of the minor child(ren) and the other parent shall have secondary residential responsibility, as set forth in paragraph 4 below. **OR** The primary residential parent shall be ( ) undesignated ( ) rotating with time sharing for the ( ) Mother ( ) Father as set forth in paragraph 4 below.

____ b. ( ) Mother ( ) Father shall have **sole parental responsibility** for the parties' minor child(ren). Shared parental responsibility would be detrimental to the child(ren)at this time because:
____
____
____.

The other parent shall have visitation with the parties' minor child(ren) as set forth in paragraph 4 below.

4. **Secondary Residential Responsibility, Visitation, or Time Sharing with Minor Child(ren).** The parent granted secondary residential responsibility, visitation, or time sharing shall have:

[√ **one** only]

____ a. **reasonable visitation or time sharing** with the parties' minor child(ren) after reasonable notice and as agreed to by the parties, subject to any limitations in paragraph 5 below. The Court reserves jurisdiction to set a specific schedule.

____ b. the following **specified visitation or time sharing** with the parties' minor child(ren), subject to any limitations set out in paragraph 5 below: *{specify days and times}* ____________________
____
____
____
____
____
____

____

____ c. **no contact** with the parties' minor child(ren) until further order of the Court, due to the existing conditions that are detrimental to the welfare of the minor child(ren). *{explain}* ________________
____
____

5. **Limitations on Parental Responsibility, Visitation, and Time Sharing.** Neither parent shall take the child(ren) from the custody of the other parent or any child care provider or other person entrusted by the other parent with the care of the child(ren) without the agreement of the other parent during the other parent's time of parental responsibility or visitation. The above reasonable (paragraph 4.a. above) or specified (paragraph 4.b. above) visitation shall be:

[√ **if** applies]

____ a. **supervised by a responsible adult** who is mutually agreeable to the parties. If the parties cannot agree, the supervising adult shall be: *{name}* ____________________________________.

____ b. at the **supervised visitation** center located at: *{address}* ________________________
____,
subject to the available times and rules of the supervised visitation center. The cost of such visits shall be paid by ( ) Mother ( ) Father ( ) Both.

6. **Communication Arrangements for Secondary Parenting, Visitation, and Time Sharing with Child(ren).**

[√ **if** applies]

____ The parties' communications to arrange visitation or time sharing and discuss issues relating to the child(ren) (if shared parenting or visitation is provided in paragraph 3 above) are restricted as follows: ( ) telephone, ( ) fax, e-mail, or letter, ( ) A responsible person shall coordinate the visitation or time sharing arrangements of the minor child(ren). If the parties cannot agree, the responsible person shall be: *{name}* ____
( ) other conditions for arrangements or discussions: *{explain}* ________________________
____
____

7. **Exchange of Minor Child(ren).** The exchange of the minor child(ren) shall be on time as scheduled and as agreed to by the parties. The following conditions, if checked below, shall also apply.

[√ **all** that apply]

____ a. The parties shall exchange the child(ren) at the following location(s): ____________________
____
____
____.

____ b. The parent granted secondary parenting, visitation, or time sharing shall not get out of the vehicle, and the other parent shall not approach the vehicle, during the time the child(ren) are exchanged

____ c. A responsible person shall conduct all exchanges of the child(ren). Neither parent shall accompany the responsible person when that person is transferring the child(ren) from one parent to the other. If the parties' cannot agree, the responsible person shall be:*{name}* ________________________

____ d. Other conditions for exchange of the child(ren) are as follows: ________________________
____
____
____
____

____ 8. **Injunction Prohibiting Removing the Child(ren).** The Court hereby prohibits and enjoins the ( ) Mother ( ) Father ( ) Both from permanently removing the minor child(ren) from the ( ) State of Florida ( ) *{specify}* ____

____

without a court order or the written consent of the other party.

____ 9. **Other Provisions Relating to the Minor Child(ren).**

____

____

____

____

____

____

____

____

____

SECTION IV. ALIMONY

1. ( ) The Court denies the request(s) for alimony **OR**
( ) The Court finds that there is a need for, and that ( ) Petitioner ( ) Respondent (hereinafter Obligor) has/had the present ability to pay, alimony as follows:

[√ **all** that apply]

____ a. **Permanent Periodic.** Obligor shall pay permanent periodic alimony to Obligee in the amount of $__________ per month, payable ( ) in accordance with Obligor's employer's payroll cycle, and in any event, at least once a month ( ) other *{explain}* ____________________________

____

beginning *{date}* ________________. This alimony shall continue until modified by court order, the death of either party, or remarriage of Obligee, whichever occurs first.

____ b. **Lump Sum.** Obligor shall pay lump sum alimony to Obligee in the amount of $____________. This amount shall be paid as follows: ____

____

____

____ c. **Rehabilitative.** Obligor shall pay rehabilitative alimony to Obligee in the amount of $________ per month, payable ( ) in accordance with Obligor's employer's payroll cycle, and in any event, at least once a month ( ) other *{explain}* ____________________________________

____

beginning *{date}* ________________. This rehabilitative alimony shall continue until modified by court order, the death of either party or until *{date/event}* ____________________________, whichever occurs first. The rehabilitative plan presented demonstrated the following: ___________

____

____

____ d. **Retroactive.** Obligor shall pay retroactive alimony in the amount of $_________ for the period of *{date}*______________, through *{date}* ______________, which shall be paid pursuant to paragraph 3 below.

2. **Reasons for ( ) Awarding ( ) Denying Alimony.** The Court has considered all of the following in awarding/denying alimony:

a. The standard of living established during the marriage;
b. The duration of the marriage;
c. The age and the physical and emotional condition of each party;
d. The financial resources of each party, the nonmarital and the marital assets and liabilities distributed to each;
e. The contribution of each party to the marriage, including, but not limited to, services rendered in homemaking, child care, education, and career building of the other party; and
f. All sources of income available to either party.
Additionally, the Court has considered the following factors in reaching its decision: ____________
____
____
____
____
____

☐ Check here if additional pages are attached.

3. **Arrearage/Retroactive Alimony.**
[√ **one** only]
____ a. There is no alimony arrearage at the time of this Final Judgment.
____ b. The ( ) Petitioner ( ) Respondent shall pay to the other party the alimony arrearage of: $__________ for retroactive alimony, as of *{date}* ________________. $_____________ for previously ordered unpaid alimony, as of *{date}* ______________________________________.
The total of $_____________________ in alimony arrearage shall be repaid in the amount of $___________ per month, payable ( ) in accordance with Obligor's employer's payroll cycle, and in any event at least once a month ( ) other *{explain}* ______________________________
____
beginning *{date}* __________________, until paid in full including statutory interest.

4. **Insurance.**
[√ **all** that apply]
____ a. **Health Insurance.** ( ) Petitioner ( ) Respondent shall be required to pay health insurance premiums for the other party not to exceed $__________ per month. Further, ( ) Petitioner ( ) Respondent shall pay any reasonable and necessary uninsured medical costs for the other party not to exceed $_____________ per year. As to these uninsured medical expenses, the party who is entitled to reimbursement of the uninsured medical expense shall submit request for reimbursement to the other party within 30 days, and the other party shall, within 30 days after receipt, submit the applicable reimbursement for that expense.
____ b. **Life Insurance (to secure payment of support).** To secure the alimony obligations set forth in this judgment, Obligor shall maintain life insurance coverage on his/her life naming Obligee as the sole irrevocable beneficiary, so long as reasonably available. This insurance shall be in the amount of at least $___________________ and shall remain in effect until the obligation for alimony terminates

5. **Other provisions relating to alimony:** ____
____
____
____.

SECTION V. CHILD SUPPORT

1. The Court finds that there is a need for child support and that the ( ) Mother ( ) Father (hereinafter Obligor) has the present ability to pay child support. The amounts in the Child Support Guidelines Worksheet, ✎ ❑ Florida Family Law Rules of Procedure Form 12.902(e), filed by the ( ) Mother ( ) Father are correct **OR** the Court makes the following findings: The Mother's net monthly income is $__________, (Child Support Guidelines __________%). The Father's net monthly income is $__________, (Child Support Guidelines __________%). Monthly child care costs are $__________. Monthly health/dental insurance costs are $__________.

2. **Amount.** Obligor shall be obligated to pay child support in the amount of $__________, per month payable ( ) in accordance with Obligor's employer's payroll cycle, and in any event at least once a month ( ) other *{explain}:* ____
____,
beginning *{date}* ________________, and continuing until

( ) the youngest of the minor child(ren) reaches the age of 18, become(s) emancipated, marries, dies, or otherwise becomes self-supporting **OR** one of the minor children reaches the age of 18, become(s) emancipated, marries, dies, or otherwise becomes self-supporting and either party files a supplemental petition to modify child support and the court enters such an order.

OR

( ) *{date/event}* ____,
{explain} ____.

If the child support ordered deviates from the guidelines by more than 5%, the factual findings which support that deviation are: ____
____
____

3. **Arrearage/Retroactive Child Support.**
[√ **one** only]
____ a. There is no child support arrearage at the time of this Final Judgment.
____ b. The ( ) Mother ( ) Father shall pay to the other party the child support arrearage of: $__________ for retroactive child support, as of *{date}* ________________. $________ for previously ordered unpaid child support, as of *{date}* ____________. The total of $__________ in child support arrearage shall be repaid in the amount of $__________ per month, payable ( ) in accordance with Obligor's employer's payroll cycle, and in any event at least once a month ( ) other *{explain}* ____
____
beginning *{date}* ________________, until paid in full including statutory interest.

4. **Insurance.**
[√ **all** that apply]
____ a. **Health/Dental Insurance.** ( ) Mother ( ) Father shall be required to maintain ( ) health ( ) dental insurance coverage for the parties' minor child(ren), so long as reasonably available. The party providing coverage shall be required to convey insurance cards demonstrating said coverage to the other party. **OR** ( ) Health ( ) dental insurance is not reasonably available at this time.
____ b. Reasonable and necessary **uninsured medical/dental/prescription drug costs** for the minor child(ren) shall be assessed as follows:
( ) Shared equally by both parents.
( ) Prorated according to the child support guideline percentages.
( ) Other *{explain}*: ____
____

As to these uninsured medical/dental/prescription drug expenses, the party who incurs the expense shall submit request for reimbursement to the other party within 30 days, and the other party, within 30 days of receipt, shall submit the applicable reimbursement for that expense, according to the schedule of reimbursement set out in this paragraph.

____ 5. **Life Insurance (to secure payment of support).** To secure the child support obligations in this judgment, ( ) Petitioner ( ) Respondent ( ) Each party shall maintain life insurance coverage, in an amount of at least $______________, on ( ) his life ( ) her life ( ) his/her life naming the ( ) minor child(ren) as the beneficiary(ies) ( ) primary residential parent as the beneficiary as Trustee for the minor child(ren), so long as reasonably available. The obligation to maintain the life insurance coverage shall continue until the youngest child turns 18, becomes emancipated, marries, dies, or otherwise becomes self-supporting.

6. **IRS Income Tax Exemption(s).** The party granted primary residential responsibility or sole parental responsibility of the minor child(ren) shall have the benefit of any tax exemption(s) for the child(ren), **OR**, if checked here, ( ) assignment of any tax exemption(s) for the child(ren) shall be as follows:
____
____.

Further, each party shall execute any and all IRS forms necessary to effectuate the provisions of this paragraph.

7. **Other provisions relating to child support:** ______________________________
____
____

SECTION VI. METHOD OF PAYMENT

Obligor shall pay court-ordered child support/alimony and arrears, if any, as follows:

1. **Central Governmental Depository.**
[√ **if** applies]
____ a. Obligor shall pay court-ordered support directly to the Central Governmental Depository in *{name}* ______________________ County, along with any depository service charge.
____ b. Both parties have requested and the court finds that it is in the best interests of the child(ren) that support payments need not be directed through the Central Governmental Depository. However, either party may subsequently apply to the depository pursuant to section 61.13(1)(d)3, Florida Statutes, to

require payments through the Central Governmental Depository.

2. **Income Deduction.**

[√ **if** applies]

___ a. **Immediate.** Obligor shall pay through income deduction, pursuant to a separate Income Deduction Order which shall be effective immediately. Obligor is individually responsible for paying this support obligation until all of said support is deducted from Obligor's income. Until support payments are deducted from Obligor's paycheck, Obligor is responsible for making timely payments directly to the Central Governmental Depository or the Obligee, as previously set forth in this order.

___ b. **Deferred.** Income deduction is ordered this day, but it shall not be effective until a delinquency of $__________, or, if not specified, an amount equal to one month's obligation occurs. Income deduction is not being implemented immediately based on the following findings: Income deduction is **not** in the best interests of the child(ren) because: *{explain}* ______________________________

____

____,

AND

there is proof of timely payment of a previously ordered obligation without an income deduction order in cases of modification,

AND

( ) there is an agreement by the Obligor to advise the central governmental depository of any change in payor and health insurance **OR** ( ) there is a signed written agreement providing an alternative arrangement between the Obligor and the Obligee.

3. **Bonus/one-time payments.** ( ) All ( ) __________% ( ) No income paid in the form of a bonus or other similar one-time payment, up to the amount of any arrearage or the remaining balance thereof owed pursuant to this order, shall be forwarded to Obligee pursuant to the payment method prescribed above.

4. **Other provisions relating to method of payment.** ______________________________

____

____

SECTION VII. ATTORNEY FEES, COSTS, AND SUIT MONEY

___ 1. ( ) Petitioner's ( ) Respondent's request(s) for attorney fees, costs, and suit money is (are) denied because ____

____.

___ 2. The Court finds there is a need for and an ability to pay attorney fees, costs, and suit money. ( ) Petitioner ( ) Respondent is hereby ordered to pay to the other party $________ in attorney fees, and $ ________ in costs. The Court further finds that the attorney fees awarded are based on the reasonable rate of $ _______ per hour and ____________ reasonable hours. Other provisions relating to attorney fees, costs, and suit money are as follows: ______________________________

____

____

SECTION VIII. OTHER PROVISIONS

1. **Former Name.** The wife's former name of *{full name}* ______________________ ______________________ is restored.

2. **Other Provisions.** ______________________
____
____
____

3. The Court reserves jurisdiction to modify and enforce this Final Judgment.

ORDERED on ______________________.

____
CIRCUIT JUDGE

COPIES TO:
Petitioner (or his or her attorney)
Respondent (or his or her attorney)
Central Governmental Depository
Other: ______________________

IN THE CIRCUIT COURT OF THE ____________________________ JUDICIAL CIRCUIT,
IN AND FOR ____________________________ COUNTY, FLORIDA

Case No.: ________________________
Division: __________________________

_____________________________________,
Petitioner,

and

_____________________________________,
Respondent.

FINAL JUDGMENT OF DISSOLUTION OF MARRIAGE WITH PROPERTY BUT NO DEPENDENT OR MINOR CHILD(REN)

This cause came before this Court for a trial on a Petition for Dissolution of Marriage. The Court, having reviewed the file and heard the testimony, makes these findings of fact and reaches these conclusions of law:

1. The Court has jurisdiction over the subject matter and the parties.
2. At least one party has been a resident of the State of Florida for more than 6 months immediately before filing the Petition for Dissolution of Marriage.
3. The parties have no minor children in common, and the wife is not pregnant.
4. The marriage between the parties is irretrievably broken. Therefore, the marriage between the parties is dissolved and the parties are restored to the status of being single.

SECTION I. MARITAL ASSETS AND LIABILITIES

A. Date of Valuation of Property. The assets and liabilities listed below are divided as indicated. The date of valuation of these assets and liabilities is, unless otherwise indicated:

____ a. date of filing petition for dissolution of marriage __________________.
____ b. date of separation ____________________________.
____ c. date of divorce trial ___________________________.

B. Division of Assets.

1. **The assets listed below are nonmarital assets.** Each party shall keep, as his or her own, the assets found to be nonmarital, and the other party shall have no further rights or responsibilities regarding these assets.

ASSETS: DESCRIPTION OF ITEM(S) (Describe each item as clearly as possible. You do not need to list account numbers.)	Current Fair Market Value	Wife's Nonmarital Property	Husband's Nonmarital Property
	$	$	$

ASSETS: DESCRIPTION OF ITEM(S) (Describe each item as clearly as possible. You do not need to list account numbers.)	Current Fair Market Value	Wife's Nonmarital Property	Husband's Nonmarital Property
Total Nonmarital Assets	$	$	$

2. **The assets listed below are marital assets.** Each party shall keep, as his or her own, the assets awarded in this section, and the other party shall have no further rights or responsibilities regarding these assets. **Any personal item(s) not listed below are awarded to the party currently in possession or control of the item(s).**

ASSETS: DESCRIPTION OF ITEM(S) (Describe each item as clearly as possible. You do not need to list account numbers.)	Current Fair Market Value	Wife Shall Receive	Husband Shall Receive
Cash (on hand or in banks/credit unions)	$	$	$
Stocks/bonds			
Notes			
Business interests			
Real estate: (Home)			
Automobiles			
Boats			
Furniture & furnishings			
Jewelry			
Life insurance (cash surrender value)			
Retirement Plans (Profit sharing, Pension, IRA, 401(k)s, etc.)			
Other assets			

ASSETS: DESCRIPTION OF ITEM(S) (Describe each item as clearly as possible. You do not need to list account numbers.)	Current Fair Market Value	Wife Shall Receive	Husband Shall Receive
Total Marital Assets	$	$	$

C. Division of Liabilities/Debts.

1. **The liabilities listed below are nonmarital liabilities** and, therefore, are owed as indicated. Each party shall owe, as his or her own, the liabilities found to be nonmarital, and the other party shall have no responsibilities regarding these debts.

LIABILITIES: DESCRIPTION OF DEBT(S) (Describe each item as clearly as possible. You do not need to list account numbers.)	Current Amount Owed	Wife's Nonmarita l Liability	Husband's Nonmarit al Liability
	$	$	$
Total Nonmarital Liabilities	$	$	$

2. **The liabilities listed below are marital liabilities** and are divided as indicated. Each party shall hold the other party harmless and pay, as his or her own, the marital liabilities awarded below.

LIABILITIES: DESCRIPTION OF DEBT(S) (Describe each item as clearly as possible. You do not need to list account numbers.)	Current Amount Owed	Wife Shall Pay	Husband Shall Pay
Mortgages on real estate: (Home)	$	$	$
(Other)			
Charge/credit card accounts			
Auto loan			
Auto loan			

LIABILITIES: DESCRIPTION OF DEBT(S) (Describe each item as clearly as possible. You do not need to list account numbers.)	Current Amount Owed	Wife Shall Pay	Husband Shall Pay
Bank/Credit Union loans			
Other			
Total Marital Liabilities	$	$	$

D. Contingent assets and liabilities will be divided as follows: ______________________________

____

____

E. The distribution of assets and liabilities in this final judgment is equitable; if each party does not receive approximately one-half, the distribution is based on the following facts and reasoning: __________

____

____

____

____

SECTION II. EXCLUSIVE USE AND POSSESSION OF HOME

[√ **all** that apply]

____ 1. ( ) Petitioner ( ) Respondent, as a condition of support, shall have exclusive use and possession of the dwelling located at: ______________________________ until *{date or event}* ______________________________

____

______________________________.

____ 2. ( ) Petitioner ( ) Respondent may make visits to the premises described in the paragraph above for the purpose of obtaining any items awarded in this Final Judgment. These visits shall occur after notice to the person granted exclusive use and possession of the dwelling and at the earliest convenience of both parties or as ordered in paragraph 4 below.

____ 3. Upon the termination of the right of exclusive use and possession, the dwelling shall be sold and the net proceeds divided ___ % to Petitioner and ___% to Respondent, with the following credits and/or setoffs being allowed: ______________________________

____

____

____ 4. Other: ______________________________

____

____

SECTION III. ALIMONY

1. ( ) The Court denies the request(s) for alimony **OR**
( ) The Court finds that there is a need for, and that ( ) Petitioner ( ) Respondent (hereinafter Obligor) has/had the present ability to pay, alimony as follows:

[√ **all** that apply]

____ a. **Permanent Periodic.** Obligor shall pay permanent periodic alimony to Obligee in the amount of $__________ per month, payable ( ) in accordance with Obligor's employer's payroll cycle, and in any event, at least once a month ( ) other *{explain}* ______________________________
____
beginning *{date}* ________________. This alimony shall continue until modified by court order, the death of either party, or remarriage of Obligee, whichever occurs first.

____ b. **Lump Sum.** Obligor shall pay lump sum alimony to Obligee in the amount of $ ___________. This amount shall be paid as follows: ______________________________________
____
____

____ c. **Rehabilitative.** Obligor shall pay rehabilitative alimony to Obligee in the amount of $________ per month, payable ( ) in accordance with Obligor's employer's payroll cycle, and in any event, at least once a month ( ) other *{explain}* ______________________________________
beginning *{date}* ________________. This rehabilitative alimony shall continue until modified by court order, the death of either party or until *{date/event}* __________________________, whichever occurs first. The rehabilitative plan presented demonstrated the following: __________
____
____

____ d. **Retroactive.** Obligor shall pay retroactive alimony in the amount of $______________ for the period of *{date}* ____________, through *{date}* ____________, which shall be paid pursuant to paragraph 3 below.

2. **Reasons for ( ) Awarding ( ) Denying Alimony.** The Court has considered all of the following in awarding/denying alimony:
a. The standard of living established during the marriage;
b. The duration of the marriage;
c. The age and the physical and emotional condition of each party;
d. The financial resources of each party, the nonmarital and the marital assets and liabilities distributed to each;
e. The contribution of each party to the marriage, including, but not limited to, services rendered in homemaking, child care, education, and career building of the other party; and
f. All sources of income available to either party.
Additionally, the Court has considered the following factors in reaching its decision: ___________
____
____
____
____
____
☐ Check here if additional pages are attached.

3. **Arrearage/Retroactive Alimony.**

[√ **one** only]

____ a. There is no alimony arrearage at the time of this Final Judgment.

____ b. The ( ) Petitioner ( ) Respondent shall pay to the other party the alimony arrearage of: $__________ for retroactive alimony, as of *{date}* ______________. $____________ for previously ordered unpaid alimony, as of *{date}* ______________. The total of $__________ in alimony arrearage shall be repaid in the amount of $____________ per month, payable ( ) in accordance with Obligor's employer's payroll cycle, and in any event at least once a month ( ) other *{explain}* ____

____

beginning *{date}* ________________, until paid in full including statutory interest.

4. **Insurance.**

[√ **all** that apply]

____ a. **Health Insurance.** ( ) Petitioner ( ) Respondent shall be required to pay health insurance premiums for the other party not to exceed $__________ per month. Further, ( ) Petitioner ( ) Respondent shall pay any reasonable and necessary uninsured medical costs for the other party not to exceed $____________ per year. As to these uninsured medical expenses, the party who is entitled to reimbursement of the uninsured medical expense shall submit request for reimbursement to the other party within 30 days, and the other party shall, within 30 days after receipt, submit the applicable reimbursement for that expense.

____ b. **Life Insurance (to secure payment of support).** To secure the alimony obligations set forth in this judgment, Obligor shall maintain life insurance coverage on his/her life naming Obligee as the sole irrevocable beneficiary, so long as reasonably available. This insurance shall be in the amount of at least $________________ and shall remain in effect until the obligation for alimony terminates.

5. **Other provisions relating to alimony:** ______________________________________

____

____

____.

SECTION IV. METHOD OF PAYMENT

Obligor shall pay court-ordered alimony and arrears, if any, as follows:

1. **Central Governmental Depository.**

[√ **if** applies]

___ a. Obligor shall pay court-ordered support directly to the Central Governmental Depository in *{name}* ____________________ County, along with any depository service charge.

___ b. Both parties have requested and the court finds that support payments need not be directed through the Central Governmental Depository. However, either party may subsequently apply to the depository pursuant to section 61.13(1)(d)3, Florida Statutes, to require payments through the Central Governmental Depository.

2. **Income Deduction.**

[√ **if** applies]

___ a. **Immediate.** Obligor shall pay through income deduction, pursuant to a separate Income Deduction Order which shall be effective immediately. Obligor is individually responsible for paying this support obligation until all of said support is deducted from Obligor's income. Until support payments are deducted from Obligor's paycheck, Obligor is responsible for making timely payments directly to the

Central Governmental Depository or the Obligee, as previously set forth in this order.

____ b. **Deferred.** Income Deduction is ordered this day, but it shall not be effective until a delinquency of $__________, or, if not specified, an amount equal to one month's obligation occurs. Income deduction is not being implemented immediately based on the following findings: There are no minor or dependent child(ren) common to the parties,

AND

there is proof of timely payment of a previously ordered obligation without an income deduction order in cases of modification,

AND

( ) there is an agreement by the Obligor to advise the central governmental depository of any change in payor and health insurance **OR** ( ) there is a signed written agreement providing an alternative arrangement between the Obligor and the Obligee.

3. **Bonus/one-time payments.** ( ) All ( ) _________% ( ) No income paid in the form of a bonus or other similar one-time payment, up to the amount of any arrearage or the remaining balance thereof owed pursuant to this order, shall be forwarded to Obligee pursuant to the payment method prescribed above.

4. **Other provisions relating to method of payment.** ____
____
____

SECTION V. ATTORNEY FEES, COSTS, AND SUIT MONEY

____ 1. ( ) Petitioner's ( ) Respondent's request(s) for attorney fees, costs, and suit money is (are) denied because ____
____.

____ 2. The Court finds there is a need for and an ability to pay attorney fees, costs, and suit money. ( ) Petitioner ( ) Respondent is hereby ordered to pay to the other party $________ in attorney fees, and $_________ in costs. The Court further finds that the attorney fees awarded are based on the reasonable rate of $__________ per hour and ________ reasonable hours. Other provisions relating to attorney fees, costs, and suit money are as follows: ____
____
____

SECTION VI. OTHER PROVISIONS

1. **Former Name.** The wife's former name of *{full name}* ______________________________
______________________ is restored.

2. **Other Provisions.** ____
____
____
____

3. The Court reserves jurisdiction to modify and enforce this Final Judgment.

ORDERED on ________________________.

____
CIRCUIT JUDGE

COPIES TO:
Petitioner (or his or her attorney)
Respondent (or his or her attorney)
Central Governmental Depository
Other: ___________________________________

IN THE CIRCUIT COURT OF THE __________________________ JUDICIAL CIRCUIT,
IN AND FOR __________________________ COUNTY, FLORIDA

Case No.: ______________________________
Division: ______________________________

__________________________________,
Petitioner,

and

__________________________________,
Respondent.

FINAL JUDGMENT OF DISSOLUTION OF MARRIAGE WITH PROPERTY BUT NO DEPENDENT OR MINOR CHILD(REN) (UNCONTESTED)

This cause came before this Court for a hearing on a Petition for Dissolution of Marriage. The Court, having reviewed the file and heard the testimony, makes these findings of fact and reaches these conclusions of law:

1. The Court has jurisdiction over the subject matter and the parties.
2. At least one party has been a resident of the State of Florida for more than 6 months immediately before filing the Petition for Dissolution of Marriage.
3. The parties have no minor or dependent children in common, and the wife is not pregnant.
4. The marriage between the parties is irretrievably broken. Therefore, the marriage between the parties is dissolved, and the parties are restored to the status of being single.
5. Marital Settlement Agreement. The parties have voluntarily entered into a Marital Settlement Agreement, and each has filed the required Family Law Financial Affidavit. Therefore, the Marital Settlement Agreement is filed as "Exhibit A" in this case and is ratified and made a part of this final judgment. The parties are ordered to obey all of its provisions.
6. The Court finds that the parties have the present ability to pay support as agreed to in the marital settlement agreement as ratified and made part of this final judgment.
7. ( ) yes ( ) no The wife's former name of *{full legal name}* __________________________ ______ is restored.
8. The Court reserves jurisdiction to enforce this final judgment.

ORDERED on ______________________.

____
CIRCUIT JUDGE

COPIES TO:
Petitioner (or his or her attorney)
Respondent (or his or her attorney)
Other: ________________________

Florida Supreme Court Approved Family Law Form 12.990(b)(2), Final Judgment of Dissolution of Marriage with Property but No Dependent or Minor Child(ren) (Uncontested) (9/00)

IN THE CIRCUIT COURT OF THE ______________________ JUDICIAL CIRCUIT,
IN AND FOR ______________________ COUNTY, FLORIDA

Case No.: ______________________
Division: ______________________

______________________,
Petitioner,

and

______________________,
Respondent.

FINAL JUDGMENT OF DISSOLUTION OF MARRIAGE WITH NO PROPERTY OR DEPENDENT OR MINOR CHILD(REN) (UNCONTESTED)

This cause came before this Court for a hearing on a Petition for Dissolution of Marriage. The Court, having reviewed the file and heard the testimony, makes these findings of fact and reaches these conclusions of law:

1. The Court has jurisdiction over the subject matter and the parties.
2. At least one party has been a resident of the State of Florida for more than 6 months immediately before filing the Petition for Dissolution of Marriage.
3. The parties have no minor or dependent children in common, and the wife is not pregnant.
4. The marriage between the parties is irretrievably broken. Therefore, the marriage between the parties is dissolved, and the parties are restored to the status of being single.
5. There is no marital property or marital debts to divide, as the parties have previously divided all of their personal property. Therefore, each is awarded the personal property he or she presently has in his or her possession. Each party shall be responsible for any debts in his or her own name.
6. ( ) yes ( ) no The wife's former name of *{full legal name}* ______________________ is restored.

7 The Court reserves jurisdiction to enforce this judgment.

ORDERED on ______________________.

____
CIRCUIT JUDGE

COPIES TO:
Petitioner (or his or her attorney)
Respondent (or his or her attorney)
Other: ______________________

Florida Supreme Court Approved Family Law Form 12.990(b)(3), Final Judgment of Dissolution of Marriage with No Property or Minor Child(ren) (Uncontested) (9/00)

CIVIL COVER SHEET

The civil cover sheet and the information contained herein neither replace nor supplement the filing and service of pleadings or other papers as required by law. This form is required for the use of the Clerk of Court for the purpose of reporting judicial workload data pursuant to Florida Statute 25.075.

NAME OF COURT: FAMILY LAW, CIRCUIT COURT

I. CASE STYLE

____
PETITIONER,

Case #: ______________

vs.

Division: ______________

____
RESPONDENT.

II. TYPE OF CASE

(Place an x in one box only. If the case fits more than one type of case, select the most definite.)

Domestic Relations	Torts	Other Civil
❐ **Simplified dissolution**	❐ **Professional Malpractice**	❐ **Contracts**
❐ **Dissolution**	❐ **Products liability**	❐ **Condominium**
❐ **Support - IV-D**	❐ **Auto negligence**	❐ **Real property/ Mortgage foreclosure**
❐ **Support - Non IV-D**	❐ **Other negligence**	❐ **Eminent domain**
❐ **UISFA - IV-D**		❐ **Challenge to proposed constitutional amendment**
❐ **UISFA - NonIV-D**		❐ **Other**
❐ **Domestic violence**		
❐ **Other domestic relations**		

III. IS JURY TRIAL DEMANDED IN COMPLAINT?

☐ Yes ☒ No

DATE______________

____
SIGNATURE OF ATTORNEY OR PARTY INITIATING ACTION:

ADDRESS ______________________
____

PHONE:________________________

FINAL DISPOSITION FORM

This form is required for the use of the Clerk of Court for the purpose of reporting judicial workload data pursuant to Florida Statute 25.075.

NAME OF COURT: FAMILY LAW, CIRCUIT COURT

I. CASE STYLE

____
PETITIONER,

Case #: __________________

vs.

Division: __________________

____
RESPONDENT.

II. MEANS OF FINAL DISPOSTION (Place an "x" in one box only.)

- ☐ Dismissed Before Hearing
- ☐ Dismissed After Hearing
- ☐ Disposed by Default
- ☐ Disposed by Judge
- ☐ Disposed by Non-Jury Trial
- ☐ Disposed by Jury Trial
- ☐ Other

DATE________________________

____
SIGNATURE OF ATTORNEY OR PARTY
INITIATING ACTION:

ADDRESS ____________________________
____

PHONE:______________________________

IN THE CIRCUIT COURT OF THE ____________________ JUDICIAL CIRCUIT,
IN AND FOR ____________________ COUNTY, FLORIDA

Case No.: ____________________
Division: ____________________

____________________,
Petitioner,

and

____________________,
Respondent.

MOTION FOR TEMPORARY SUPPORT WITH DEPENDENT OR MINOR CHILD(REN)

The ( ) Petitioner ( ) Respondent requests that the Court enter an order granting the following temporary support:

[√ **or complete all** that apply]

1. **Assets and Liabilities.**

___ a. **Award temporary exclusive use and possession of the marital home.** *{address}* ______
____

The Court should do this because: ____________________
____
____

___ b. **Award temporary use and possession of marital assets.** *{Specify}* ____________________
____
____
____

The Court should do this because: ____________________
____
____

___ c. **Enter a temporary injunction** prohibiting the parties from disposing of any marital assets, other than ordinary and usual expenses. *{Explain}* ____________________
____
____
____

The Court should do this because: ____________________
____
____

___ d. **Require temporary payment of specific marital debts.** *{Explain}* ____________________
____
____
____

The Court should do this because: ____________________
____
____
____

2. **Child(ren).**

____ a. Enter a temporary custody order for the parties' minor child(ren). It is in the best interests of the child(ren) that the primary residential parent be ( ) Petitioner ( ) Respondent ( ) undesignated ( ) rotating because: ____

____

____

____

___ b. Enter a temporary injunction prohibiting the parties from permanently removing the child(ren) from the jurisdiction of the Court. The Court should do this because: ______________________

____

____

3. **Support.**

____ a. Award temporary child support of $ _______ per month.

____ b. Award temporary spousal support/alimony of $ ___________ per month.

The Court should do this because: ____

____

____

4. **Attorney's fees and costs.**

____ a. Award temporary attorney's fees of $ ___________.

____ b. Award temporary costs of $ ____________.

The Court should do this because: ____

____

____

5. **Other Relief.** *{specify}* ____

____

____

____

____

6. A completed Uniform Child Custody Jurisdiction and Enforcement Act (UCCJEA) Affidavit, ✎ ❑ Florida Supreme Court Approved Family Law Form 12.902(d), is filed with this motion or has already been filed with the Court.

7. A completed Certificate of Compliance with Mandatory Disclosure, ✎ ❑ Florida Family Law Rules of Procedure Form 12.932, is filed with this motion or has already been filed with the Court.

8. A completed Notice of Social Security Number, ✎ ❑ Florida Supreme Court Approved Family Law Form 12.902(j), is filed with this motion or has already been filed with the Court.

I request that the Court hold a hearing on this matter and grant the relief specifically requested and any other relief this Court may deem just and proper.

I certify that a copy of this document was [√ **one** only] ( ) mailed ( ) faxed and mailed ( ) hand delivered to the person(s) listed below on *{date}* ______________________________.

Other party or his/her attorney:

Name: ______________________________

Address: ______________________________

City, State, Zip: ______________________________

Fax Number: ______________________________

Dated: ______________________________

____
Signature of Party
Printed Name: ______________________________
Address: __________________________________
City, State, Zip: ____________________________
Telephone Number: __________________________
Fax Number: _______________________________

IF A NONLAWYER HELPED YOU FILL OUT THIS FORM, HE/SHE MUST FILL IN THE BLANKS BELOW: [✍ fill in **all** blanks]
I, *{full legal name and trade name of nonlawyer}* ____,
a nonlawyer, located at *{street}* __________________________________, *{city}* ____________________,
{state} ____________________, *{phone}* __________________, helped *{name}* ___________________,
who is the [√ **one** only] ___ petitioner **or** ___ respondent, fill out this form.

IN THE CIRCUIT COURT OF THE __________________________ JUDICIAL CIRCUIT,
IN AND FOR __________________________ COUNTY, FLORIDA

Case No.: ____________________________
Division: ____________________________

____________________________________,
Petitioner,

and

____________________________________,
Respondent.

TEMPORARY ORDER OF SUPPORT WITH DEPENDENT OR MINOR CHILD(REN)

This cause came before this Court for a hearing on a Motion for Temporary Support with Dependent or Minor Child(ren). The Court, having reviewed the file and heard the testimony, makes these findings of fact and ORDERS as follows:

The Court has jurisdiction over the subject matter and the parties.

SECTION I. MARITAL ASSETS AND LIABILITIES

A. Injunction.

1. ( ) Petitioner ( ) Respondent is (are) prohibited and enjoined from disposing of any marital assets without the written permission of the other party or a court order. If checked here ( ), the person(s) prohibited and enjoined from disposing of any marital assets may continue to pay all ordinary and usual expenses.

2. The Court may enforce compliance with the terms of this injunction through civil and/or indirect criminal contempt proceedings, which may include arrest, incarceration, and/or the imposition of a fine.

3. Violation of this injunction may constitute criminal contempt of court.

4. Bond. This order is conditioned upon ( ) Petitioner ( ) Respondent posting bond in the sum of $__________________ with the clerk of this Court.

B. Temporary Use of Assets.

1. The assets listed below are temporarily determined to be marital assets. Each party shall temporarily have the use of, as his/her own, the assets awarded in this section, and the other party shall temporarily have no further use of said assets. **Any personal property not listed below shall be for the use of party currently in possession of that item(s), and he or she may not dispose of that item(s) without the written permission of the other party or a court order.**

ASSETS: DESCRIPTION OF ITEM(S)	Wife Shall Have Temporary Use	Husband Shall Have Temporary Use
Automobiles		
Furniture & furnishings in home		

ASSETS: DESCRIPTION OF ITEM(S)	Wife Shall Have Temporary Use	Husband Shall Have Temporary Use
Furniture & furnishings elsewhere		
Jewelry		
Business interests		
Other Assets		

C. Temporary Responsibility for Liabilities/Debts.

1. The liabilities listed below are temporarily determined to be marital. Each party shall pay as his or her own the marital liabilities indicated below and shall keep said payments current. The other party shall temporarily have no further responsibility for the payment of these debts.

LIABILITIES: DESCRIPTION OF DEBT(S)	Current Amount Owed	Wife Shall Pay	Husband Shall Pay
Mortgages on real estate: (home)	$	$	$
Charge/credit card accounts			
Auto loan			
Auto loan			
Bank/Credit Union loans			
Money owed (not evidenced by a note)			
Other			

SECTION II. TEMPORARY EXCLUSIVE USE AND POSSESSION OF HOME

[√ **all** that apply]

____ 1. ( ) Petitioner ( ) Respondent shall have temporary exclusive use and possession of the dwelling located at: *{address}* ____
____
until *{date or event}* ____
____.

____ 2. ( ) Petitioner ( ) Respondent may make a visit to the premises described in the paragraph above for the purpose of obtaining his or her clothing and items of personal health and hygiene and to obtain any items awarded in this order. This visit shall occur after notice to the person granted temporary exclusive use and possession of the dwelling and at the earliest convenience of both parties.

____ 3. Other: ____
____
____

SECTION III. TEMPORARY CUSTODY OF AND VISITATION WITH DEPENDENT OR MINOR CHILD(REN)

1. **Jurisdiction.** The Court has jurisdiction to determine temporary custody of and visitation with the parties' minor child(ren) listed in paragraph 2 below.

2. **The parties' dependent or minor child(ren) is (are):**

Name	Birth date

3. **Temporary Parental Responsibility for the Minor Child(ren).**

[√ **one** only]

____ a. The parties shall have temporary **shared parental responsibility** for the parties' minor child(ren). ( ) Mother ( ) Father shall have temporary **primary residential responsibility** of the minor child(ren) and the other parent shall have temporary secondary residential responsibility, as set forth in paragraph 4 below. **OR** The temporary primary residential parent shall be ( ) undesignated ( ) rotating with time sharing for the ( ) Mother ( ) Father as set forth in paragraph 4 below.

____ b. ( ) Mother ( ) Father shall have temporary **sole parental responsibility** for the parties' minor child(ren). Temporary shared parental responsibility would be detrimental to the child(ren) at this time because: ____
____
____.

The other parent shall have temporary visitation with the parties' minor child(ren) as set forth in paragraph 4 below.

4. **Temporary Secondary Residential Responsibility, Temporary Visitation, or Temporary Time Sharing with Minor Child(ren).** The parent granted temporary secondary residential responsibility, visitation, or time sharing shall have:

[√ **one** only]

___ a. **reasonable visitation or time sharing** with the parties' minor child(ren) after reasonable notice and as agreed to by the parties, subject to any limitations in paragraph 5 below. The Court reserves jurisdiction to set a specific schedule.

___ b. the following **specified visitation or time sharing** with the parties' minor child(ren), subject to any limitations set out in paragraph 5 below: *{specify days and times}* ____________________
____
____
____
____
____
____
____
____
____
____
____
____

___ c. **no contact** with the parties' minor child(ren) until further order of the Court, due to the existing conditions that are detrimental to the welfare of the minor child(ren). *{explain}* ______________
____
____

5. **Limitations on Temporary Parental Responsibility, Visitation, and Time Sharing.** Neither parent shall take the child(ren) from the custody of the other parent or any child care provider or other person entrusted by the other parent with the care of the child(ren) without the agreement of the other party during the other party's time of temporary parental responsibility or temporary visitation. The above reasonable (paragraph 4.a. above) or specified (paragraph 4.b. above) temporary visitation shall be:

[√ **if** applies]

___ a. **supervised by a responsible adult** who is mutually agreeable to the parties. If the parties cannot agree, the supervising adult shall be: *{name}* ______________________________.

___ b. at a **supervised visitation** center located at: *{address}* ______________________________
____,
subject to the available times and rules of the supervised visitation center. The cost of such visits shall be paid by ( ) Mother ( ) Father ( ) Both.

6. **Communication Arrangements for Temporary Secondary Parenting, Visitation, and Time Sharing with Child(ren).**

[√ **if** applies]

___ The parties' communications to arrange visitation or time sharing and discuss issues relating to the child(ren) (if temporary shared parenting, time sharing or visitation is provided in paragraph 3 above) are restricted as follows: ( ) telephone, ( ) fax, e-mail, or letter, ( ) a responsible person shall coordinate the visitation or time sharing arrangements of the minor child(ren). If the parties cannot agree, the responsible person shall be: *{name}* ______________________________
( ) other conditions for arrangements or discussions: *{explain}* ______________________
____
____
____

7. **Exchange of Minor Child(ren).** The exchange of the minor child(ren) shall be on time as scheduled and as agreed to by the parties. The following conditions, if checked below, shall also apply.

[√ **all** that apply]

____ a. The parties shall temporarily exchange the child(ren) at the following location(s): ____________
____.

____ b. The parent granted temporary secondary parenting, visitation, or time sharing shall not get out of the vehicle, and the other parent shall not approach the vehicle, during the time the child(ren) are exchanged.

____ c. A responsible person shall conduct all exchanges of the child(ren). The parent granted temporary secondary parenting, temporary visitation, or time sharing shall not be present during the exchange. If the parties' cannot agree, the responsible person shall be: *{name}* ____________________

____ d. Other conditions for exchange of the child(ren) are as follows: ____________________
____
____
____
____
____

___ 8. **Injunction Prohibiting Removing the Child(ren).** The Court hereby temporarily prohibits and enjoins the ( ) Mother ( ) Father ( ) Both from permanently removing the minor child(ren) from the State of Florida without a court order or the written consent of the other party.

____ 9. **Other Temporary Provisions Relating to the Minor Child(ren).**
____
____
____
____
____
____
____
____
____

SECTION IV. TEMPORARY ALIMONY

1. ( ) The Court denies the request(s) for temporary alimony. **OR**
( ) The Court finds that there is a need for, and that ( ) Petitioner ( ) Respondent, hereinafter Obligor, has/had the present ability to pay temporary alimony as follows:

[√ **all** that apply]

____ a. **Temporary Periodic.** Obligor shall pay temporary periodic alimony to Obligee in the amount of $__________ per month, payable ( ) in accordance with Obligor's employer's payroll cycle, and in any event, at least once a month ( ) other *{explain}* ____________________
____,
beginning *{date}* __________. This temporary periodic alimony shall continue until modified by court order, the death of either party, or until, *{date/event}* ____________________, whichever occurs first.

____ b. **Lump Sum.** Obligor shall pay temporary lump sum alimony to Obligee in the amount of $ __________. This amount shall be paid as follows: ____________________
____
____.

____ c. **Rehabilitative.** Obligor shall pay temporary rehabilitative alimony to Obligee in the amount of $__________ per month, payable ( ) in accordance with Obligor's employer's payroll cycle, and in any event, at least once a month ( ) other *{explain}* ____________________
____
beginning *{date}* ____________________. This temporary rehabilitative alimony shall continue until

modified by court order, the death of either party or until *{date/event}* ______________________, whichever occurs first. The temporary rehabilitative plan presented demonstrated the following:
____
____
____
____.

____ d. **Retroactive.** Obligor shall pay retroactive alimony in the amount of $_________ for the period of *{date}* _______________ through *{date}* ___________, which shall be paid pursuant to paragraph 3 below.

2. **Reasons for Awarding/Denying Temporary Alimony Award.** The reasons for awarding/denying temporary alimony are as follows:
____ a. length of the marriage of the party receiving temporary alimony: ____________ years;
____ b. age of party receiving temporary alimony: __________;
____ c. health of party receiving temporary alimony: ( ) excellent ( ) good ( ) poor ( ) other ____;
____ d. other factors ____
____
____
____

☐ Check here if additional pages are attached.

3. **Retroactive Alimony.** ( ) Petitioner ( ) Respondent shall pay to the other party the temporary retroactive alimony of $___________, as of *{date}* ___________. This amount shall be paid in the amount of $_________ per month, payable in accordance with Obligor's employer's payroll cycle, and in any event at least once a month ( ) other *{explain}* ______________________________
____
beginning *{date}* __________________, until paid in full including statutory interest.

4. **Insurance.**
[√ **all** that apply]
____ a. **Health Insurance.** ( ) Petitioner ( ) Respondent shall temporarily be required to pay health insurance premiums for the other party not to exceed $_____________ per month. Further, ( ) Petitioner ( ) Respondent shall pay any uninsured medical costs for the other party not exceed $_____________ per year. As to these uninsured medical expenses, the party who is entitled to reimbursement of the uninsured medical expense shall submit request for reimbursement to the other party within 30 days, and the other party shall, within 30 days after receipt, submit the applicable reimbursement for that expense.
____ b. **Life Insurance (to secure payment of support).** To secure the temporary alimony obligations set forth in this order, the Obligor shall temporarily maintain life insurance coverage on his/her life naming the Obligee as the sole irrevocable beneficiary, so long as reasonably available. This temporary insurance shall be in the amount of at least $__________ and shall remain in effect until this temporary obligation for alimony terminates.

5. **Other provisions relating to temporary alimony:** ______________________________
____
____

SECTION V. TEMPORARY CHILD SUPPORT

1. The Court finds that there is a need for temporary child support and that the ( ) Mother ( ) Father (hereinafter Obligor) has the present ability to pay child support. The amounts in the Child Support

Guidelines Worksheet, ✎ ❑ Florida Family Law Rules of Procedure Form 12.902(e), filed by the ( ) Mother ( ) Father are correct **OR** the Court makes the following findings: The Mother's net monthly income is $__________.
The Father's net monthly income is $__________. Monthly child care costs are $__________.
Monthly health/dental insurance costs are $__________.

2. **Amount.** Obligor shall be obligated to pay temporary child support in the amount of $__________ per month payable ( ) in accordance with Obligor's payroll cycle, and in any event at least once a month ( ) *{explain}* ____

____

beginning *{date}* ______________________, and continuing until further court order or until *{date/event}* ____,
{explain} ____.
If the temporary child support ordered deviates from the guidelines by more than 5%, the factual findings which support that deviation are: ____

____

____.

3. **Retroactive Child Support.**
[√ **if** applies]
____ ( ) Mother ( ) Father shall pay to the other party the temporary retroactive child support of $__________, as of *{date}* ______________. This amount shall be paid in the amount of $ __________ per month, payable in accordance with Obligor's employer's payroll cycle, and in any event at least once a month ( ) other *{explain}* ____

____

beginning *{date}* ________________, until paid in full including statutory interest.

4. **Insurance.**
[√ **all** that apply]
____ a. **Health/Dental Insurance.** ( ) Mother ( ) Father shall be required to temporarily maintain ( ) health ( ) dental insurance coverage for the parties' minor child(ren), so long as reasonably available. The party providing coverage shall be required to convey cards showing coverage to the other party. **OR** ( ) Health ( ) dental insurance is not reasonably available at this time.
____ b. Reasonable and necessary **uninsured medical/dental/prescription drug costs** for the minor child(ren) shall temporarily be assessed as follows:
( ) Shared equally by both parents.
( ) Prorated according to the child support guideline percentages.
( ) Other *{explain}*: ____

____

As to these uninsured medical/dental/prescription drug expenses, the party who incurs the expense shall submit request for reimbursement to the other party within 30 days, and the other party, within 30 days of receipt, shall submit the applicable reimbursement for that expense, according to the schedule of reimbursement set out in this paragraph.

5. **Life Insurance (to secure payment of support).** To secure the temporary child support obligations in this order, ( ) Petitioner ( ) Respondent ( ) Each party shall temporarily maintain life insurance coverage, in an amount of at least $__________, on ( ) his life ( ) her life ( ) his/her life naming the ( ) minor child(ren) as the sole irrevocable beneficiary(ies) ( ) primary residential parent as the sole irrevocable beneficiary as Trustee for the minor child(ren), so long as reasonably available. The obligation to maintain the life insurance coverage shall continue until the Court orders otherwise or until *{date/event}* ____

____.

6. **IRS Income Tax Deduction(s).** The party granted temporary primary residential responsibility or temporary sole parental responsibility of the minor child(ren) shall have the benefit of any tax deductions for the child(ren), **OR**, if checked here, ( ) assignment of any tax deduction for the child(ren) shall be as follows: ____
____

7. **Other provisions relating to temporary child support:** ______________________
____

SECTION VI. METHOD OF PAYMENT

Obligor shall pay any temporary court-ordered child support/alimony and arrears, if any, as follows:

1. **Central Governmental Depository.**

[√ **if** applies]

____ a. Obligor shall pay temporary court-ordered support directly to the Central Governmental Depository in *{name}* ____________________ County, along with any depository service charge.

____ b. Both parties have requested and the court finds that it is in the best interests of the child(ren) that temporary support payments need not be directed through the Central Governmental Depository. However, either party may subsequently apply to the depository pursuant to section 61.13(1)(d)3, Florida Statutes, to require payments through the Central Governmental Depository.

2. **Income Deduction.**

[√ **if** applies]

____ a. **Immediate.** Obligor shall pay through income deduction, pursuant to a separate Income Deduction Order which shall be effective immediately. Obligor is individually responsible for paying this temporary support obligation until all of said support is deducted from Obligor's income. Until temporary support payments are deducted from Obligor's paycheck, Obligor is responsible for making timely payments directly to the Central Governmental Depository or the Obligee, as previously set forth in this order.

____ b. **Deferred.** Income deduction is ordered this day, but it shall not be effective until a delinquency of $____________, or, if not specified, an amount equal to one month's obligation occurs. Income deduction is not being implemented immediately based on the following findings: Income deduction is **not** in the best interests of the child(ren) because: *{explain}* ______________________
____
____,

AND

there is proof of timely payment of a previously ordered obligation without an income deduction order in cases of modification,

AND

( ) there is an agreement by the Obligor to advise the central governmental depository of any change in payor and health insurance **OR** ( ) there is a signed written agreement providing an alternative arrangement between the Obligor and the Obligee.

3. **Bonus/one-time payments.** ( ) All ( ) __________% ( ) No income paid in the form of a bonus or other similar one-time payment, up to the amount of any arrearage or the remaining balance thereof owed pursuant to this order, shall be forwarded to Obligee pursuant to the payment method prescribed above.

4. **Other provisions relating to method of payment.** ______________________
____
____

SECTION VII. TEMPORARY ATTORNEY FEES, COSTS, AND SUIT MONEY

____ 1. ( ) Petitioner's ( ) Respondent's request(s) for temporary attorney fees, costs, and suit money is (are) denied because ____ ____.

____ 2. The Court finds there is a need for and an ability to pay temporary attorney fees, costs, and suit money. ( ) Petitioner ( ) Respondent is hereby ordered to pay to the other party $__________ in temporary attorney fees, and $__________ in costs. The Court further finds that the temporary attorney fees awarded are based on the reasonable rate of $__________ per hour and ________ reasonable hours. Other provisions relating to temporary attorney fees, costs, and suit money are as follows: ____
____
____

SECTION VIII. OTHER PROVISIONS

Other Provisions: ____
____
____
____

ORDERED on *{date}* ______________________, at *{time}* ____________________.

____
CIRCUIT JUDGE

COPIES TO:
Petitioner (or his or her attorney)
Respondent (or his or her attorney)
Central Governmental Depository
Other: ______________________________

IN THE CIRCUIT COURT OF THE ____________________________ JUDICIAL CIRCUIT,
IN AND FOR ____________________________ COUNTY, FLORIDA

Case No.: ______________________
Division: ______________________

______________________________________,
Petitioner,

and

______________________________________,
Respondent.

MOTION FOR TEMPORARY SUPPORT WITH NO DEPENDENT OR MINOR CHILD(REN)

( ) Petitioner ( ) Respondent requests that the Court enter an order granting the following temporary support:

[√ **or complete all** that apply]

1. **Assets and Liabilities.**

___ a. **Award temporary exclusive use and possession of the marital home.** *{address}* ______
____
The Court should do this because: ____
____
____.

___ b. **Award temporary use and possession of marital assets.** *{Specify}* ______________
____
____
____
The Court should do this because: ____
____
____.

___ c. **Enter a temporary injunction** prohibiting the parties from disposing of any marital assets, other than ordinary and usual expenses. *{Explain}* ______________________________
____
____
____.
The Court should do this because: ____
____
____.

___ d. **Require temporary payment of specific marital debts.** *{Explain}* ______________
____
____
____.
The Court should do this because: ____
____
____.

2. **Support.** Award temporary spousal support/alimony of $__________ per month. The Court should do this because: ____
____

____.

3. **Attorney's fees and costs.**
____ a. Award temporary attorney's fees of $___________.
____ b. Award temporary costs of $___________.
The Court should do this because: ____

4. **Other Relief.** *{specify}* ____

5. A completed Certificate of Compliance with Mandatory Disclosure ✎ ❑ Florida Family Law Rules of Procedure Form 12.932, is filed with this motion or has already been filed with the Court.

6. A completed Notice of Social Security Number, ✎ ❑ Florida Supreme Court Approved Family Law Form 12.902(j), is filed with this motion or has already been filed with the Court.

I request that the Court hold a hearing on this matter and grant the relief specifically requested and any other relief this Court may deem just and proper.

I certify that a copy of this document was [√ **one** only] ( ) mailed ( ) faxed and mailed ( ) hand delivered to the person(s) listed below on *{date}* ____________________________________.

Other party or his/her attorney:
Name: ________________________________
Address: ________________________________
City, State, Zip: ____________________________
Fax Number: ______________________________

Dated: ________________________

____
Signature of Party
Printed Name: ____________________
Address: ________________________
City, State, Zip: __________________
Telephone Number: _________________
Fax Number: _____________________

IF A NONLAWYER HELPED YOU FILL OUT THIS FORM, HE/SHE MUST FILL IN THE BLANKS BELOW: [✍ fill in **all** blanks]
I, *{full legal name and trade name of nonlawyer}* ____________________________,
a nonlawyer, located at *{street}* _______________________, *{city}* ________________,
{state} __________________, *{phone}* ____________, helped *{name}* ________________,
who is the [√ **one** only] ___ petitioner **or** ___ respondent, fill out this form.

IN THE CIRCUIT COURT OF THE ____________________ JUDICIAL CIRCUIT,
IN AND FOR ____________________ COUNTY, FLORIDA

Case No.: ____________________
Division: ____________________

____________________,
Petitioner,

and

____________________,
Respondent.

TEMPORARY SUPPORT ORDER WITH NO DEPENDENT OR MINOR CHILD(REN)

This cause came before this Court for a hearing on a Motion for Temporary Support with No Dependent or Minor Child(ren). The Court, having reviewed the file and heard the testimony, makes these findings of fact and ORDERS as follows:

The Court has jurisdiction over the subject matter and the parties.

SECTION I. MARITAL ASSETS AND LIABILITIES

A. Injunction.

1. ( ) Petitioner ( ) Respondent is (are) prohibited and enjoined from disposing of any marital assets without the written permission of the other party or a court order. If checked here ( ), the person(s) prohibited and enjoined from disposing of any marital assets may continue to pay all ordinary and usual expenses.

2. The Court may enforce compliance with the terms of this injunction through civil and/or indirect criminal contempt proceedings, which may include arrest, incarceration, and/or the imposition of a fine.

3. Violation of this injunction may constitute criminal contempt of court.

4. Bond. This order is conditioned upon ( ) Petitioner ( ) Respondent posting bond in the sum of $__________ with the clerk of this Court.

B. Temporary Use of Assets.

1. The assets listed below are temporarily determined to be marital assets. Each party shall temporarily have the use of, as his/her own, the assets awarded in this section, and the other party shall temporarily have no further use of said assets. **Any personal property not listed below shall be for the use of party currently in possession of that item(s), and he or she may not dispose of that item(s) without the written permission of the other party or a court order.**

ASSETS: DESCRIPTION OF ITEM(S)	Wife Shall Have Temporary Use	Husband Shall Have Temporary Use
Automobiles		
Furniture & furnishings in home		

ASSETS: DESCRIPTION OF ITEM(S)	Wife Shall Have Temporary Use	Husband Shall Have Temporary Use
Furniture & furnishings elsewhere		
Jewelry		
Business interests		
Other Assets		

C. Temporary Responsibility for Liabilities/Debts.

1. The liabilities listed below are temporarily determined to be marital. Each party shall pay as his or her own the marital liabilities indicated below and shall keep said payments current. The other party shall temporarily have no further responsibility for the payment of these debts.

LIABILITIES: DESCRIPTION OF DEBT(S)	Current Amount Owed	Wife Shall Pay	Husband Shall Pay
Mortgages on real estate: (home)	$	$	$
Charge/credit card accounts			
Auto loan			
Auto loan			
Bank/Credit Union loans			
Money owed (not evidenced by a note)			
Other			

SECTION II. TEMPORARY EXCLUSIVE USE AND POSSESSION OF HOME

[√ **all** that apply]

____ 1. ( ) Petitioner ( ) Respondent shall have temporary exclusive use and possession of the dwelling located at: *{address}* ____

____

until *{date or event}* ____

____.

____ 2. ( ) Petitioner ( ) Respondent may make a visit to the premises described in the paragraph above for the purpose of obtaining his or her clothing and items of personal health and hygiene and to obtain any items awarded in this order. This visit shall occur after notice to the person granted temporary exclusive use and possession of the dwelling and at the earliest convenience of both parties.

____ 3. Other: ____

____

____

SECTION III. TEMPORARY ALIMONY

1. ( ) The Court denies the request(s) for temporary alimony. **OR**
( ) The Court finds that there is a need for, and that ( ) Petitioner ( ) Respondent, hereinafter Obligor, has/had the present ability to pay, temporary alimony as follows:

[√ **all** that apply]

____ a. **Temporary Periodic.** Obligor shall pay temporary periodic alimony to Obligee in the amount of $__________ per month, payable ( ) in accordance with Obligor's employer's payroll cycle, and in any event, at least once a month ( ) other *{explain}* ______________________________

____,

beginning *{date}* _________. This temporary periodic alimony shall continue until modified by court order, the death of either party, or until, *{date/event}* ______________________________, whichever occurs first.

____ b. **Lump Sum.** Obligor shall pay temporary lump sum alimony to Obligee in the amount of $__________. This amount shall be paid as follows: ______________________________

____

____

____ c. **Rehabilitative.** Obligor shall pay temporary rehabilitative alimony to Obligee in the amount of $__________ per month, payable ( ) in accordance with Obligor's employer's payroll cycle, and in any event, at least once a month ( ) other *{explain}* ______________________________

____

beginning *{date}* __________________. This temporary rehabilitative alimony shall continue until modified by court order, the death of either party or until *{date/event}* ____________________, whichever occurs first. The temporary rehabilitative plan presented demonstrated the following:

____

____

____

____

____.

____ d. **Retroactive.** Obligor shall pay retroactive alimony in the amount of $________ for the period of *{date}* _______________ through *{date}* __________, which shall be paid pursuant to paragraph 3 below.

2. **Reasons for Awarding/Denying Temporary Alimony Award.** The reasons for awarding/denying

temporary alimony are as follows:

____ a. length of the marriage of the party receiving temporary alimony: ____________ years;
____ b. age of party receiving temporary alimony: _________;
____ c. health of party receiving temporary alimony: ( ) excellent ( ) good ( ) poor ( ) other ____;
____ d. other factors ____
____
____
____

☐ Check here if additional pages are attached.

3. **Retroactive Alimony.** ( ) Petitioner ( ) Respondent shall pay to the other party the temporary retroactive alimony of $___________, as of *{date}* ___________. This amount shall be paid in the amount of $________ per month, payable in accordance with Obligor's employer's payroll cycle, and in any event at least once a month ( ) other *{explain}* ____, beginning *{date}* __________________, until paid in full including statutory interest.

4. **Insurance.**

[√ **all** that apply]

____ a. **Health Insurance.** ( ) Petitioner ( ) Respondent shall temporarily be required to pay health insurance premiums for the other party not to exceed $___________ per month. Further, ( ) Petitioner ( ) Respondent shall pay any uninsured medical costs for the other party not exceed $_____________ per year. As to these uninsured medical expenses, the party who is entitled to reimbursement of the uninsured medical expense shall submit request for reimbursement to the other party within 30 days, and the other party shall, within 30 days after receipt, submit the applicable reimbursement for that expense.

____ b. **Life Insurance (to secure payment of support).** To secure the temporary alimony obligations set forth in this order, the Obligor shall temporarily maintain life insurance coverage on his/her life naming the Obligee as the sole irrevocable beneficiary, so long as reasonably available. This temporary insurance shall be in the amount of at least $_________ and shall remain in effect until this temporary obligation for alimony terminates.

5. **Other provisions relating to temporary alimony:** ______________________________
____
____

SECTION IV. METHOD OF PAYMENT

Obligor shall pay any temporary court-ordered alimony and arrears, if any, as follows:

1. **Central Governmental Depository.**

[√ **if** applies]

____ a. Obligor shall pay temporary court-ordered support directly to the Central Governmental Depository in *{name}* ______________________ County, along with any depository service charge.

____ b. Both parties have requested and the court finds that it is in the best interests that temporary support payments need not be directed through the Central Governmental Depository. However, either party may subsequently apply to the depository pursuant to section 61.13(1)(d)3, Florida Statutes, to require payments through the Central Governmental Depository.

2. **Income Deduction.**

[√ **if** applies]

____ a. **Immediate.** Obligor shall pay through income deduction, pursuant to a separate Income Deduction Order which shall be effective immediately. Obligor is individually responsible for paying this temporary support obligation until all of said support is deducted from Obligor's income. Until support payments are deducted from Obligor's paycheck, Obligor is responsible for making timely payments directly to the Central Governmental Depository or the Obligee, as previously set forth in this order.

____ b. **Deferred.** Income deduction is ordered this day, but it shall not be effective until a delinquency of $__________, or, if not specified, an amount equal to one month's obligation occurs. Income deduction is not being implemented immediately based on the following findings: there are no minor child(ren) common to the parties,

AND

there is proof of timely payment of a previously ordered obligation without an income deduction order in cases of modification,

AND

( ) there is an agreement by the Obligor to advise the central governmental depository of any change in payor and health insurance **OR** ( ) there is a signed written agreement providing an alternative arrangement between the Obligor and the Obligee.

3. **Bonus/one-time payments.** ( ) All ( ) ________% ( ) No income paid in the form of a bonus or other similar one-time payment, up to the amount of any arrearage or the remaining balance thereof owed pursuant to this order, shall be forwarded to Obligee pursuant to the payment method prescribed above.

4. **Other provisions relating to method of temporary payment:** ____________________
____
____

SECTION V. TEMPORARY ATTORNEY FEES, COSTS, AND SUIT MONEY

____ 1. ( ) Petitioner's ( ) Respondent's request(s) for temporary attorney fees, costs, and suit money is (are) denied because ______________________________
____.

____ 2. The Court finds there is a need for and an ability to pay temporary attorney fees, costs, and suit money. ( ) Petitioner ( ) Respondent is hereby ordered to pay to the other party $__________ in temporary attorney fees, and $__________ in costs. The Court further finds that the temporary attorney fees awarded are based on the reasonable rate of $__________ per hour and ________ reasonable hours. Other provisions relating to temporary attorney fees, costs, and suit money are as follows: ______________________________
____
____

SECTION VI. OTHER PROVISIONS

Other Provisions: ______________________________
____
____
____

ORDERED on *{date}* ____________________, at *{time}* ____________________.

____
CIRCUIT JUDGE

COPIES TO:

Petitioner (or his or her attorney)
Respondent (or his or her attorney)
Central Governmental Depository
Other: ________________________________

IN THE CIRCUIT COURT OF THE ________________________ JUDICIAL CIRCUIT,
IN AND FOR ________________________ COUNTY, FLORIDA

Case No.: ____________________
Division: ____________________

__________________________________,
Petitioner,

and

__________________________________,
Respondent.

MOTION FOR CIVIL CONTEMPT/ENFORCEMENT

( ) Petitioner ( ) Respondent requests that the Court enter an order of civil contempt/enforcement against ( ) Petitioner ( ) Respondent in this case because:

1. A final judgment or order *{title of final judgment or order}* ____________________ in this case was entered on *{date}*________________, by *{court, city, and state}*__________ ____.

   □ Check here if the judgment or order is not from this Court and attach a copy.

2. This order of the Court required the other party in this case to do or not do the following: *{Explain what the other party was ordered to do or not do.}* ______________________________
   ____
   ____
   ____
   ____
   ____
   ____

   □ Check here if additional pages are attached.

3. The other party in this case has willfully failed to comply with this order of the Court: *{Explain what the other party has or has not done.}* ______________________________________
   ____
   ____
   ____
   ____
   ____
   ____
   ____
   ____

   □ Check here if additional pages are attached.

4. I respectfully request that the Court issue an order holding the above-named person in civil contempt, if appropriate, and/or providing the following relief:
   ____ a. enforcing or compelling compliance with the prior order or judgment;
   ____ b. awarding a monetary judgment;
   ____ c. if a monetary judgment was included in the prior order, issuing a writ of execution or garnishment or other appropriate process;
   ____ d. awarding prejudgment interest;
   ____ e. requiring the other party to pay costs and fees in connection with this motion;
   ____ f. if the other party is found to be in civil contempt, ordering a compensatory fine;
   ____ g. if the other party is found to be in civil contempt, ordering a coercive fine;

____ h. if the other party is found to be in civil contempt, ordering incarceration of the other party;

____ i. issuing a writ of possession for real property, writ for possession of personal property, or other appropriate writ;

____ j. issuing a writ of bodily attachment if the other party fails to appear at the hearing set on this motion;

___ k. requiring the other party to make payments through the central governmental depository;

____ l. requiring the support payments to be automatically deducted from the other party's income or funds;

____ m. requiring the other party to seek employment;

____ n. awarding make-up visitation with minor child(ren) as follows *{explain}*: ____________
____
____
____
____
____; and

____ o. awarding other relief *{explain}*: ____
____
____
____
____
____
____.

I certify that a copy of this document was [√ one only] ( ) mailed ( ) faxed and mailed ( ) hand delivered to the person(s) listed below on *{date}* ______________________________________.

Other party or his/her attorney:
Name: ______________________________
Address: _____________________________
City, State, Zip: ________________________
Fax Number: __________________________

I understand that I am swearing or affirming under oath to the truthfulness of the claims made above and that the punishment for knowingly making a false statement includes fines and/or imprisonment.

Dated: ___________________________

____
Signature of Party
Printed Name: ______________________________
Address: __________________________________
City, State, Zip: ____________________________
Telephone Number: __________________________
Fax Number: _______________________________

STATE OF FLORIDA
COUNTY OF ______________________

Sworn to or affirmed and signed before me on ___________________ by __________________.

____

NOTARY PUBLIC or DEPUTY CLERK

____
[Print, type, or stamp commissioned name of notary or clerk.]

___ Personally known
___ Produced identification
Type of identification produced ____________________

IF A NONLAWYER HELPED YOU FILL OUT THIS FORM, HE/SHE MUST FILL IN THE BLANKS BELOW: [✍ fill in **all** blanks]
I, *{full legal name and trade name of nonlawyer}*________________________________,
a nonlawyer, located at *{street}*__________________________, *{city}* ________________,
{state} ___________, *{phone}* ______________, helped *{name}* ______________________,
who is the [√ **one** only] ___ petitioner **or** ___ respondent, fill out this form.

Index

A

B

C

D

F

G

H

N

O

P

R

S

T

U

V

W